ReFocus: The Films of Rakhshan Banietemad

ReFocus: The International Directors Series

Series Editors: Robert Singer, Stefanie Van de Peer, and Gary D. Rhodes

Board of advisors:
Lizelle Bisschoff (Glasgow University)
Stephanie Hemelryck Donald (University of Lincoln)
Anna Misiak (Falmouth University)
Des O'Rawe (Queen's University Belfast)

ReFocus is a series of contemporary methodological and theoretical approaches to the interdisciplinary analyses and interpretations of international film directors, from the celebrated to the ignored, in direct relationship to their respective culture—its myths, values, and historical precepts—and the broader parameters of international film history and theory. The series provides a forum for introducing a broad spectrum of directors, working in and establishing movements, trends, cycles, and genres including those historical, currently popular, or emergent, and in need of critical assessment or reassessment. It ignores no director who created a historical space—either in or outside of the studio system—beginning with the origins of cinema and up to the present. *ReFocus* brings these film directors to a new audience of scholars and general readers of Film Studies.

Titles in the series include:

ReFocus: The Films of Susanne Bier
Edited by Missy Molloy, Mimi Nielsen, and Meryl Shriver-Rice

ReFocus: The Films of Francis Veber
Keith Corson

ReFocus: The Films of Jia Zhangke
Maureen Turim and Ying Xiao

ReFocus: The Films of Xavier Dolan
Edited by Andrée Lafontaine

ReFocus: The Films of Pedro Costa: Producing and Consuming Contemporary Art Cinema
Nuno Barradas Jorge

ReFocus: The Films of Sohrab Shahid Saless: Exile, Displacement and the Stateless Moving Image
Edited by Azadeh Fatehrad

ReFocus: The Films of Pablo Larraín
Edited by Laura Hatry

ReFocus: The Films of Michel Gondry
Edited by Marcelline Block and Jennifer Kirby

ReFocus: The Films of Rachid Bouchareb
Edited by Michael Gott and Leslie Kealhofer-Kemp

ReFocus: The Films of Andrei Tarkovsky
Edited by Sergey Toymentsev

ReFocus: The Films of Paul Leni
Edited by Erica Tortolani and Martin F. Norden

ReFocus: The Films of Rakhshan Banietemad
Edited by Maryam Ghorbankarimi

edinburghuniversitypress.com/series/refocint

ReFocus:
The Films of Rakhshan Banietemad

Edited by Maryam Ghorbankarimi

Edinburgh University Press is one of the leading university presses in the UK. We publish academic books and journals in our selected subject areas across the humanities and social sciences, combining cutting-edge scholarship with high editorial and production values to produce academic works of lasting importance. For more information visit our website: edinburghuniversitypress.com

© editorial matter and organization Maryam Ghorbankarimi, 2021, 2023
© the chapters their several authors, 2021, 2023

Edinburgh University Press Ltd
The Tun—Holyrood Road
12 (2f) Jackson's Entry
Edinburgh EH8 8PJ

First published in hardback by Edinburgh University Press 2021

Typeset in 11/13 Ehrhardt MT by
IDSUK (DataConnection) Ltd

A CIP record for this book is available from the British Library

ISBN 978 1 4744 7761 1 (hardback)
ISBN 978 1 4744 7762 8 (paperback)
ISBN 978 1 4744 7763 5 (webready PDF)
ISBN 978 1 4744 7764 2 (epub)

The right of the contributors to be identified as authors of this work has been asserted in accordance with the Copyright, Designs and Patents Act 1988 and the Copyright and Related Rights Regulations 2003 (SI No. 2498).

Contents

List of Figures and Tables	vii
Acknowledgments	ix
Notes on Contributors	x
Note on Transliteration and Style	xiii

Part I Introduction

An Overview of Banietemad's Career and Films   3
Maryam Ghorbankarimi

A Conversation with the Director   12
Maryam Ghorbankarimi

Part II Aesthetics, Politics, and Narrative Structure

1. From Black Comedies to Social Realism: Rakhshan Banietemad's Early Feature Films   27
   Farshad Zahedi
2. Under the Skin of Society: Rakhshan Banietemad's Social History of Post-revolutionary Iran   42
   Matthias Wittmann
3. *Tales* and the Cinematic *Divan* of Rakhshan Banietemad   57
   Michelle Langford
4. The Artistic and Political Implications of the Meta-cinematic in Rakhshan Banietemad's Films   79
   Zahra Khosroshahi

Part III Gender, Love, and Sexuality

5. "Modes of Expression not Subject to the Law of Male Desire": Considering the Role of Voice-over and Enunciation in the Work of Rakhshan Banietemad   97
   Rosa Holman

6. Affective Listening, Sonic Intimacy, and the Power of
   Quiet Voices in Rakhshan Banietemad's *The May Lady*:
   Towards a Cinema of Empathy   115
   Laudan Nooshin
7. *The Blue-veiled*: A Semiological Analysis of a Social Love Story   140
   Asal Bagheri
8. Masculinities in Banietemad's *Tales*: Reshuffling Gender
   Dynamics under Socio-economic Pressures   159
   Nina Khamsy
9. Representing Sexuality on Screen in Walled Societies:
   A Comparative Analysis of Iranian Film (*The May Lady*) and
   Chinese Film (*Army Nurse*)   173
   Yunzi Han

Part IV Fact, Fiction, and Society
10. Rakhshan Banietemad's Art of Social Realism:
    Bridging Realism and Fiction   189
    Maryam Ghorbankarimi
11. Embracing *All My Trees*: An Ecocritical Reading   206
    Fatemeh-Mehr Khansalar
12. Hidden Transcripts of Subordinates and the Art of Resistance
    in *Our Times*   219
    Bahar Abdi

Filmography   233
Bibliography   235
Index   247

Figures and Tables

FIGURES

I.1	Banietemad on the set of *Gilane*	12
I.1	Banietemad on the set of *Canary Yellow*	28
2.1	*Under the Skin of the City*	42
2.2	Forugh giving up the project of finding the best mother in *The May Lady*	48
2.3	*Under the Skin of the City*	54
3.1	On-screen embrace in *Tales*	72
4.1	The opening shot of *Tales*: through the viewfinder of a camera operated by a fictional documentary filmmaker	80
4.2	The bus scene through the hand-held camera of the filmmaker showing the workers in *Tales*	90
5.1	Banietemad on the set of *Gilane*	109
6.1	*The May Lady* (20′47″)	120
6.2	*The May Lady* (24′53″)	121
6.3	*The May Lady* (25′53″)	122
6.4	*The May Lady* (43′48″)	130
6.5	*The May Lady* (53′20″)	130
6.6	*The May Lady* (1:00′37″)	132
6.7	*The May Lady* (1:18′45″)	133
7.1	Exchanging glances in *The Blue-veiled*	146
7.2	Abortive gestures in *The Blue-veiled*	147
7.3	Children as animate "objects" in *The Blue-veiled*	148
7.4	The off-screen in *The Blue-veiled*	151
10.1	The Azadi Tower in *Centralization*	192

10.2	Banietemad in Seyyed's house, behind the scenes of *To Whom Do You Show These Films?*	200
10.3	Banietemad at the rehabilitation center, behind the scenes of *Under the Skin of the City*	203
11.1	Mahlagha Mallah among her friends and colleagues in *All My Trees*	207
12.1	*Our Times*, Arezoo explaining why she decided to become a candidate	222

TABLE

7.1	From "Les Relations homme/femme dans le cinéma iranien postrévolutionnaire" (Bagheri 2012)	145

Acknowledgments

I am pleased to see the first English-language book on Rakhshan Banietemad has finally come together. I would like to thank Rakhshan Banietemad herself for dedicating a lifetime to her art and making some of the most remarkable films of Iranian cinema. This project would not be possible without her endorsement and support, and especially the long hours she dedicated to speaking with me in preparation for the interview chapter. I am also indebted to Ms Banietemad for making her digital library of works available to us, as this especially facilitated our explorations of her documentaries.

This project has been made possible through the incredible work of this book's contributors. I thank them for their patience and dedication to their work, even through the difficult times we have faced during the Covid-19 pandemic. Their shared passion for Banietemad's films has made this book possible.

At ReFocus and Edinburgh University Press, I wish to thank my dear friend and colleague Stefanie Van de Peer for her continuous support and encouragement beyond the call of duty, along with Robert Singer and Gary Rhodes for their invaluable input at various stages of the book's production. I am also grateful for Gillian Lesley and Richard Strachan for ensuring the smooth and friendly process of acceptance and publication during the Covid-19 pandemic.

I would also like to acknowledge the generous support and encouragement of my friends and family, especially my mother, Mahvash Tehrani, and my father, Hosseinali Ghorbankarimi, who dedicated their lives to cinema and have always been a source of inspiration for me.

Notes on Contributors

Bahar Abdi, educated in Iran and Scotland, holds a BA in Persian Language and Literature from the University of Tehran and an MLitt in Middle Eastern Literary and Cultural Studies from the University of St Andrews. She has taught Persian literature and culture, published articles in Persian, and presented her research at international conferences. Her current research is on women's everyday life in post-revolutionary Iran.

Asal Bagheri holds a PhD in Semiology and Linguistics, with a specialization in Iranian cinema. She is author of the thesis *Men and Women's Relationships in Post-revolutionary Iranian Cinema: Directors' Strategies and Semiotic Analysis* (2012). She has also written several articles in French, English, and Persian. She teaches Linguistics, Semiology, Communication, and French language courses in different universities in France: Sorbonne Paris Descartes, Paris Est Créteil, Paris Est Marne La Vallée, Rennes 1, Sorbonne University, and Catholic Institute. She is currently completing her book in French entitled *Feelings, Love and Sexuality: Cinema's Dilemma in the Islamic Republic of Iran*.

Maryam Ghorbankarimi is a Lecturer in Film at Lancaster University. Born and raised in Tehran, she moved to Canada in 2001 to continue her education in film at Toronto's Ryerson University. She completed her PhD in Film Studies at the University of Edinburgh in 2012. Her book, *A Colourful Presence; The Evolution of Women's Representation in Iranian Cinema*, was published in 2015. Maryam is also a filmmaker and has made award-winning shorts in both documentary and fiction formats. Her current research is on transnational cinema and culture, specifically the representation of gender and sexuality in Middle Eastern cinemas.

Yunzi Han is a PhD candidate at SOAS University of London, studying Representing Sexuality on Screen in a Walled Society: A Comparative Reading of Contemporary Arthouse Cinema from China and Iran Since the Late 1980s. She holds an MA in Film Studies from University College London and an MA in Cultural and Creative Industries from King's College London. She was awarded her BA degree in Film Production from the Communication University of China (CUC).

Rosa Holman holds a PhD from the University of New South Wales, Sydney, which focused on the themes of authorship, voice, and lyricism in the work of various female Iranian filmmakers. Her research has primarily investigated the cultural politics and aesthetic practices of Iranian national and diasporic cinema, with particular emphasis on women's cinema, the influence of poeticism, and representations of disability. Her research on Iranian cinema has appeared in cinema journals *Senses of Cinema* and *Screening the Past*, with contributions specifically on Iranian women's filmmaking published in titles by Intellect and Wallflower Press.

Nina Khamsy is a PhD candidate at the Department of Anthropology and Sociology of the Graduate Institute in Geneva. She specialized in the politics of Iranian cinema in her MA and later on in her work at SOAS University of London, where she organized masterclasses. She gained practical skills in ethnographic research in her MSc in Social Anthropology at Oxford University and has co-published on female pilgrimage in Mashhad, Iran. Her PhD research keeps a focus on mobility and looks at Afghan migration in the digital age.

Fatemeh-Mehr Khansalar holds an MLitt in Middle Eastern Cultural and Literary Studies from the University of St Andrews. She has worked as the director of an Iranian language and cultural institute for several years and undertaken active roles for two major Iranian periodicals. She has published two short story collections, as well as several literary reviews and short stories in Persian literary magazines. At present, whilst she is preparing her novel for publication, she is working on ecocritical essays on Iranian cultural products for her next book project.

Zahra Khosroshahi recently completed her PhD at the University of East Anglia, focusing on Iranian filmmaker Rakhshan Banietemad's body of work as a gateway into important discussions around gender, femininity, and the taboo in Iran. More generally, her work explores the ways in which the visual medium challenges systems of power, and how film specifically functions as a form of resistance in Iran. Her research interests include world cinema, Iranian cinema, gender politics, and resistance.

Michelle Langford is a Senior Lecturer in Film Studies at the University of New South Wales in Sydney. Her research on Iranian cinema has been published in leading film studies journals including *Screen*, *Camera Obscura*, and *Screening the Past*. She is the author of *Allegory in Iranian Cinema: The Aesthetics of Poetry and Resistance* (2019). She has also published extensively on German cinema and is currently researching the German films of Iranian director Sohrab Shahid Saless.

Laudan Nooshin is Professor of Music and Head of the Music Department at City University London. She has research interests in creative processes in Iranian music; music and youth culture in Iran; urban sound; music in Iranian cinema; and music and gender. Her publications include *Iranian Classical Music: The Discourses and Practice of Creativity* (editor, 2015); *Music and the Play of Power in the Middle East, North Africa and Central Asia* (editor, 2009); and *The Ethnomusicology of Western Art Music* (editor, 2013). Between 2007 and 2011, Laudan was co-editor of the journal *Ethnomusicology Forum*.

Matthias Wittmann is a film and media scholar, film critic, film curator, and research assistant at the Seminar for Media Studies at the University of Basel. He is focusing on Afterimages of Revolution and War: Trauma and Memory Escapes in Post-revolutionary Iranian Cinema as part of an ongoing project supported by the Swiss National Science Foundation. He is the author of *MnemoCine: Die Konstruktion des Gedächtnisses in der Erfahrung des Films* (2016) and has organized international conferences on Iranian cinema.

Farshad Zahedi is a lecturer at the University of Carlos III in Madrid, where he teaches Moving Image History and Film Studies. He is an associate member of the Centre for Iranian Studies at SOAS University of London, and has published widely on Iranian cinema. He has written articles for *Quarterly Review of Film and Video* and *Film International*.

Note on Transliteration and Style

For the transliteration of Persian terms and names, the full range of vowels is used: ā, a, e, i, o, u; and the diphthong "ow" (as in Nowruz). Proper and personal names, wherever possible, are given in conventional forms. Film titles are always—at least in the first instance in each chapter—given in transliterated Persian and in English, along with the date of their release, but from the second mention onward, only the English title is used. Where there is more than one English translation or spelling, the most commonly used form of the English title is given.

Rakhshan Banietemad has recently changed the spelling of her last name, previously seen as "Bani-Etemad." Most previous scholarly works have used the old spelling, but in this new book we have chosen to use the new preferred spelling.

PART I

Introduction

An Overview of Banietemad's Career and Films

Maryam Ghorbankarimi

Throughout the history of cinema, women have tirelessly negotiated their position, despite all the existing obstacles: both those unique to women in the film industry in general, and those unique to women in the Iranian context. Whilst the prominence of female filmmakers is evident to those working on, or otherwise familiar with, Iranian cinema, it is my belief that many pioneering figures, such as Pouran Derakhshandeh, Rakhshan Banietemad, and Tahmineh Milani, have not received the recognition they deserve in this field of study. Works like the present volume are essential for developing and promoting a fuller understanding of the contributions made by filmmakers such as these, not only to their respective national cinemas, but to world cinema as a whole.

The 1990s were the decade in which Iranian cinema began its grand global appearance, coinciding with a growing number of female directors in this realm. In an early article, Bill Nichols wrote about the twelve Iranian films representing post-revolutionary Iranian cinema that he had watched at the Toronto Film Festival in 1992. Through this intensive but limited experience with Iranian cinema at large, he defined and praised Iranian cinema as a cinema free from most of the qualities present in Hollywood films (Nichols 1994: 21). The Iranian style of filmmaking, with its long takes, long shots, and minimal editing, offering a sense of "realism," remained for years the formal definition of New Iranian cinema. But among these twelve films was *Nargess* (1992), the seminal work by Rakhshan Banietemad. This female-centric film does, in fact, for the most part, follow the classical Hollywood narrative structure combined with social realist traits, which—along with melodramatic storytelling and the employment of professional actors—very much defies this definition. Perhaps the only convention that *Nargess* follows that befits the definition of New Iranian cinema is the incorporation of an open-ended narrative. Nichols writes the following about *Nargess*:

> Similarly, questions of gender identity and subjectivity receive little emphasis. The bulk of central characters are male, and most issues pertain primarily to them. These issues seldom pit the masculine against the feminine but rather provide an arena for the exploration of proper conduct for members of either sex. Only *Nargess* presents central women characters. Made by a woman director, it helps throw a light on questions of gender in relation to proper conduct that the other films may very well finesse. (Nichols 1994: 21)

Unfortunately, this somewhat sparse analysis, along with a couple of other short comments referring to the film as "unusual," is unsurprising, mainly because the film does not really seem to fit the article's thesis. The article is based on a generalized idea and tries to offer a definition that actually overlooks the uniqueness of this film, as well as the fact that it embodies many features claimed to be lacking in Iranian cinema. Iranian cinema is not one single "thing" that can be defined easily by someone who is not immersed in it, but rather a complex and diverse creative culture that deserves and requires deeper study of its pioneers: in particular, of course, its female pioneer, Banietemad.

In fact, one could read all these different ways of filmmaking as achievements specific to the experience and creativity of Banietemad, a pioneering director in Iran, in Iranian cinema. Most of her films have female protagonists and address topical social issues in Iranian society. Yet, in spite of the many awards and accolades that her films have earned in Iran and globally, the fact remains that Banietemad, along with other fellow female directors, is yet to receive the recognition she truly deserves (Dabashi 2018).

Nichols's article on the "festival phenomenon" of Iranian cinema is an invaluable piece of work, and an excellent starting point for transnational cinema studies. In the context of film festival studies, he analyzes how "we" watch and comprehend international films outside of their contexts. However, the article ultimately perpetuates the general and global expectations surrounding Iranian cinema at the time. It must have been difficult to go against the grain, watching and accepting critical work from female filmmakers who, according to media depictions, lived in a society in which oppressive measures against women were widely practiced. Perhaps the very existence of those female filmmakers was contradicting this one-dimensional view of Iran. Whilst I am not denying the issue of their living under an oppressive rule, ignoring their achievements and the contributions they have made in spite of all this is, in itself, another form of oppression. This is evident in the fact that the only celebrated works of Iranian female directors in this period were those which, in one way or another, dealt with controversial topics, such as women's rights: films that confirmed the general view of Iran. Such examples include *Sib* (*The Apple*, Samira Makhmalbaf, 1998) and *Roozi Ke Zan Shodam* (*The Day I Became a Woman*, Marziyeh Meshkini, 2000). Tahmineh Milani's *Nimeh-ye Penhan* (*The Hidden Half*, 2001)—which was deemed controversial and led to her two-week detainment under suspicion of promoting counter-revolutionary ideas—was her first film to attract global attention. Although it is significant in her œuvre and forms the second part of an unofficial trilogy, one could venture the opinion that it attracted attention for the wrong reasons.

It is only really since the latter part of the 2000s that global audiences are ready to see, and interested in seeing, different films from Iran, and not only those with minimal dialogue and rural settings. Asghar Farhadi's films with their long list of international awards, including two Oscars, are a case in point. In an interesting and fairly recent article on Asghar Farhadi, Daniele Rugo argues that Farhadi's style is a hybrid between realism and Hollywood, confirming the persistence of the old definition of Iranian cinema. He asserts: "Farhadi stands as an exception to the accepted canon of post-revolutionary Iranian cinema" (Rugo 2016: 175). This exception to the so-called "canon" is a long-running tradition in Iranian cinema: one that, it could be argued, was elevated to higher ground by Banietemad and further finessed by Farhadi. Unfortunately, however, Rugo's article fails to mention the contributions of Banietemad, further proof that she has been left out of the conversations on Iranian cinema's "canon." The platform provided by the ReFocus series can help to decolonize the so-called "canons" associated with global cinemas.

In the larger context of English-language studies on Middle Eastern cinema, Iranian cinema has generally been very well represented. And whilst some of the pioneering female directors have often been included in anthological works on Iranian cinema or global women's cinema, the focus is usually on their most influential works. In contrast, this book approaches Banietemad as a filmmaker dedicated to the representation of socio-cultural issues that we do not often find in other studies of her work or in Iranian cinema by women. Among the first books published on the history of Iranian cinema in English are the works by Rose Issa and Sheila Whitaker (1999), Hamid Dabashi (2001), Richard Tapper (2002), and Hamid Reza Sadr (2006). More recently, Hamid Naficy, the most prominent Iranian cinema scholar, published a four-volume book called *A Social History of Iranian Cinema* (2011–12). These books all include studies and discussions of many of the films by Iranian female directors, and they continue to be referenced, including in many of the following chapters. As interest in Iranian cinema globally has increased over the years, scholarship on Iranian cinema has grown as well. Some of the more recent books and edited volumes that dedicate considerable sections to women filmmakers are by Saeed Zeydabadi-Nejad (2009),

Parviz Jahed (2012), Peter Decherney and Blake Atwood (2014), Michelle Langford (2019), and Gönül Dönmez-Colin (2019), to name just a few. Rakhshan Banietemad is also included in chapters within books looking more broadly at women in world cinemas, such as two recent chapters by Laura Mulvey (2019). Whilst all of this work enlivens the study of women in global cinema and in Iranian film, it does remain necessary to dedicate more work to important filmmakers such as Banietemad, to reveal their substantial impact on filmmaking, both locally and internationally.

Born in Tehran in 1954, Rakhshan Banietemad came from an educated family and planned to study architecture after high school. However, after completing a nine-month training program at National Iranian Radio and Television (NIRT), which would guarantee her paid employment and the chance to become a script supervisor, she fell in love with cinema and all that it could do. Whilst working at the NIRT, she pursued a degree in film at the Faculty of Dramatic Arts at the University of Tehran. She continued to work for television until after the Revolution. During this time, she also worked as assistant director on several feature films and made a number of short documentaries. Among the directors she worked with are the likes of Mehdi Sabbaghzadeh, Rasul Sadrameli, and Kianoush Ayari, to name just a few. In "A Conversation with Rakhshan Banietemad," which follows this introduction, the filmmaker explains in detail how she made the transition from television to film, and the regulations and requirements involved in the process.

Because of the difficulty in acquiring state approval for her own scripts, she made her debut with three preapproved scripts, all with subject matters that were particularly appealing to her. Banietemad's early documentaries were largely concerned with urbanization and the migration of people from the provinces to cities like Tehran. Among these are *Mohājerin-e Rustāi dar Shahr* (*Occupation of Migrant Peasants in the City*, 1980) and *Tamarkoz* (*Centralization*, 1986). Her first three films—*Khārej az Mahdudeh* (*Off Limits*, 1988), *Zard-e Ghanāri* (*Canary Yellow*, 1989), and *Pul-e Khāreji* (*Foreign Currency*, 1989)—also deal with similar issues, but in slightly more comedic fashion.

During the Iran–Iraq War (1980–8), only very specific types of film were granted permission to be made. Priority was given to films that would help to mobilize the people to support the war, in addition to patriotic war films that depicted Iranian soldiers as heroes and martyrs. The other genre that was supported was comedy, in an effort to help keep up morale. The scripts that Banietemad selected, whilst still addressing real issues in Iranian society, were categorized as comedies. Her choice to work on *Off Limits* and *Foreign Currency* was the beginning of a long-standing working relationship with writer Farid Mostafavi. Indeed, he went on to work with her on several of her future scripts, including *Zir-e Pust-e Shahr* (*Under the Skin of the City*, 2001), *Khun Bāzi* (*Mainline*, 2006), and *Ghesseh-hā* (*Tales*, 2014). The first script she wrote on her own was initially called *Tooba*, named for its female protagonist. *Tooba* would much later become the feature film *Under the Skin of the City*, produced in 2001.

But her first film as sole writer–director was *Nargess*. I have previously argued that not only is this film a turning point in Banietemad's career; it also marks the beginning of a significant shift in the representation of female characters in Iranian cinema (Ghorbankarimi 2015). This film earned her first prize at the Fajr International Film Festival in Iran in 1992, the first time that a female director had ever won this award. Since then, she has been given six more awards at the same festival.

After *Nargess*, Banietemad continued to make films with prominent female protagonists—by now a signature trait—but also pursued documentaries, which she emphasizes are socially committed works that she is equally proud of, even if they travel less well on the global festival network. Surveying both her feature films and her documentaries, it is clear to see that she has had a vibrant and full career. Her films tend to depict snapshots of society, and she incorporates stories that were developed in her documentaries into her feature fiction films. The interplay between reality and fiction is best embodied in her film *Bānu-ye Ordibehesht* (*The May Lady*, 1998). In this film, Forugh Kia, a documentary filmmaker, works on a project to find the perfect mother for a program for Mother's Day. She blends elements from her documentaries, such as *In Film-hā ro beh ki Neshun Midin?* (*To Whom Do You Show These Films?*, 1993), with fictional documentary interviews with actors. In *The May Lady*, we see both Nargess from the film of the same name, and Nobar from Banietemad's *Rusari Ābi* (*The Blue-veiled*, 1995). This intertextuality not only connects *The May Lady* to her earlier films; it also foreshadows characters in her future work. In one of the factual scenes, we see a mother taking care of her injured war-veteran son. Gilāneh's character in Banietemad's later film *Gilāneh* (*Gilane*, 2005) is inspired by that mother.

This type of intertextuality is evident not only in her characters, but in the subject matter and the topic of her films too. Her half-hour documentary *Under the Skin of the City* deals with addiction and the challenges of overcoming it. This is an issue she returns to years later in her film *Mainline*. She explains in the interview that, although she had worked on this topic in the past, for her research she still went and lived with a family who were dealing with addiction, in order to learn about and understand it in more detail.

In more recent years, Banietemad has become a public figure and advocate, working with countless charities and non-governmental organizations to help them bring positive change to Iranian society. She is also a mentor for younger filmmakers and has helped many to develop their career in Iranian cinema over the years. One of her most productive initiatives has been the establishment of the Karestan film project in collaboration with Kara Film Studio and fellow veteran documentary filmmaker and producer, Mojtaba Mirtahmasb. Through this studio, "a group of professional Iranian filmmakers express their common concerns regarding humanistic, social and cultural issues through documentary films" (Karestan). One of the documentaries made under this initiative, *Hame-ye Derakhtān-e Man* (*All My Trees*, 2015), is discussed in Chapter 11.

Banietemad's latest feature, *Tales*, comes after a long interlude. A compilation of several short films she had produced, this is her most poignant and arguably darkest film, in which she brings the diverse layers of her career as a filmmaker together. She revives some of her beloved protagonists from previous work, from her very first film *Off Limits* to the more recent *Mainline*. Amazingly, as an audience, we get to follow the lives of these characters even after their respective films have ended. This also speaks of a confidence that audiences will remember, recognize, and know her characters, and of a presumption that people will have seen her films.

Banietemad has an extraordinary style of filmmaking that is both palatable for untrained spectators and enjoyable for trained eyes. The first chapter in each section of this book offers a different auteuristic reading of her works. Although, due to a lack of recognition of the inherently collaborative aspect of film, there are many arguments against the auteurist approach, it is still a valid means to evaluate the œuvre of a writer–director such as Banietemad. Just because we have only begun studying the works of women in cinema does not mean that we cannot evaluate them using the same methods we have used for decades to evaluate male directors. This is especially necessary when we put the scholarship on her work alongside the existing scholarship on her male counterparts in Iranian cinema. She deserves more attention in the study of Iranian and global cinema, in particular in a world that still needs to pay attention to its female filmmakers and the ways in which they have helped to develop different forms of cultural expression. In what follows I give an overview of what this book offers in terms of an in-depth study of this prolific filmmaker.

After this brief introduction, the book starts with Rakhshan Banietemad's own words, based on a series of interviews by Maryam Ghorbankarimi, conducted over four sessions in July 2019. In this chapter, Banietemad speaks articulately and at length about her life and work, relating memories and anecdotes concerning her childhood and her individual path to filmmaking. She also offers insightful reflections on the decisions and circumstances behind the making of some of her most prominent works, and emphasizes the endless inspiration she gets from the many different people in her country, and the social and cultural issues they have always faced.

"Part II: Aesthetics, Politics, and Narrative Structure" begins with Farshad Zahedi's chapter: "From Black Comedies to Social Realism: Rakhshan Banietemad's Early Feature Films." This offers an analytical study of Banietemad's first films, none of which has previously been addressed in detail. Zahedi contextualizes the historical, political, and social factors that led to the birth of a social genre in Iran, and examines the ways in which Banietemad, as an auteur, negotiated the systematic constraints and censorship she faced in her early career with efficient strategies in selecting and staging apparently non-problematic narratives.

Matthias Wittmann's "Under the Skin of Society: Rakhshan Banietemad's Social History of Post-revolutionary Iran" picks up seamlessly from where Zahedi leaves us. Surveying Banietemad's films, beginning with *Nargess*, Wittman argues that Banietemad's urban ballads not only show "the people who are missing," uncovering suppressed, silenced voices; they also illustrate how ordinary people are organizing themselves into communities, networks, and grassroots movements. He further asserts that, in doing so, the films expose the emptiness of the official claims made by the Islamic Republic of Iran. At the same time, they destabilize stereotypes regarding Iran emerging outside of the country, especially the image of "fatalistic Muslim masses," "the passive poor", and the "disoriented marginal."

Michelle Langford's chapter, "*Tales* and the Cinematic Divan of Rakhshan Banietemad," considers the film in the context of Banietemad's other works, analyzing the ways in which its style creates a delicate balance between social realism and poetic cinema. This chapter discusses how the theme of love and its structural treatment within the film evokes classical Persian traditions of love poetry known as *ghazal*, constituting evidence of the emergence of what she has previously termed the "cinematic *ghazal*."

Zahra Khosroshahi's chapter, "The Artistic and Political Implications of the Meta-cinematic in Rakhshan Banietemad's Films," explores the centrality of the recurring theme of the meta-cinematic and the film-within-the-film as an artistic and political tool in Banietemad's body of work. She argues that, through the meta-cinematic, Banietemad comments directly on the very concept of cinema; the films allude to their own form and this is especially significant in the way in which they challenge censorship laws. This chapter also focuses on where visualization and use of the camera as a theme and a technique can lead us. The author shows that the double-camera function not only serves as a vivid reminder of the cinematic form, but also, inevitably, tells stories.

"Part III: Gender, Love, and Sexuality" begins with Rosa Holman's chapter, "'Modes of Expression not Subject to the Law of Male Desire': Considering the Role of Voice-Over and Enunciation in the Work of Rakhshan Banietemad." Holman argues that voicing encompasses not only the aesthetic practices associated with the literal, acoustic voice in Banietemad's films, but also the process of inscribing authorship. Referencing feminist film scholarship of the 1980s concerning voice-over and the positioning of the female subject beyond the gaze of the spectator in experimental women's cinema, this chapter looks at how Banietemad's social melodramas and documentaries have played with the notion of voice, disembodiment, and enunciation.

Laudan Nooshin's chapter, "Affective Listening, Sonic Intimacy, and the Power of Quiet Voices in Rakhshan Banietemad's *The May Lady*: Towards a Cinema of Empathy," smoothly transitions from Holman's chapter, as it goes beyond the purely metaphorical deployment of female voice as a symbol of agency. This chapter focuses on the variety of ways in which sound plays a pivotal role in *The May Lady*. Nooshin analyzes the act of listening as portrayed and provoked by the protagonist of the film, examining how the purely sonorous material qualities of the spoken voice, such as timbre, texture, and contour—often presented as being outside of referential meaning—in fact communicate a great deal to the listener "beyond words." She argues in particular how sounds facilitate a new kind of filmic intimacy, affective subjectivity, and embodied listening that she terms "cinema of empathy."

Asal Bagheri's chapter, "*The Blue-veiled*: A Semiological Analysis of a Social Love Story," explores how, through formal filmic grammar, Banietemad has depicted love and relations between men and women in this film. This chapter also demonstrates how Iranian cinema chastely explores love and expresses its own "Iranian form" regarding relationships between man and woman, through constructing space in the way that traditional Iranian architecture does (external spaces for guests and internal spaces for family and private activities), but also through using stylistic devices reminiscent of classical Persian poetry.

Nina Khamsy's chapter, "Masculinities in Banietemad's *Tales*: Reshuffling Gender Dynamics under Socio-economic Pressures," shows how Banietemad exposes social crisis in its reordering of gender relations. By examining the vignettes of everyday life which make up *Tales*, Khamsy discusses how Banietemad's camera lyrically conveys gender reshuffling, thereby confronting the bigger question of imbalance in studies of gender in Iranian cinema.

Yunzi Han's chapter, "Representing Sexuality on Screen in Walled Societies: A Comparative Analysis of Iranian Film (*The May Lady*) and Chinese Film (*Army Nurse*)," offers a comparative study of contemporary Iranian and Chinese cinema since the late 1980s from a trans-Asia perspective. Through a close reading of the two films, Han discusses how they situate their protagonists in their respective societies and analyzes the similarities between the two films' aesthetic approaches in the representation of the sacrificing mother and single motherhood.

"Part IV: Fact, Fiction, and Society" focuses on Banietemad's documentary films. Maryam Ghorbankarimi's chapter, "Rakhshan Banietemad's Art of Social Realism: Bridging Realism and Fiction," offers a survey of her documentary works in search of a unique social realist approach to filmmaking. The chapter argues that, although Banietemad's auteurship might be evident in her films through their recurring links and themes, it is in her self-reflexive documentaries that we really see her artistic and critical approach to telling stories about ordinary people in society.

Fatemeh-Mehr Khansalar's chapter, "Embracing *All My Trees*: An Ecocritical Reading," offers a unique ecocritical perspective on Banietemad's documentaries and filmmaking. In particular, the chapter considers the independent Karestan project that Banietemad co-established and undertakes a close reading of the documentary *All My Trees*, which portrays Mahlagha Mallah, mother of Iran's environment.

Bahar Abdi's chapter, "Hidden Transcripts of Subordinates and the Art of Resistance in *Our Times*," employs James Scott's theory of hidden transcript as a mode of resistance, and demonstrates how, in her polemic documentary *Our Times*, Banietemad has subtly managed to give voice and agency to youth in general and, in a more specific sense, to female presidential candidates.

With these varied contributions to the study of Banietemad's work, it is hoped that this volume will add significantly to existing scholarship on Iranian cinema and on women in world cinema. These chapters open up some of Banietemad's less accessible titles to a wider readership of students and scholars interested in her work, and in Iranian cinema at large. By focusing on both the aesthetics of her work and on their socio-political context, these pieces reveal the social impact of Banietemad's films, an important aim she has strived for throughout her career. The diverse angles of study offered by the chapters in this book also reflect the multi-faceted outlook of the filmmaker's work, as she lays out so eloquently in the interview in the following chapter.

A Conversation with the Director

Maryam Ghorbankarimi

I was born on 3 April 1954 in a clinic in Tajrish, north Tehran. My father was a skilled accountant working for Sāzmān-e Barnāmeh va Budjeh [Planning and Budget Organization], who also had a keen interest in poetry and literature. When I was only four, he used to teach me poetry and encourage me to memorize one of Hafiz's most well-known *ghazals*. I have treasured memories of my dad, although I unfortunately lost him at the age of nine. For a time, we lived in Mashshad, the birthplace of my dad, and for a time in Shiraz, where

Figure I.1 Banietemad on the set of *Gilane* (2005)

my mother was born. But I began school in Tehran. My favorite memory of my first nine years is set at the house where my aunt and grandmother lived. It was, in my imagination, the quintessential representation of the house where the protagonist of Simin Daneshvar's novel *Suvashun*[1] lived. I often dream of that large courtyard: the small chamomile flowers peeking through the cobblestones and the round pond in the middle, shaded by the orange blossoms; the large rooms and the stained-glass windows. I remember I fell in the pond one cold winter. These distant memories are always with me; exactly why, I'm not sure. When I was reading *Suvashun*, I always thought that, if there was going to be an adaptation made, it had to be shot in that house. Unfortunately, the plot of that beautiful house has now been taken over by a huge ugly parking lot.

I went to primary school in Narmak, a neighborhood in the northeast of Tehran. After my dad's sudden passing, our lives were shaken and completely transformed. We moved from that beautiful home which my dad had built with love, to a much smaller house. I did not have a "childhood" in the general sense of the word; the good times were when my father was alive. His departure had a huge emotional impact on me. Still, perhaps the sudden change of fortune and moving to the small house was a blessing in disguise. This unwanted change introduced me, a teenager with a certain emotional sensitivity, to a new environment and condition which was to have an enormous impact on my future career.

So, you want to know why film, why me, how and when . . . These questions are perhaps easier to reflect on now, after four or five decades of work in cinema. Because when you are young, you simply start out following the path, not knowing where it will take you. It is difficult, even impossible, to explain why and how. But as time goes by and you look back, that is when you can start to unpick these questions.

I was not supposed to end up in cinema: my plan was to become an architect. I was studying mathematics,[2] and I was a good student, with a real passion for architecture. Architecture was the profession I loved, but destiny introduced me to storytelling through images. I became acquainted with communication through images during my work at National Television, which motivated me to pursue filmmaking.

The sudden changes in my childhood, as I mentioned earlier, exposed me to certain vulnerable layers of society which I would not have had a chance to encounter otherwise. In our neighborhood, there was a family whose father, Amu jan, worked for the Sherkat-e Vāhed [United Bus Company of Tehran] and was an active member of the drivers' union. He was a man with little education, but he sought to do what was right and just. Back then, I was tutoring the neighborhood kids and also ended up teaching Amu jan how to read and write. I became closer to him and more acquainted with his activism. I used to write some of the letters that they had to write for the union. Like many girls in Iran, I was well versed in literature and poetry and I had a knack for writing. I also began reading the constitution and would use quotes from it in the letters. This helped me understand labor rights and the issues the working classes were dealing within their day-to-day lives. I learned that most of these families had come from the provinces. They did not have good living conditions and were facing real hardship. I became their petitioner for the court and the union. As a fourteen-year-old, I did not understand that I was participating in the process of political struggle. Later on, even when I was involved in other types of activism, I always knew I was more of social activist than a political activist; and it had all started when I was fourteen. So, fighting for one's civil rights was mixed into my life from my teenage years. Many of the letters they sent to the Shah, the Prime Minister and the bus company were written entirely by me. All this made me very perceptive to people's social conditions, and I never experienced those carefree teenage years like other girls my age. My world view was shaped in those formative years.

I am happy I was exposed to all this; even though the movement was oppressed and Amu jan was captured. I also faced some friction with Vezārat Sāvāk [National Organization for Security and Intelligence, the Iranian secret police]. I still did not understand that what we were doing could have such consequences. Through all this, I learned about resistance, strength, and fighting back. This stayed with me when I was studying and thinking I would pursue architecture. But working at National Television helped me to realize that I could address the concerns of my teenage years through the medium of film.

Although I am telling you all this, it is not that at the age of eighteen, when I went to study cinema, I went to fight. It was not like that at all. Rather, all these concerns which were latent in my memory unconsciously directed me to study cinema. This is why I always say that, for me, cinema is a tool and device, not the endpoint. I have been criticized for this controversial view, but I truly believe it. I know cinema with all its capabilities and dimensions, and I love it. More than anything, though, I like cinema because, in a society like Iran, it can make a difference. Many see art as separate from society. Of course, for some, art may only be created for art's sake, but that is not my point of view. This idea also changes from one society to another. I won't deny that, first and foremost, I look at the impact of my works in Iran, and then perhaps in the larger global context. Of course, like any other filmmaker, I am delighted at the thought of my films being shown at international festivals and winning awards. But, receiving the positive or negative reactions after my films are screened in Iran, which reflects a real impact on the Iranian audience, is my main mission. That is why I was never happy about the idea of one of my films being banned and unable to be screened in Iran. I have always waited to receive permission to show my film in Iran before sending it to the festivals abroad, even if that meant waiting years, as was the case with *Ghesseh-hā* [*Tales*, 2014].

A film is never just a film, you are right. Thinking about the depiction of reality in film is a sensitive and delicate issue. The journalistic idea that audiences want to see the reality of a society on the screen is incorrect. It is true that cinema is the mirror of reality, but it is never the entire reality. What is reality, anyway? If you stand here, you see reality one way, and if I move my camera a meter in that direction, this reality becomes another. It is my point of view that I am witnessing from my individual perspective, not that of an entire society. You can never truly understand a society by watching a film. But you can get to know a part of it. As a filmmaker, you would never claim that what you are depicting of society is society as a whole; it's the aspect you choose to focus on. For example, if a film depicts the issue of addiction in a society, this does not mean that everyone in this society is an addict; however, it could mean that it is a significant issue in this particular society.

Straight after high school, I was accepted on the architecture program of Dāneshgāh-e Meli [The National University]. I knew I wanted to work and study at the same time. The economic circumstances in which my mother raised us were nothing out of the ordinary. I always wanted to begin work and help support the family. During my high school years, I worked as a tutor. I wanted to reach financial independence sooner rather than later, so my higher education expenses would not fall on my family. Whilst in search of a job before university started, I learnt that National Iranian Radio and Television [NIRT] had a nine-month training program which would lead to the position of script supervisor. After completing this program, you would be hired by National TV. I was planning to do this whilst studying architecture. After I got onto the program, my situation changed again, and I found myself unable to go to university. I thought to myself that I would first finish this nine-month training and then, when I was hired, I would pursue the study of architecture. But by the time I had finished the training and became a script supervisor, and having seen the social impact of the programs I was involved with, my plans had completely changed again. The following year I went to Dāneshgāh Honar [Tehran University of Art], where I studied cinema alongside my work at National Television. Once I had completed my studies, I began making films.

When I look at young people now with all the possibilities before them—which is obviously not comparable to what we had access to growing up—I still think our generation was happier. We could have a goal, and for a girl from an ordinary background it was not impossible to both study and work and build a future. For the youth today, this goal is not self-determined, and so much of what dictates their future is out of their control, especially in Iran's current social, economic, and political situation.

As for the film industry in Iran, one could say it is much easier now to get into it, but remaining in it is difficult. About ten years ago, when I was the head of Kānun Kārgardānān-e Cinemā-ye Irān [Guild of Iranian Directors], we took a census and found that there were about 450 directors in Iran. Of this number, about 200 had only made one film, regardless of their gender, and 80 had only made two films. The digital revolution has truly made cinema widely accessible, much more accessible than it used to be. Today there are many more possibilities than we had in our time. When I was at university, even obtaining a roll of 8mm film was not cheap or easy. Now, you can use your mobile phone to make a film. But this level of accessibility has changed the definition of cinema. I am not saying it is now better or worse; it is just a different language, which is the necessity of this day and age. On the one hand, all this has made different experimentations possible, so at least from this perspective it has become much easier to enter the world of filmmaking. On the other hand, this wide accessibility has helped to develop a simplistic approach to cinema; not just anyone with camera equipment is a filmmaker. Anyone can record something and say that it is their point of view, but this is a world apart from professional filmmaking. I worked on gaining experience for about six or seven years before I made my first film. I worked as a script supervisor, an assistant director, and a writer to understand how everything worked before I began to make my own films. I tried to climb the ladder step by step, not by fighting my way in. Something I see in your generation, in my children's generation, is that they are not happy with the possibilities available to them. It is important to aim high, but it is also important to enjoy the smaller steps that bring you to that greater goal. When I was a script supervisor, I do not think my joy and satisfaction were any less than when I was making my own films. When I was an assistant director, I truly enjoyed the commitment and the work. I knew I wanted to direct my own films, but I did not spoil my path to getting there by yearning so much that I would be blind to what I had already achieved. I learned so much from the directors I worked with. I learned what I should and should not do, and what it means to be a novice director. All these experiences helped me want to make my own films.

Up until that point, no feature films had been made by a woman. In order to make a feature film, you needed permission from the Vezārat Farhang va Ershād-e Islāmi [Ministry of Culture and Islamic Guidance, MCIG]. They had set three conditions, two of which required you to get a permit. Firstly, you needed to have formal education in film; secondly, you needed to have had two credits as an assistant director; and thirdly, you needed to have made at least one short fiction or documentary film as a sample of work. I applied once I had fulfilled all three requirements. Although nowhere in the terms and conditions had it stipulated that the director had to be a man or woman, it nonetheless came as a surprise to them when I made the request, seeing as no other woman had ever done it before. The issue was finding a producer and an investor. The private company who wanted to invest in making *Khārej az Mahdudeh* [*Off Limits*, 1988] asked me to have a male consultant. I told them that if it was really necessary, I would consult with a man. But they told me that I needed a full-time male consultant on set, explaining that, because I was a woman, I might feel shy in asking my crew to do things. A man could therefore act as liaison between myself and the crew. I assured them that I had no problem in communicating, but it took them a while to accept this. A lot of my works were shot in public locations like coffee houses, a rehabilitation center, and so on, and many people thought that my husband, Jahangir Kosari, who was a TV producer at that time, had made those films. When he was once asked about this at a festival, he responded that he would not dare enter the locations I chose for my films!

I have always been against any kind of gender segregation, especially in professional realms. As one of the first female directors in Iran, I have been asked to create a women's society of filmmakers and so on. But I do not see why such a distinction is necessary, the same way that I do not want to be recognized only as a woman. It is important that film festivals, for instance, select films without bias and regardless of the filmmaker's gender. I don't think that recognitions based only on "female" status are helping women, because that means they are still seen differently and are not awarded equal respect. As a jury member at festivals, I always try to look at the film without considering who made it, making a judgment based on the quality of the film only.

In the past, my point of view has been misunderstood to the point where people called me "anti-women." But I believe that society should provide for all its members and should not give privilege to one cross-section without good reason. This should be true for both men and women. There should be an environment created in which women can grow and receive an equal education, in which the job market is inclusive; all these are rights that women deserve, and we need to fight for these rights. But patronizing and labeling women as people to be pitied is both disrespectful and insulting.

Because television in Iran became very strict after the Revolution, a huge wave of highly professional and skilled filmmakers and crew members, both male and female, migrated to cinema. In Iranian National Television, female directors, cinematographers, editors, script supervisors, and so on were not such a strange phenomenon, and they also began to migrate to cinema after the Revolution. This is also true in terms of some technology. For example, whilst using sync sound was a common practice in TV, Iranian cinema was still mostly using dubbing. This shifted after the Revolution, because the technical crew who had moved from television to cinema brought with them their skills, revolutionizing the industry. You could say that one of the reasons for the expansion and growth of cinema was the migration of these professionals from television. I remember when we (women) were coming to Europe for festivals in the 1990s, and everyone was shocked to see women representatives from Iran, especially with us wearing headscarves. The number of female filmmakers in

Iran was comparable with much more progressive countries in the West. Statistics released a few years ago stated that Iran actually has a higher percentage of female filmmakers than America.

What I am trying to say is that those of us who came from television brought with us the ideology and concepts that we had been practicing there for years. We were not women who all of a sudden were given permission to work in cinema, but we were educated and skilled in our profession and just carried on our work alongside male colleagues in a new environment. Soon, this culture also took over the film industry, and we did not allow belittling views on women in film to imprint on us. This situation was not only confined to cinema: women continued their work in all other professional realms as well.

Right now, it is important for me to focus on what satisfies me most. I have to admit that at times I do miss being on set for a feature film; it is a completely different experience to making low-budget documentaries. But I tell myself I should be true to myself: if I start that, then I would be neglecting all those other projects that bring me joy, even if they are only seen by a small audience. For instance, the result of making the documentary *Ay, Adamhā* [*Hey, Humans*, 2016] was the building of a specialist children's hospital with a capacity of 140 patients, the largest of its kind in the region. This film helped to create the circumstances to build this hospital. It was screened in France, which is what motivated them to support this project. The screenings were not at festivals, but what matters is that it helped to take the project to the next level. This was much more fulfilling for me than awards I could have won with a feature film. In *Rusari Ābi* [*The Blue-veiled*, 1995], there is a line by the protagonist in which he states: "Happiness is not what people see from the outside; happiness is in one's *del* (heart)."

It is true that social cinema does not always have to include non-professional actors or be shot in real-life locations. What I try to do, which is the foundation of my directorial approach, is to incorporate authenticity and realism into all aspects of my films: from the script and directing actors to the look, mise-en-scène, and sound, which is very important. Realism for me is not restricted to working with non-professional actors, but instead I want to try to employ all the techniques and the art of the actor so that they can fit into their role and the viewer can forget it is being acted altogether, and believe them completely. In most of my films, the locations are believed to be real locations, but they are all set up in advance, down to the finest details.

In each film we only see part of the life of a character: the part that comes to life from the moment the script writing begins. But all the characters have a back story that could turn into a big book, some of which I have written out and some of which I have kept in my mind. I tend to begin rehearsals with the main actors before the script is completed. Through this practice a character like Tooba, performed by Golab Adineh, was born, becoming a memorable figure. If you speak to Golab, she can talk to you for hours and tell you about the backstory of this character, including things you never get to see in the film. Through this backstory, Golab began her rehearsals with me. This is why the longest period of the production for me is before the actual shooting. During shooting, I usually have very little to say to my actors; all the discussions and exchanges of ideas take place beforehand. On set we only rehearse with the camera to get the technicality of the shots right; we never have any input for the acting.

My characters do not only exist on paper or on screen. I have lived with each one of them in their situations for some time. For example, for Khun Bāzi [*Mainline*, 2006], although I had worked on addiction for years, I went and lived with a family dealing with addiction for a month. I would go to bed after them and wake up before them to truly witness this devastating condition, and to see how they would continue to inject into veins that had become severely damaged due to excessive misuse. I wanted to understand what it meant when they said that they cannot quit. Combining all these results in the moment when you create your character, they come into being, as though they have blood coursing through their veins. This is why these characters do not finish for me; Tooba does not end with Zir-e Pust-e Shahr [*Under the Skin of the City*, 2001]. When I was making *Bānu-ye Ordibehesht* [*The May Lady*, 1998], I had not yet conceived of *Under the Skin of the City*. But Tooba and Abbas, from *The May Lady*, were already living with me. Many of my characters were inspired by people who featured in documentaries I made thirty or thirty-five years ago. It is painful to see that, when I look at them now, they are in an even worse situation. I will never forget them; I have kept my connection with them through my connection with making social documentaries. Filmmaking is not a profession you can leave behind when you leave the office. It is always with you. The characters I have developed did not appear out of thin air. They are made up, but they are still inspired by real people in real situations.

I always decide on suitable actors whilst I am still writing the script. Some of the actors were well known or became well known afterwards. I never selected them based on their popularity, but rather on their ability. Having said that, in many of my films the main actors were cast in a role that no one would ever expect of them. I remember when one of the co-producers came to see the make-up test for the film *Nargess* [1992] and saw Farimah Farjami's make-up, he was totally shocked. He said: "Everyone casts her for her beauty; you are taking that away!"

I am always after new experiments in my films, like a curious, inquisitive child. After all these years, every film for me is a new experience and I still get nervous before the first public screening, regardless of the film's length or type. None of it has become second nature to me: I still get goose bumps when I watch one of my films with the cast and crew and general audience for the first time. But I love it, I love this suffering. I still love this sensitivity, the fact that cinema has not got old or normal for me. Looking back at every film I have made, there was always something fresh and new in them for me.

I have a beautiful memory from *Nargess* which I would like to share. *Nargess* was made at the time in which the lamp of cinema projectors was like a bicycle lamp, very weak. The equipment in many cinemas had not been updated since the Revolution. The condition and quality of screenings were really poor. For months before the shoot, we were discussing the look and color of the film with Hossein Jafarian (director of photography) and Amir Esbati (production designer). We did several tests because *Nargess* had to have a cold, low-key, and dark setting. At that time, we were facing extreme shortages of film stock. Only Fuji film was available, which had a high color sensitivity. But we wanted the film to have a monotone, mute color and a gray look. Hossein Jafarian asked me if I wanted to risk it and make the film that dark, and I said that that is exactly how I wanted it to be. I remember that due to the screening conditions in lots of cinemas across Iran the film looked too dark. Many reviews even wrote that the cinematography was terrible. But that year we were invited by Fuji to Japan, where the film received the award for best cinematography. They were shocked at how one could achieve such an aesthetic using Fuji film stock. I really saw the color and brilliant lighting of the film, watching it at the Lincoln Center in New York. Back in the day in Iran, we did not have the facilities for chemical color grading which other film industries had access to. These limitations did not just affect my films; all Iranian filmmakers were facing the same issue.

Back then, when a film was released, they would paint banners and hang them in the marquees of the cinemas. I had prepared the image I wanted painted for *Nargess*. I was away when the film opened, and when I came back it had already been in the cinema for a week. I went to Shahr-e Farang cinema in Tehran. When I saw the banner, I was shocked to see it depicted the profile of a beautiful girl and a beautiful boy on opposite sides, with a bunch of flowers and a hut in the middle and the name *Nargess* on top. With my glasses on, I began crying. A soldier guarding the building I was standing next to came and asked me if someone had stolen my purse. I said no, look at the cinema! He asked: What is it? I could not explain what had happened. There were no mobiles back then; I went and found a phone and called the distributor to ask what this was. Why did you not use what I gave you? I asked. He said: "Mrs Banietemad, you have made a black and white film and have chosen a dark-skinned actress (he was really against casting Atefeh Razavi because she did not have fair skin and blue eyes) and the pretty actress you have made ugly. We have to do something so the film can make a dime!" We had to deal with these kinds of attitudes and viewpoints, and this was still not the worst of it, because at least he had agreed to distribute the film. But I can say, even after all these years, that the look and cinematography of *Nargess* is still fascinating.

I always search to find the link or connection between the cinematography, set design, and mise-en-scène. Because all these aspects have to work together, along with the actors and characters, for the film to reach its ultimate visual structure. For example, in *Mainline*, we wanted to desaturate the colors. We kind of wanted the film to be in black and white, with only certain elements remaining in red and yellow colors. We tested several times to achieve this look. By then we made digital transfers and worked on the colors, but still the technology we had access to was not what it is today. We processed the tests outside of Iran, but thankfully, once we had found the look, we managed to complete the film in Iran. Studio Roshana was one of the pioneering studios that did this.

My first experience with digital editing and digital sound was on *The May Lady*. After the digital edit, the film was to be edited based on the digital track. We were working with several systems that were much more complex than those of today. Sometimes the numbers would not match on the negative with the digital transfers. I remember once we had to sit and manually go through every inch of the negative to find the matching numbers!

Although, in one way or another, all my works look at women and their situations from different angles, at no point did I ever resolve to always make films about women's issues. I believe there are cultural, civil, and economic issues in any society, and these affect men and women equally. But obviously when it comes to women, whose human rights have historically been denied, with only some societies acknowledging this in recent times—and especially in societies like Iran that are even further away from fulfilling this goal—I felt I had to speak out for their human and civil rights. Failing women's rights reflects fundamental injustice latent in a society. For this reason, due to my first-hand knowledge of life as a woman and my studies in this field, women's issues became a priority, but not the sole topic that I would limit myself to.

When I began to make feature films, I wanted to focus on women's issues, but receiving permission to shoot a script was very difficult back then. Today, there are ways to get around the restrictions a little, but not previously. None of the scripts I had written were given permits. My first script was called *Tooba*, which later turned into *Under the Skin of the City*. That is why I began with scripts that were written by Farid Mostafavi and Behnam Zarrinpour, which had already received permission to be filmed. I have collaborated with Farid Mostafavi on many of my other films as well. These scripts addressed the same concerns that I had: the inequalities in society. Although they were not female-centric stories, they did focus on topics that were among my most serious concerns, such as the issue of the big city, migration, and urbanization. I had already made the documentary *Tamarkoz* [*Centralization*, 1986] and done research on the subject of urbanization. *Off Limits* addresses, in a comic way, the issue of city expansion that not based on any proper planning. *Zard-e*

Ghanāri [*Canary Yellow*, 1989] and *Pul-e Khāreji* [*Foreign Currency*, 1989] both focus on the economic pressures of the middle classes. By the time I made *Nargess*, which I had written before making those films, the topic was a lot closer to me and my vision of society.

But I always say, regardless of the type of film I make, it is the topics that pick me, not the other way around. If a particular issue in society continues to occupy my thoughts, then that is the subject I am drawn to. For example, I made *Mainline* when the rate of addiction in society was particularly high; or I made *Gilāneh* [*Gilane*, 2005] to show the scars the war had left behind, scars that never really leave the affected society. I chose not to make any films about the war during the war, because its effect on society is perpetual and I wanted to portray that.

During the second round of Mohammad Khatami's presidential election I made the documentary *Ruzegār-e Ma* [*Our Times*, 2002]. At one point, I was accused of making films with expiry dates, and this judgment did not bother me at all. In fact, in each of my works I think I have been able to register the impact of the time in history beyond mere reporting. When I look back, I see what a strong record of every period my films have left behind. The effect of social conditions is evident in all my films. I always say that you cannot create a revolution with one work of art, but through works of art you can impact the culture of a society and change the social condition in the long run. It's like a drop of water falling on a huge rock. In the first instance, the drop seems unable to do anything to the rock, but over time it can create a huge crevice and give birth to transformation. That is why I think that if we look for the immediate impact of a film—mine or any other filmmakers'—we won't find anything. But the impact of an intellectual or political movement can be studied with the passage of time.

At times the relationship between my work and social issues is indirect. I employ cinematic language for increasing awareness. To give you an example, I began making *Mā Nimi az Jame'yat-e Irānim* [*We Are Half of Iran's Population*, 2009] when we were entering the second round of Ahmadinejad's presidential election. During his first presidential term, many serious and fundamental incidents with regard to the condition of women had taken place. Half of the voting population are women, so they would play a key role in the political destiny of society. These women had their own needs and requests, and their condition had worsened during the first four years of his presidency. Television was producing programs to address these issues, but female activists, non-governmental organizations, and women's organizations were not given any space to bring their concerns to the table. They had even shut down women's magazines. I thought cinema could be an outlet. Usually, right before every election, a semi-open environment is created where people from all walks of life can raise their concerns in public gatherings. I took advantage of this opportunity. Some amazing events occurred that had never happened and have not happened since: for example, the coalition of a whole spectrum of female activists with different ideologies was formed. This was a very significant moment in that, through coming together, they managed to raise their voice loud enough that it was heard. The film helped to gather all the different viewpoints together and deliver it to the people. The structure I chose for the film was experimental and participatory. Once the section with the women activists' requests was completed, I contacted each candidate's campaign and invited them to watch them and share their opinions, so that people could be in a position to decide how to vote. I created an equal condition for the four candidates who had begun their political campaigns. I knew the candidates might have been traveling from other provinces and would be extremely busy, so we planned to have the studio for forty-eight hours; that way they could come whenever they could manage. Three out of the four candidates (Mohsen Rezai, Mirhossein Mousavi, and Mehdi Karroubi) turned up, saw the film, and expressed their views and plans on camera.

If you ask me what I like or dislike about what has been written about my work, in fact I would say that I appreciate the interest. I know a lot is written about my films and how they are made and their standing in the world cinema, but to tell you the truth, what is more important to me is the social impact of my work. I'm not trying to feign modesty, but all the ceremonies, retrospectives, and celebrations associated with the film industry do not really appeal to me. I try to avoid the commemorations and retrospectives which have been organized for me. The only one that really humbled me was the invitation from Firuze Saber for a celebration at the *Bonyād-e Tose'e Kār Afārini-ye Zanān va Javānān* [The Entrepreneurship Development Foundation for Women and Youth]. In short, if your book addresses the social impact of my work, I would be so pleased.

Looking back at my professional life, I have always been in search of what would be most impactful. At times, the impact was best achieved by making documentaries; at other times by making feature films; and at times I just resorted to social activism. I always wanted to take advantage of my position as a filmmaker and expend this privilege in areas where it could help to make a change, not simply on the red carpet. For example, I spent three years making a film with the charity organization Zanjireh Omid, which helps to care for sick and underprivileged children in Iran. I knew the value of the work they were doing was worthy of the time I spent making the film, and by doing so I could help increase the support they received. I could probably have made two feature films in that time which would have had a wider international reach. But they would not have had the same impact.

People always ask me: when will you make your next film? And I reply that I am never without work. Work is not only when I make a feature film. I am always working in one way or another. I never accept commissions either, only the short film *Bārān va Bumi* [*Baran and the Native*, 1999], which became part of the feature film *Kish Stories*, was commissioned. I usually commission myself; apart from that film, every other film I have made, from one-minute to feature-length, has been a reflection of my own concerns at the time. I do spend a lot of time on my projects. When looking in from the outside, one could say that I might have been more successful, had I gone for another feature film instead. But for me, the definition of satisfaction is something else.

You asked me what I would like to achieve, or where I am headed next. I have always said that, for me, the route is as satisfying and enjoyable as the destination. I will not sacrifice the journey in order to reach the endpoint sooner. I live within the process and on the road. For this reason, I am not headed anywhere *per se*. Where I am at the moment has the feel and sense of documentaries, much more than fictional films. But I am also working on a story and, if I am happy with it, I may make it one day. What I care about right now is ensuring that I am making full use of what remains of my life to leave behind something worthy of preservation and something impactful, something that can make a change. I am not simply talking about a legacy for myself. Right now, I am working closely with some charities and non-governmental organizations, using my name and my connections as much as possible to try and help them in their endeavors.

NOTES

1. *Suvashun* is the acclaimed novel by the prominent writer Simin Daneshvar (b. Shiraz, 1921; d. Tehran, 2012), and the first novel in Persian written by a female author.
2. In order to study architecture in Iran, you have to take the mathematics route in high school, as opposed to natural sciences or humanities.

PART II

Aesthetics, Politics, and Narrative Structure

CHAPTER I

From Black Comedies to Social Realism: Rakhshan Banietemad's Early Feature Films

Farshad Zahedi

INTRODUCTION

Rakhshan Banietemad's œuvre strikingly encapsulates the complexity of women's cinema. If we survey the initial phase of her career in the 1980s, however, we note that the first three films she made did not deal directly with women as social subjects. Indeed, the emergence of Banietemad as an auteur of women's cinema was recognized only after the impact of her fourth feature film, *Nargess* (1992)—a film that resounded with historical feminist and socialist concerns. In light of this apparent transition, this chapter will pose the following question: why does Banietemad not portray women with the same socio-political commitment in her first three films as she does in the films she made after *Nargess*?

Iranian cinema of the 1980s was palpably affected by a period of political interstice. On the one hand, films were required to be ideologically in accordance with the new guidance overseen by the Ministry of Culture and Islamic Guidance (MCIG); on the other hand, they needed to entertain the masses. This controversial juxtaposition had its economic reasonings: the films made in the new, so-called "purified" Iranian cinema needed to fill the void that had been left by largely ceasing the massive import of popular foreign films—from Hollywood productions to Hong Kong martial arts films—had left behind. This is why, after a few years of uncertainty in late 1980s, social comedies such as *Ejāreh-neshinhā* (*The Tenants*, Dariush Mehrjui, 1986), and a number of successful war films that followed Hollywood-style narrative structure, such as *Oghābhā* (*The Eagles*, Samuel Khachikian, 1985), paved the way for the inception of a new model for popular genre films in Iranian cinema. This demand for new productions consequently smoothed the path into the industry for

Figure 1.1 Banietemad on the set of *Canary Yellow* (1989)

novice filmmakers. It was against this background that Rakhshan Banietemad found the opportunity to pursue filmmaking and went on to produce her first three feature films: *Khārej az Mahdudeh* (*Off Limits*, 1988), *Zard-e Ghanāri* (*Canary Yellow*, 1989; Figure 1.1), and *Pul-e khāreji* (*Foreign Currency*, 1989).

The transitional period in Iran from the mid-1980s until the early 1990s therefore witnessed opportunities for a new generation of filmmakers, in addition to some of the veteran filmmakers who had managed to reinitiate their careers. As Hamid Naficy argues: "the transformation from Pahlavi to Islamicate cinema was not rapid or unidirectional, but was impacted by major cultural and ideological shifts, contestations, negotiations and transformations" (2012a: 117). The irony of this historical period is that, as a result of a series of structural shifts to foster an ideological cinema according to the newly established religious values, women were given the space and the opportunity to participate fully in the film industry. It could even be argued that, in this period of refashioning of the governmental system of supervision and control of cinema, some of the masterpieces of Iranian cinema flourished.

With these paradoxical coincidences in mind, the next issue to be addressed in this chapter is how the first three films of Rakhshan Banietemad are key examples of auteurial negotiations within the systemic constraints imposed during this important transitional period of Iranian cinema. Although they are not generally considered to be examples of women's cinema, this chapter will also examine how the first feature films of Banietemad demonstrate the pivotal social concerns of the filmmaker in their plots—concerns that would be developed in her later films and perceived by many film critics and scholars as her signature trait. Furthermore, given that these three films have been broadly neglected by critics and scholars for not representing a Deleuzian minor cinema, this chapter will argue for their significance in Banietemad's œuvre. It will demonstrate to what extent these films constituted essential first negotiations with the new cinematic system, without which the next phase of her filmmaking would hardly have existed. In other words, the three films under scrutiny here can be considered as transitional as Iranian cinema itself in the late 1980s. This transition, in Banietemad's case, is materialized in her movement from films that encompass marginal social subjects, to films that focus on women as doubly marginal social subjects.

THE GOLDEN AGE OF IRANIAN CINEMA

As previously mentioned, a series of political decisions during the 1980s paved the way for the development of a new cinema in Iran. This new cinema grew from the very kernel of the paradoxical concept of Islamic cinema. Cinema at large and a purified system of filmmaking became an important issue for the Iranian government. This was to the extent that in 1984, for the first time in Iranian film history, the President, Prime Minister, Parliamentary Speaker, and Minister of Culture and Islamic Guidance unanimously expressed the importance of cinema for the interests of the Islamic Republic (Omid 2004: 218–31). Since 1983, cinema had been significantly harnessed as an apparatus for educating, informing, and entertaining people. In this regard, Iranian cinema borrowed anti-imperialist terminologies of Third Cinema to take it into the boundaries of an imaginary and not yet fully defined "Islamic cinema." Thus, the initial concept of the restitution of the film industry was born—one that was now protected economically and ideologically by the state. The first step of this "Islamized cinema" was forged at the same time as Ayatollah Khomeini entered Tehran, a few days before the victory of the Revolution in February 1979. In his speech, he spoke in favor of cinema as an educational tool, but against a cinema which corrupts youth (Naficy 1995: 4).

It was not an easy task to achieve this desired educational cinema, however. The first years after the Revolution were marked by a limited practice of filmmaking and an erratic system of cinematic supervision. By the mid-1980s, this system was deemed inefficient. The blatant ideological propaganda films with a didactic agenda resulted largely in financial failure; the response of the box office to this type of national film was much less favorable than had been anticipated. As a consequence, film production stopped being attractive for private investors. With the number of film producers gradually decreasing, the number of national productions followed suit.

At the same time, another issue that the new Iranian cinematic authorities were confronted with was the fact that Hollywood productions—which never completely disappeared from Iranian screens—were overwhelmingly more popular than the so-called *sinema-ye enghelabi* (revolutionary national cinema) (Omid 2004: 366–7). Moreover, the increasing but illegal networks of VCRs and videotapes—particularly distributing recent Hollywood films—were considered a great cultural evasion, the eradication of which could not be achieved through a simple ban. The industry was in dire need of a much more functional solution (Zeydabadi-Nejad 2016). The prohibition of video clubs was never a realistic solution since the great demand for foreign films generated an uncontrollable urban black market of videotape exchange. The tangible influence of cinema on the Iranian middle class forced the Iranian authorities toward serious consideration of filmmaking as an entertainment industry. In this regard, the need for structural decisions about cinema to curb the influence of foreign films created an opportune space for both genre and arthouse films to flourish. Gradually, within the margins of this system of production and protection, there arose an arguably independent cinema, or a cinema of resistance, among which a promising emergence of women's cinema was to be observed (Zeydabadi-Nejad 2011: 104–5).

According to Jamal Omid (2004: 46), in 1981 the General Department of Cinematic Affairs (GDCA) in the MCIG was established to be an official entity for supporting and supervising all filmic activities in the Islamic Republic of Iran (IRI). Many historians argue that this coincided with the circumstances that took the film industry in post-revolutionary Iran into the governmental arena. In 1983, new Prime Minister Mir Hossein Moussavi appointed Mohammad Khatami as Minister of the MCIG (Omid 2004; Naficy 2012a, 2012b; Atwood 2016). In the Khatami-led MCIG, Fakhreddin Anvar was appointed as a new Deputy Minister for leading the GDCA (Anvar 2014: 54). Soon after, the Farabi Cinema Foundation (FCF) was created as a para-governmental organism for executing ministerial decisions concerning the film industry. Mohammad Beheshti, the nephew of an influential revolutionary cleric, was appointed to oversee the organization. Hamid Naficy has reflected on the history of the friendships within this group and their film and theatre activities since the late 1970s, arguing that they were following the ideal of revolutionary ideology introduced by Ali Shariati (Naficy 2012a: 121–7). All (with the exception of Khatami) were architects educated during the 1970s within the ideological framework of Shariati's Islamic nativism.

What this new cinematic group encountered was a devastated industry in terms of production and exhibition. They faced tenuous political decisions concerning the purification of the film industry and cinematic screens from what were considered to be the corrupted films of the Pahlavi era. In addition, they had to deal with the effects of a total end to international film imports and find new methods of reorganizing the hitherto unpredictable system of censorship. From 1979 until 1983, there was no clear official position on cinema: on the one hand, cinema was rejected for its capacity to show obscenities; on the other hand, cinema was perceived as an *arma più forte*, a weapon for the new IRI authorities. Whilst the use of cinema as an educational device was emphasized, there was no clear idea of how it could also be made entertaining and attractive for audiences. The noticeable decline in the number of films produced during this period points to the existence of a fundamental crisis in Iranian cinema. The situation was naturally further complicated by the impact of the Iran–Iraq War (1980–8). The industry faced wide-scale shortages of raw materials and cinematic supplies. In this volatile climate and on the ruins of the industry, this new group—in particular the GDCA and the FCF—were tasked with creating a new model of production, distribution, and exhibition.

By early 1984, after months of continuous meetings, the new IRI's cinematic authorities had devised an urgent program for reanimating Iranian cinema. Among its most important goals, the need for a growing national film production in order to achieve cultural and material independence from foreign films was underscored (Omid 2004: 217). They similarly highlighted the pressing need for the creation of a so-called "clean" environment for production and for the film industry in general. In the official literature of this period, the terms "cleansing" and "purification," borrowed from Shi'a terminology, are abundant. This "clean" environment was to be applied both in front of and behind the camera, connoting the practice of modesty in particular with regard to contact between men and women. The ideological lines were also defined thus: "the films must show the world the Iranian quest for justice [and at the same time] they have to produce healthy attractions for the audience in order to offer a human spiritual transcendence" (cited by Omid 2004: 217). The political backdrop of Iran in 1983 and 1984 translated into different governmental definitions of a national film industry and subsequent promises of centralized policies. In this regard, Mir Hossein Moussavi's wartime policies, include rationing of the public's basic necessities, were extended to film production, supplying filmmakers with only the raw materials within a broader framework of *hemāyat* (support), *hedāyat* (guidance), and *nezārat* (supervision) (Omid 2004; Naficy 2012a, 2012b; Zeydabadi-Nejad 2011; Atwood 2016). In summary, the experience of Soviet-style cinematic policies was implemented in Iran in the 1980s. However, substantial differences between these two public service-based cinemas are to be observed and, as will be argued, the issue of women was at the forefront.

In 1984, Mohammad Beheshti, the first director of the FCF, identified the lack of women's presence in cinema as a matter which required the attention of the new authorities. This was among an extensive list of issues transpiring from his diagnosis of national cinema and suggestions to increase the widespread appeal of films. In terms of the industry, Beheshti proposed that a quality cinema could be achieved through not only systematically supporting filmmakers and producers, but also by encouraging auteur filmmakers to experiment. This would also mean producing films which followed a classical narrative structure and employed star actors. For Beheshti, film genres such as action, thriller, melodrama, and comedy, in addition to nostalgic historical films, were the key to ending the film production deadlock. On the particular topic of women, he asserted:

> [We should] find a solution for the presence of women in the cinema, not only due to their desirability in terms of gender diversity but also by taking into consideration the fact that a story will only be complete and expressed adequately, when there are possibilities for the inclusion of women, as human beings, not as a [mere] sexual object. (Beheshti 1984, cited by Omid 2004: 231)

The IRI's new policy of filmmaking amounted to some important changes: the veteran directors of the New Iranian cinema of the 1970s, such as Bahram Beyzaie, Masud Kimiai, and Dariush Mehrjui, among others, again found opportunities to make films and, additionally, a space for the emergence of new directors had been created. As a consequence of the aforementioned focus on both commercial genre films and auteur art films, there gradually emerged more possibilities for the presence of women on both sides of the camera, as expressed by Naficy: "women have had fewer problems attending film schools and working behind cameras as film directors" (Naficy 1995: 551). These changes affected the position of female actors in a similar way: whilst the main protagonists of Iranian cinema of the early 1980s were largely middle-aged males such as Ali Nasirian, Ezattollah Entezami, and Mohammad Ali Keshavarz (Sadr 2006: 223), towards the end of this decade women's representation on screen went from background noise to center stage (Naficy 1995: 550).

Economic factors are also crucial for understanding this atmosphere of transformation and adaptation. An array of non-official manifestos about ideal Islamic cinema pointed finally to the need for economic support through the creation of cooperative structures of production. Regulation of censorship policies was also encouraged as a deterrent to erratic decision-making and as an offer of certainty to private producers. As Naficy aptly concludes, the political decisions from 1984 that pushed Iranian cinema toward a new stage of production

> steadily encouraged local production and reduced destructive competition from imports. Municipal taxes on local films were reduced; long-term bank loans were made available; a film-rating system to encourage quality films was instituted; foreign exchange funds for importing equipment and supplies were allocated; and a social security system for film workers was implemented. Since this point, many Iranian films

have been entered in, and received high praise from, international film festivals. (1995: 550)

As a consequence of this regime of support and supervision, since the mid-1980s the number of national productions has gradually increased (Saberi 2003). As mentioned before, some veteran auteurs found opportunities for directing new feature films. The war film genre known as *sinema-ye defa' moghaddas* (sacred defense films), and *komedi ejtema'i* (social comedies), took over Iranian screens. This apparently controversial auteurial commercial trend responded to the psychological needs of wartime and to socio-economic instability. The re-emergence of social comedies was a phenomenon epitomized in the great success of *Tenants* in 1987. This slapstick comedy was made by a member of New Iranian cinema, Dariush Mehrjui, who, having emigrated to France after the Revolution, returned to Iran after obtaining permission for filmmaking and restarted his career. The film not only broke the box-office record in Iranian cinema; it also illuminated the new possibilities for competing with the overwhelming popularity of foreign films.

RAKHSHAN BANIETEMAD: FROM TV TO CINEMA

It is within this lively context that we first observe Rakhshan Banietemad entering the filmmaking arena. As it stands today, her first feature film, *Off Limits*, constitutes a striking example of both this transitory period in Iranian film history, and the filmmaker's personal preoccupations with various social realities. Far from being an example of women's cinema in terms of representability, it portrays downtrodden lives within a comedic framework and without crossing any ideological red lines. The film is especially significant as a fulfilment of a unique opportunity for a young woman willing to make films in the Iran of the 1980s: it follows the official ideology of support for the dispossessed and lower classes, yet avoids a focus on women from a dramatic or technical perspective.

The film narrates the story of a middle-aged man's bureaucratic burden a few years before the Revolution. He suffers from being part of the invisible lower classes, forgotten by Pahlavi representational policies. His home is allegorically in a zone that is not represented by official urban maps; that is, the entire neighborhood in which he just purchased a house has been erased from the maps because of a technical error on the part of the ministerial cartographers. This renders his house "non-existent"—and the same happens to the man himself as a social subject, his family as a social entity, and finally the region itself as a space for a certain social class. Like many Iranian films since the mid-1980s, *Off Limits* sees a return to the urban margins to pursue the proclaimed quest for social justice and an urgent need for social reconstruction within the confines of comedy and dark humor.

This tendency in Banietemad's works to return to the marginalized was not formed *ex nihilo*. Although it was her first feature film, *Off Limits* was not her first attempt to portray the living conditions of the lower class. Her experience of making social documentaries during the years she spent working for Iranian National TV (after the Revolution, Islamic Republic of Iran Broadcasting, IRIB) indicates that this trend most likely originated as a result of these first professional encounters with social realities. As she recounts about her time in television, she started working as a script supervisor for different departments like TV-Theater or the Department for Children and Adolescents, but soon after the Revolution was moved to the Department of Workers and finally, in 1980, to the Department of Economy. In her final years of working as a film director in IRIB, she considered the Department of Economy an ideal space to begin working "seriously" on making documentaries. Banietemad points to an environment in which cinema was seen as a "social responsibility" and film as a "social commitment" for filmmakers and other TV crew during those fresh years of the "revolutionary" era (Banietemad 2020). In her last documentary for IRIB, *Tamarkoz* (*Centralization*, 1986), Tehran appears as the central matter of concern: a megacity that attracts emigration but does not guarantee equal opportunity, in terms of health and education, to its massive and dramatically increasing population. She underscores that this documentary's script was written by Farid Mostafavi, who became her main collaborator for her first three feature films.

In 1987, Rakhshan Banietemad left the TV industry because of—as she puts it—some serious problems with new policies introduced at IRIB, which constrained her even more and took away her creative freedom (Banietemad 2020). Her decision to leave TV coincided with the emergence of the previously discussed new Iranian film production policies which offered a space for aspiring filmmakers. However, her path to filmmaking had been gradual. Her collaboration in some film projects since 1980, particularly during her last years working at the IRIB, was crucial for her entry to the industry as a film director in 1987. Her name had appeared on celebrated films of the 1980s such as *Aftab Neshinha* (*Sun Dwellers*, Mehdi Sabbaghzadeh, 1980), *Golhaye Davoodi* (*Chrysanthemums*, Rasul Sadralemi, 1985), and *Tanoureh-ye Deev* (*Beast's Chimney*, Kianoush Ayari, 1986), as script supervisor and later as programmer and assistant director. Ayari's film, as Banietemad observes, was a masterclass that she attended just before her first experience of directing a feature film (Banietemad 2020). In 1987, she made *Off Limits*, a project produced by Goruh-e Ta'āvoni-ye Filmsāzān (Filmmaking Cooperative Group) and Bonyād-e Mostaz'afān (Foundation of the Oppressed). As well as being based on a script written by Banietemad's colleague and collaborator at IRIB, Farid Mostafavi, the project included another familiar name for Banietemad: her husband, Jahangir Kosari, as assistant director.

Banietemad's first film received two types of reactions from Iranian critics and scholars. The first group dismissed the film by measuring it against certain women's cinema criteria that her later films would subscribe to: films made by women, concerning women's issues. The second group framed the film within its genre structure, its narrative, its aesthetic functionality, and its capacity to reflect social reality (Omid 2004: 648–52). The film received a B grade for distribution in the GDCA rating system. This meant distribution to a wide network of cinemas, in which the film met with outstanding box-office success, rendering it the twelfth highest-grossing film of Iranian cinema in 1988 (Annual 1988). The most important reason behind this success was, according to some critics, its being a social comedy featuring beloved actor Mehdi Hashemi, the protagonist of the very popular TV series *Afsaneh Soltan va Shaban* (*The Legend of the Sultan and the Shepherd*, Dariush Farhang, 1984), in the lead role. The cinematography, by Alireza Zarrindast, was also praised and added to the film's aesthetic quality (Aghighi 2016: 63–5). Banietemad herself received contradictory responses: some saw her as a promising and pioneering filmmaker, and some—particularly in the more conservative press—discouraged her from continuing her career in film (Omid 2004: 647–52).

Mr Halimi, the protagonist of the film, is a simple, honest, and disciplined civil servant. Along with his wife, he has recently moved to a new house in a neighborhood on the city's periphery. On the first night, they are shocked to find a thief sleeping in their new home. Mr Halimi detains the thief and his wife cries out for help. Some neighbors come along, but no one is surprised, and the thief behaves as if nothing has happened. When the thief is brought to the police station, they find out that their neighborhood is outside urban police control limits and, worse still, that the entire neighborhood is not registered on any official map. The bureaucratic labyrinth makes its re-registration impossible. These journeys of Mr Halimi with the thief turn from comedic to more absurdist territory. The thief tags along from one office to another, obeying Mr Halimi's orders.

The novelty of the film can be clearly perceived in its portraits of masculinity. The proto-*jahel* figure of the thief, evincing the dominant masculine characteristics of the pre-revolutionary "tough guy," is deconstructed here. Although he apparently maintains the traditional notions of maleness in being "good, brave, loyal and benevolent" (Gerami 2003: 258), he is also a criminal, who produces a deep sense of unsafety in the urban space and makes others suffer. Behind the comical surface of this character, one can find a reflection of cultural and even political privileges that are granted to this masculine figure, which translate into tragedies that go unpunished by social justice. The thief considers his criminal activities as ordinary and even necessary.

Mr Halimi, on the other hand, can be considered a depiction of the "other men": the third male category of Shahin Gerami's study of post-revolutionary social prototypes of masculinity (Gerami 2003). He is a simple *karmand* (civil servant), whose attitude lingers at the margins of the standardized homosocial male culture. At the beginning, the audience finds him in the house, doing some domestic chores with his wife. His role as protector of the family is not particularly emphasized. He finally resists the authorities and the thief, not through being physically powerful, but through being a resilient, honest, and disciplined man who respects social commitment and has a personal sense of duty. He is endowed with an arguably subversive sense of non-normative masculinity that conveys visible contrasts with the hypermasculine male figures of the Iranian propaganda films of the late 1980s.

Neither is the film completely lacking in female representation. Although it is not highlighted, in the last sequence, Mr Halimi's wife is crucial in mobilizing the entire neighborhood to confront the thieves. Altogether, men and women, they cooperate to construct a protective wall. They also take advantage of their situation of being, officially and paradoxically, outlaws "out-maps" to take justice into their own hands. They arrest the thieves and begin to educate them. The very final scene of the film is particularly memorable, in which a woman is teaching a group of thieves the alphabet. As Saeed Aghighi argues:

> the journey of the main character is designed on this step-by-step quest for a caricaturized bitter reality, which nevertheless … [finally] becomes an idealized sweet caricature. In this transformation, the film achieves an adequate ending in accordance with the cliché of national cinema's narratives. (2016: 38)

Banietemad's subsequent feature film, *Canary Yellow*, followed a similar pattern. Bahman Zarrinpour's script—re-edited and adapted by Banietemad and Farid Mostafavi—portrays the conflict between rural émigrés and the city within a black comedy framework and shows the evident influence of neorealism. Outstanding documentary-type shots depict Tehran as a place of social conflict. The dreams of Nasrollah, an energetic and cheerful shoemaker's assistant, turn into a nightmare when he discovers that he is the victim of fraud. The land that he bought with his savings to start his own farm had already been sold to another person; meanwhile, the fraudster has escaped abroad. There is no other option for him than to relocate to Tehran with his wife, Golab, to begin a new life. But in Tehran, this provincial simpleton once again becomes ensnared by a new ruse. His brother-in-law offers him the opportunity to purchase a car and work as a taxi driver. However, immediately after this transaction, the car is stolen. Nasrollah begins desperately seeking the car throughout the city. His journey ends up in the downtrodden margins of the city, where again he suffers deception and fraud. He finally realizes that the car theft has been one huge set-up by his brother-in-law: the car had been sold to different victims and stolen several times, all of whom were fresh émigrés like him. Finally, they all confront the brother-in-law in a slapstick comedic scene. Nasrollah and Golab return home to the provinces, and he decides once again to restart his interrupted career as shoemaker.

Canary Yellow depicts Tehran from two different angles and establishes a dual relationship with the city. On the one hand, some urban locations are framed as the background to a particular social landscape; on the other hand, interior spaces, such as houses and stores, are depicted without clear references to the actual city. As Hamid Naficy argues, this hybrid relation shows another instance of experimentation by Iranian auteurs with "neorealism's philosophic and stylistic tenets" (2012c: 233). However, in *Canary Yellow*, the poetic and ethical commitments of neorealism, with the reality of quotidian life narrated in sober tones, is nuanced with a sense of humor. The reality here is nothing but a natural stage on which a tragicomedy of human relations takes place. Naficy considers a systemic hybridity to be the result of the application of new governmental policies in Iranian cinema during the 1980s to foster and control film production: "films were produced according to the logic not only of the hybrid production mode (consisting of public and private sector funding and semi-industrialized and artisanal practices) but also of a hybrid textual mode consisting of realist and counter-realist narrative strategies" (2012c: 233).

The social realism of Rakhshan Banietemad demonstrates this hybridity by merging documentary and genre film conventions: *Canary Yellow* follows the pattern set in *Off Limits* by picturing the real city alongside fictional characters and situations. This hybridity should be considered a strategy for negotiating the harsh ideological and economical constraints of the film industry. That is to say, the humor here is a necessary addition to the proto-documentary realist pictures, in order to make the auteurs' reading of reality tolerable for both the systemic eye of censorship and the audience itself. Although this strategy might be considered by some critics as "conservative," the positive audience response to the film nonetheless designated it a success that could secure a future for Banietemad as an emerging film director (Omid 2004). *Canary Yellow* also received a B grade for distribution and was scheduled for the *Nowruz*—Iranian new year—program in cinemas. It overtook *Off Limits* in terms of box-office gross and stood as the eighth highest-grossing film of 1989 (Annual 1989).

It could perhaps be argued that, due to this efficient negotiation strategy, Banietemad's first three films have avoided examination by critics and scholars as serious pieces of art with a clear authorial signature. A new historical reading of these preliminary films, however, shows to what extent they aesthetically encompass the director's concerns with social realities, and particularly with Tehran as a place of social conflict.

Canary Yellow also showed a correspondence with *Off Limits* in its gender portrayal. Although the main protagonist—a male character—bears the burden of moral service, resiliently triumphing over greed and vice (Naficy 2012b: 158), his character, in a similar way to the protagonist of *Off Limits*, is not tainted by stereotypical homosocial behaviors. In this regard, as Naficy highlights, Banietemad's film evinces a second phase concerning representations of women. One particular example is the mother-in-law of Nasrollah, who is "strong, mature and level-headed, ruling through the force of her personality and teaching the men who are naïve, unscrupulous or weak" (Naficy 2012b: 158). Golab and her sister are also given a voice and play a positive role in encouraging their husbands to be civilized and resilient. Both crucially remind the men of their family commitments and ethical responsibilities.

Foreign Currency, Banietemad's next feature film, marks the end of the trilogy of "simple men and the city" (Aghighi 2016: 39). Dariush Moaddabian and Farid Mostafavi's script depicts the economic burden of a civil servant called Olfat, and his dreams and endeavors to find a way out from his existential and family crisis. He accidentally stumbles across a bag full of American dollars in the middle of the black market for foreign currency exchange in the center of Tehran. Olfat's stroke of luck, however, transitions into a miserable ordeal when he finds himself unable to exchange the dollars on the illegal market. Finally, he loses the money in a similar way to how he found it: in the street, in the middle of a crowd negotiating the price of foreign currencies when the police suddenly arrive and the ensuing chaos provokes a stampede. Despair sends him into madness, and he is finally sectioned in a psychiatric hospital.

Foreign Currency captures the essence of the Iran of the 1980s: the wartime and rationing policies; the black market; a weakened middle class who witness their income being gradually devalued in a harsh economic crisis. Banietemad's camera again tries to register pieces of historical reality as the background to the character's attempt to find a safe place in the midst of the chaos. However, the documentary style of *Foreign Currency* is much more marked, in a way which casts the city as a central character. Olfat repeatedly embarks on his erratic journeys into the manic city to resolve his problems, yet there is no possible way to exist for a man like him, who—in a similar fashion to the two previous films' main characters—has a great sense of morality and social responsibility. The hidden part of the city, the place of dominant speculative economy, causes him deep confusion and eventually drives him to insanity. For Saeed Aghighi, these dominant proto-documentary scenes in the film—shot broadly with telephoto lenses—become a turning point in Banietemad's career, since they make the film less dramatized than previous works, and at the same time transport the storytelling technique much closer to that of Persian narrative traditions (2016: 39). As to this return-to-the-vernacular trend mentioned by Aghighi, the social documentary shooting techniques and the neorealist aesthetics of the film deserve consideration. However, *Foreign Currency*, with its plain and circular story, and perhaps because of what was mentioned above regarding its lack of dramatic demarcations, failed at the box office. Although it also received a B grade for distribution, it grossed only around a half the amount of *Canary Yellow* and *Off Limits* (Omid 2004: 1085). In Aghighi's terms, Banietemad would gradually abandon the fictional comic scenarios to put her stamp on a certain social realism in her next works (2016: 80–1).

CONCLUSIONS: TOWARD PORTRAYING WOMEN

Banietemad points to this first phase of her cinematic career as the only chance she had for filmmaking:

> During the TV years I had written some scripts, none of which were approved [by the GDCA]. Among those texts was a piece called *Tooba*, which was the result of my long-term research on the situation of women workers, and which I had written with Farid Mostafavi. It was about a woman called Tooba who works in a textile factory. [Fourteen] years later I found the chance to make a film based on this script. It was revised four times meanwhile and finally was entitled *Zir-e Pust-e Shahr* [*Under the Skin of the City*, 2001] . . . *Tooba* might have been my first feature film, but it did not receive the production permit. Then Farid Mostafavi proposed making his already approved script, *Off Limits*. Although I never imagined making a comedy, the social aspect of the text was attractive—particularly that of how an ethically responsible person could become a victim of a chaotic social system. (Banietemad 2016a: 18)

By the time Banietemad encountered the failure of *Foreign Currency* at the box office, some important changes had taken place in the Iranian political sphere, as well as in the GDCA. The most important event was the end of the devastating eight-year Iran–Iraq War in 1988. A new era of Iranian history was initiated, and Iranian cinema would react to these historical circumstances. Rakhshan Banietemad calls those initial transitional years of the post-war era "the golden years of Iranian cinema," particularly because of the establishment of new conditions for the control and censoring of film productions. According to her, certain changes in the supervision system were announced: "if a film was qualified with high grades for distribution, the director of said film needed only three other filmmakers whose films had already been highly rated to approve the script for their next film project" (Banietemad 2016: 20). Thanks to this stipulation, *Nargess*, a pioneering work of Iranian women's cinema, received a production license in 1991 and met with positive receptions, both in festivals and at cinema screenings.

The emergence of women's cinema in the 1990s was a new phenomenon in Iranian cinema. An extensive historical process of female presence, both behind and in front of the cameras, finally resulted in the fact that, just a few years after the 1980s, more women filmmakers were operating than in any previous decades (Naficy 1995: 550). Maryam Ghorbankarimi considers *Nargess* as a turning point in this process: a film that put the name of Banietemad, and consequently Iranian women's cinema, on the world film map (2012: 11). The reason for this proliferation of women filmmakers can be found in factors such as demographic and educational evolutions; the establishment of the previously mentioned pseudo-national film industry during the 1980s with its policies of support, guidance, and supervision; and finally in the universal trends of global women's cinema (Ghorbankarimi 2015). These factors broadly responded to a historical need for the emergence of a new Iranian national cinema that was officially measured by auteurial qualities. The increasing number of films and governmental economic support of so-called "qualified" films promised the emergence of new arthouse—and ideologically supervised—films. In this complex atmosphere of film production and consumption there emerged a "unique and unexpected . . . significant and signifying role of women both behind and in front of the camera" (Naficy 2000: 560). Women filmmakers gradually found the medium of cinema to be a perfect space to manifest their concerns. As the case of Rakhshan Banietemad shows, making films that represent women was not an easy task until the early 1990s, when the new socio-political circumstances of the post-war period made it possible.

Nargess drew widespread attention to Banietemad as a film auteur. Some critics and scholars deem the film a product of filmmaking experiences that have gradually matured for reflection on women's social issues, alongside an outstanding use of realist techniques. In this regard, Hamid Dabashi's analysis is significant when he compares Banietemad's aesthetic strategies for approaching social realities with those of Kiarostami and Makhmalbaf. The specific style of Banietemad, for Dabashi, is "of an entirely different sort . . . She is not trying to tease any virtuality out of reality. She wants to overemphasize its actuality" (2001: 223). Dabashi considers that this emphasis on actuality should be seen in the light of the auteur's preoccupation with societal peripheral marginalities "to locate the centre and reveal its territoriality, and the fact that we have deliberately opted to live and locate it as the territory of our moral imagination" (Dabashi 2001: 226).

In *Nargess*, women as the doubly marginal subjects displace the male main characters of the previous three films. Shahla Lahiji observes in *Nargess* a sign of an auteur at her "climax of maturity," after three feature films where "there were no traces of the femininity of filmmaker" (2012: 191–2). Nevertheless, a close examination of these three films, in comparison to *Nargess*, shows us that there is enough evidence to demonstrate the existence of a subtle feminine resistance to Hamid Dabashi's "metaphysical violence of the culture" (2001: 234). Although all three plots have male protagonists, this overly masculine representation is subtly subversive. The male characters do not adhere to clichés of patriarchal figures as the head of a politically and culturally constituted family. The relationships between men and women in the three films are not defined by stereotypical hierarchies of power. The weakened masculine authorities as the protectors of the family—stoked by a highly unstable and inflationary economy—finally require both the emotional and the logical support of their wives to overcome their existential and even schizophrenic impasses. This portrait of masculinity could arguably be understood as the counterpart of the hypermasculine male depictions in both genre and propaganda films throughout Iranian film history. Although in Banietemad's first feature films women are not cast in leading roles, and are portrayed as traditional female subjects within the confines of their homes, they are socially active subjects—within ideologically permitted limits—and are, without a doubt, psychologically stronger than their husbands. In short, it was simply a matter of time before Banietemad brought a powerful female performance out of the background and into the foreground. This was not just a personal endeavor. It required structural changes. In the context of the slight openness surrounding censorship during the 1990s, Banietemad was in the right place at the right time to become the flagbearer for a significant shift in Iranian cinema in terms of women's self-representability. This opportunity, coupled with her own resistance, efficiency, and resilience, enabled Banietemad to negotiate strategies by which, after making her first few feature films, she could successively turn Iranian filmmaking into more of a female-centric art than ever before.

CHAPTER 2

Under the Skin of Society: Rakhshan Banietemad's Social History of Post-revolutionary Iran

Matthias Wittmann

> True history is always contemporary history.
> Benedetto Croce

WHO DO YOU SHOW THESE FILMS TO ANYWAY?

Let me begin with an ending: Rakhshan Banietemad's film *Zir-e Pust-e Shahr* (*Under the Skin of the City*; Figure 2.1), which was released in 2001 to wide

Figure 2.1 *Under the Skin of the City* (2001)

acclaim from audiences and critics, ends with a resistance speech act by Tooba (Golab Adineh), the blue-collar worker from south Tehran who had already appeared in Banietemad's film *Bānu-ye Ordibehesht* (*The May Lady*, 1998) and would appear again in *Ghesseh-hā* (*Tales*, 2014). Tooba's final statement is set against the backdrop of the parliamentary elections in the year 2000, three years after the presidential vote that saw the unexpected victory of Mohammad Khatami and the Reform movement. This movement was also called, with reference to the date of Khatami's election, the Second Khordad movement—a movement that sought to reformulate the political rhetoric and cover the harsh realities with varnished terms like *jāme'eh-ye madani* (civil society) and *goftegu-ye tamaddon-hā* (dialogue amongst civilizations). When the semi-diegetic[1] film crew asks Tooba about her voting motivation and her message to the public, Tooba looks to the camera and conveys her political manifesto:

> Message? What message, sir? There was a time when we complained but you said we were fighting a war. It was the truth, so we accepted it. After the war, you asked us for patience because the country was in ruins, so once again, we put up with it all . . . Now there is someone who wants to save us, so I'm here to vote . . .

After being interrupted by the reporter due to technical problems ("Please start all over again!"), Tooba delivers a final statement:

> Just forget about it! I just lost my house, my son ran away, and people are filming all the time. I wish someone would come and film what's going on right here. Right here! Who do you show these films to anyway [In Film-hā ro beh ki Neshun Midin?]?

Hence it is Tooba who has the last word in the film, and her statement, which actually refers to *To Whom Do You Show These Films?*, a documentary made by Banietemad in 1992, interrogates the authority of the documentary medium and its alleged ability to capture human suffering whilst reaching wide audiences. Although complicating the distinction between documentary and narrative mode, since the camera that has created her diegetic reality suddenly turns out to be the reporters' perspective, Tooba also brings out her own notion of cinematic realism: "I wish someone would come and film what is going on right here," she says, pointing to her heart and, thereby, to a certain tension in the history of Iranian cinema—a tension between an epistemological and an aesthetic conception of realism that Iranian film theorist and critic Mazyar Eslami captures accurately:

> We can say that the conception of Iranian cinema of realism has been an epistemological and not an aesthetic one; which means that film is

considered by the Iranian people as a medium to convey a social message, and this medium must be an honest, bold reflection of reality. Reality for them is an objective constituent, a unified reality without any void, gaps or subjective distortions. This conception of realism has no similarities with notions of realism as an aesthetic form reflected by film theorists from Kracauer and Bazin to Bordwell and Deleuze. (Eslami 2017: n.p.)

The demand for a realism that reflects sentiments and social issues like a polished mirror—this is precisely what is expressed by Tooba. Furthermore, her final contentious question—"Who do you show these films to anyway?"—seems to echo some crucial demands we can find in the manifestos of Third Cinema and *cinéma vérité*, especially with respect to the role of the observer and the development of a cinema that is based on collaboration, participation, and what Jean Rouch would have called "shared ciné-anthropology." "For whom, and why, do I take the camera among mankind?" is the question that Jean Rouch raises in *The Camera and Man: Studies in the Anthropology of Visual Communication* (1974; *La Caméra et les hommes: Pour une anthropologie visuelle*) in order to formulate and demand a new relationship between "camera and men," based on techniques like "feedback" and "audiovisual reciprocity":

Finally, then, the observer has left the ivory tower; his camera, tape recorder, and projector have driven him, by a strange road of initiation, to the heart of knowledge itself. And for the first time, the work is judged not by a thesis committee but by the very people the anthropologist went out to observe. This extraordinary technique of "feedback" (which I would translate as "audiovisual reciprocity") has certainly not yet revealed all of its possibilities. But already, thanks to it, the anthropologist has ceased to be a sort of entomologist observing others as if they were insects (thus putting them down) and has become a stimulator of mutual awareness (hence dignity) . . . But at the same time, it is obviously absurd to condemn ethnographic film to such a closed information circuit. That is why my response to the question "For whom, and why?" is "For everyone, for the largest viewing public possible." (Rouch 2003: 44)

Similarly to Rouch, who sought to unshackle the "closed information circuit", Banietemad also makes films with a commitment to a certain closeness to the people: "I want to see the effect of my films on people both at the Enghelab Square cinema (Iran's largest cinema in Tehran) and in the smallest town" (Banietemad 2016b: 137). Social realism, according to Banietemad, becomes a question of effect: a form "that is influenced by, whilst at the same time consciously influencing reality" (Brecht 1990: 356, author's translation). One could also connect Banietemad's longing for contact and exchange with the people to the *Sinamāye Azad* (Free Cinema) movement during the early 1970s: "The young filmmakers of Free Cinema [for example, Kianoush Ayyari] wanted to remove all the barriers that distanced the masses from the cinema" (Najd-Ahmadi 2018).

Consequently, Banietemad not only reactivates a "pre-revolution ethnographic filmmaking," which reacts to the "rapid modernization and the resulting population displacements and psychic and social restructuring" (Naficy 2013: 114), but also recovers the traces of a movement towards a Third Cinema (Solanas and Getino 1970–1): a Third Cinema that has not been hijacked, monopolized, and sedated by "state-controlled postcolonial cinema" (Atwood 2016: 11), but one that keeps the revolutionary fervor alive by reflecting the post-revolutionary disappointments. This is undertaken by reassembling elements that are able to show, firstly, how the people are still missing or, rather, missing once again (Deleuze 1989: 215), and secondly, how their voices are suppressed through officially fabricated success stories of revolution and *sinemā-ye defā'-ye* moqaddas (sacred defense) and, above all, by totalizing categories like *mustaz'afin*: "the term "mustaz'afin" entered Khomeini's discourse only during the height of the Revolution, when he used it merely to repudiate the communists and attempted to offer an alternative (Islamic) and non-communist conceptualization of the poor" (Bayat 1997: 43).

If enlightenment, according to Michel Foucault, is an ethos, "in which the critique of what we are is at one and the same time the historical analysis of the limits that are imposed on us and an experiment with the possibility of going beyond them" (Foucault 1984: 32–50), then Banietemad's socio-critical attempts to question the categories and promises of propaganda can certainly be called an ongoing project of enlightenment. Such a project is not linear; it unfolds within a network of power relations and (counter-)agencies. Whilst the clergy regarded Muslims as social agents and labor as a manifestation of God, casting and engulfing the *tabaghe ye kargar* (working class) under the umbrella of *mustaz'afin*, Banietemad reframes this narrative through a consistent materialist view of claims for justice that went unheard.

EMPTY PROMISES AND COUNTER-MEMORIES

Instead of presenting a third way between east and west, and communism and capitalism, like Khomeini did, Banietemad revitalizes a third cinema between state-supported mainstream genre (like sacred defense cinema) and the symbolism of art movies, retracing the lives of ordinary people missing from the official politics of representation and uncovering their suppressed voices, often silenced by power effects and epistemic oppression. At the same time, her films try to carve out how these ordinary people organize themselves in communities, networks, and grassroots movements. She explores "the great possibility of constructing a 'liberated personality' with each people as the starting point, in a word—the decolonization of culture," as advocated by Octavio Getino and Fernando Solanas (1970–1: 3). In so doing, Banietemad's films not only expose the emptiness of the revolutionary semiotics established by the ideological architects of the Islamic Republic of Iran, but also destabilize stereotypes coming from outside Iran, especially the image of fatalistic Muslim masses, passive poor people, and disoriented marginals.

Banietemad's social history, especially of *Jonub-e shahr* (southern Tehran), is congruent with the "slums of hope" described by Asef Bayat in his book, *Street Politics* (1997). The history of the slums, as written by Bayat, whose family emigrated to Tehran in the 1960s and settled in a lower-class area in the southern part of the city, is a history that reaches back to before the Revolution and to the hypocrisy of what was then called the White Revolution: a reform program launched by Shah Mohammad Reza Pahlavi in the 1960s that, in fact, preserved traditional power patterns, enforced a "modernization without modernity" (Mirsepassi 2003: 73) from above, and strengthened the officially fabricated success story of industrialization. This White Revolution, a blend of interventions to prevent and pre-empt a red revolution in the long run, paved the way for the Islamic Revolution.

Banietemad's cinematic "counter-memories" (Foucault 1977: 160) not only produce frictions between political promises and social realities, but they also articulate correspondences between pre- and post-revolutionary experiences and promises (never to be redeemed), thus manifesting a kind of solidarity between silenced, resisting voices from before and after 1979. In this respect, as Foucault would remind us, they are not to be confused with counter-revolutionary memories. Banietemad, who is still committed to the uniqueness of a post-revolutionary, socio-critical realism—"our society needed a cinema with a different point of view" (Banietemad 2016b: 130)—positions her counter-memories in continuity with revolutionary trajectories, albeit with different means: remembering official versions of history against the grain, destabilizing the mainstream uniform memories shaped by epistemic oppression, red lines, and power effects, and maintaining a demand for justice against the traps of what is called "reform".

The special concern in Banietemad's films for the repercussions of the post-revolutionary housing crisis (Bayat 1997: 82) on living conditions, particularly in southern Tehran, can be seen against the backdrop of the empty promises made by the "clerico-engineers" (Tavakoli-Targhi 2012: 14) of the Islamic Republic of Iran.

"This Islamic revolution is indebted to the efforts of this class, the class of shanty dwellers," declared Ayatollah Khomeini. "These South Tehranies, these footbearers, as we call them, they are our masters [*vali-ne'mat*] . . . They were the ones who brought us to where we are." To the dismay of Prime Minister Mehdi Bazargan, Khomeini declared only a few days after the revolution that "everyone must have access to land, the divine endowment," that "no one must remain without a dwelling of this country," and that water and electricity should be supplied free of charge to the poor. (Bayat 1997: 99)

As a consequence of the aforementioned promises, many rural migrants came to Tehran with high expectations of free housing and high-income jobs. One image allegorizes accurately all those expectations and promises: thousands of people occupying a building on 110 Freedom Street in Tehran that was at the time under construction but no longer exists. The revolutionary act of occupation was filmed and photographed from different perspectives by several camera operators, including Mahmoud Kalari, whose images spread virally and would become icons of the 1979 Islamic Revolution. After the building had been appropriated by the revolting people, the images of this occupation have been *appropriated* a second time in the aftermath of the Revolution by state propaganda and its pervasive success stories. Banietemad's films in a way unfold the multiple stories that might be hidden in those images—stories of resistance, always singular and diverging. She re-enacts a revolution under construction and reopens allegedly concluded stories. In this respect, Banietemad's approach can be compared to Sepideh Karami's experiment in "performative writing," undertaken in her recently published book, *Interruption*, in which she tries to deconstruct the iconic image of the "freedom building 1979" by breaking it down into close-ups and zoom-ins in an attempt to reopen possibilities and imagine alternative paths. She calls her procedure a method of exhaustion: "i.e. to exhaust all of the possible stories, and at that point of exhaustion, arrive at new potentials and latencies" (Karami 2018: 66).

Thus, the decisive question is how to turn the grand narratives, the "cacophony of state propaganda" (Karami 2018: 348), into minor stories of refusal and dissidence. Banietemad's documentary and feature films constantly deal with this question and confront us with crucial ethical dilemmas of ethno-sociography: How to keep in touch with multiple layers of society? What does it mean to pick up one individual case, one case study, and transform it into a category, an exemplary case for society, whilst thousands of other singularities have been deselected? How can one avoid turning the act of photography or the gesture of filming into an act of symbolic violence through representation and contextualization, cutting off all other conflicting realities and possible worlds?

Figure 2.2 Forugh giving up the project of finding the best mother in *The May Lady* (1998)

These are the questions that drive Banietemad's anthropological films, all crossing in a highly compressed form in her self-reflexive meta-film *The May Lady*. The film tells the story of the forty-two-year-old documentary film director Forugh Kia (Minoo Farshchi): a divorced single mother having a liaison with a man to whom she is not married—he is visually absent but present through telephone, letters, and voice-over poetry—and living with her teenage son, who behaves like a jealous lover. Forugh starts a film project about an exemplary mother in Iranian society. The problem: during her research, she is confronted with such a diversity of single mothers from different social classes that she increasingly finds herself incapable of making a decision and selecting one exemplary mother (Figure 2.2).

Forugh becomes completely drowned in a plethora of collected interviews, portrait photos, and documentary snippets, which to some extent refer to real women, like Faezeh Hashemi, Majlis representative and daughter of former Iranian President Akbar Hashemi Rafsanjani. On the other hand, fake interviews can be found as well in the film, such as one with Tooba and another with Nargess Safarkhani (Atefeh Razavi), from whom we learn what has happened in the intervening years since *Nargess* (1992). Nargess's husband is in prison and she cannot forget Afaq (Farimah Farjami), the secret protagonist of *Nargess*: "According to Afaq, all pains, except the pain of being forlorn, can be overcome," she tells the diegetic documentary filmmaker Forugh, who, of course, does not know to whom Afaq refers. Thus, Banietemad brings into position a kind of long-time seriality principle.

BANIETEMAD'S REVOLUTIONARY REALISM

What does it mean, according to Banietemad, to look under the skin of Tehran's society, a skin that is, first and foremost, a second nature fabricated by the compulsions and dictates of a clerically engineered society? Many films from Banietemad are likened to neorealism, poetic realism, or even symbolism. In my view, those links and parallels do not do justice to the complexity of Banietemad's urban realism, even though the latter is evidently influenced by Italian neorealism and can even be traced back to Lionel Rogosin's *On the Bowery* (1956) or *Come Back Africa* (1959). Be that as it may, I am more interested in carving out the crucial cultural differentiations than the similarities.

If censorship is a set of permanently shifting, partly unwritten red lines that compel filmmakers to play a game of hide-and-seek called symbolism, then Banietemad's semi-fictional, semi-documentary approach can be considered as a set of strategies to avoid pursuing this game. Instead, her post-revolutionary "street level perspectives" (Atwood 2016: 77) make visible and audible the materiality of tensions between conflicting social realities that are produced by the censorship of Tehran itself: a topology of boundaries, class differences, and social limitations, or rather exclusions, a system of all sorts of unequally distributed capital—social, cultural, economic, symbolic—and of incorporated rules, schemes of perception, and classifications. This is what Bourdieu would call "habitus" or "hexis" (with Aristotle; see, for example, Bourdieu 1977).

It should be noted that Bourdieu's notion of habitus is very closely intertwined with considerations about censorship. It is a restricted and constrained space of possibilities shaped by codes and a matrix of actions, perceptions, and judgments. According to Bourdieu, a social field functions as a kind of censorship structuring the distribution of different sorts of capital, as well as the forms of more or less possible interactions. And therefore, realism according to Bourdieu, who refers to Gustave Flaubert, Gustave Courbet, and Édouard Manet's realism, is everything that transgresses the ethical–aesthetic doxa and "threaten[s] the moral order" (Bourdieu 1992: 75) produced by censorship.

This does not relate only to the shifting red lines of cinema censorship. Several censorship codes, even contradicting ones, are immanent to conflicting social realities outside the cinema, and cinema's realism, according to Banietemad, consists in finding a form for those contradictions and showing the gaps between them. Consequently, alternative films gain their shape under contradicting conditions, which at the same time are exposed in those films:

> Even in the government there isn't a single, fixed point of view; so existing censorship does not necessarily comply with the government's own laws! . . . It is within the gaps between these different points of view, ideologies and "tastes" that we find the space to realize our films. (Banietemad 2016b: 132)

In a country where different fictions are quarreling about the right to represent reality, only forms of friction and contradiction can approach the lived experience of social reality.

It is a leitmotif of Iranian Sufism that truth would be a perfectly polished mirror in which light is given shape (Corbin 1971: 86, 151), yet this mirror has been broken into pieces. I would like to borrow the image of the broken mirror to open up several possible perspectives on the relation between image and reality. One perspective could emphasize the way of searching for the truth as being more important than truth itself. Another perspective could focus on the deficit inherent in the reality of the image, which always refers to a multiplicity of other mirror fragments all longing for completion; this perspective still presumes a universal truth. Furthermore, the broken mirror image could be interpreted in the sense that the measure of universal truth is lost, and artists are committed to a particular shape of the mirror fragment. This is reflected, for example, in Kianoush Ayari's *Abadaniha* (1994) or in the films of Abbas Kiarostami. According to the latter, the shortest way to truth is a lie since the image is a means of producing a certain reality in cooperation with the imagination of its recipient and his own mirror fragments. Fiction is where truth lies, in the double sense of the word (Kiarostami 2016: 75). Yet another style of realism, by confusing the clear cut between fact and fiction, juxtaposes contrasting versions of reality, a specific Iranian form of Sergei Eisenstein's intellectual collision and conflict montage. As Blake Atwood (2016) has shown, this specific form of producing tensions between contradicting statements has been elaborated before 1979 by Kamran Shirdel, whose films, including *Tehrān, Pāyetakht-e Irān Ast* (*Tehran is the Capital of Iran*, 1966) and Ān Shab ke Bārun Āmad (The Night it Rained, 1967), stand at the beginning of a whole tradition of dialectical, socio-critical movies. This tradition was carried on and diversified after 1979 by Massoud Bakhshi, in *Tehrān Anār Nadārad* (*Tehran Has No More Pomegranates*, 2006), and Banietemad, among others.

> If my camera looked at life in Zargandeh Street where I live and then a daily life in Zafar Street, which is only ten minutes away, you'd see two completely different worlds—the former is more like a street in a small town—almost a village—with a smaller middle-class population, whereas the latter is a highly urbanized street in a highly affluent area. And there are many dramatic disparities between the two, particularly the differences in people's behaviour. (Banietemad 2016b: 139)

One main feature of Banietemad's socio-critical art of squeezing the spectator in between contradicting layers of society—and by doing so, forcing him to plunge under the skin of society—can be found in *Rusari Ābi* (*The Blue-veiled*, 1995): Rasul Rahmani (Ezzatolah Entezami), grand-bourgeois widower and owner of a tomato sauce factory, is praying and mourning with his family in the dining room of their luxury property ("Ya Ali! Ya Ali! Cleanse our hearts with your bounty. If the people have faith in the poor . . ."). In the meantime, their domestic workers, including Nobar (Fatemeh Mottamedarya), the factory worker and widower's secret love, have to wait in the side room until they are allowed to serve tea once the endless prayer is over. Banietemad thereby unmasks the hypocrisy of religious rituals (especially those dictated by the state) and lays open the empty remains of the promises of what was once called liberation theology: a revolutionary political stance and an anti-hegemonic utopia based on freedom, social justice, spirituality, and what Ali Shari'ati called *bāzgasht be khishtan*, or return to the religious self (Davari 2014).

ON THE STREETS OF TEHRAN

In *Under the Skin of the City*, it is the restless mobility of Abbas (Mohammad Reza Forutan), the delivery boy riding the motorbike, that is developed by Banietemad as a socio-topological vehicle to drive us through Tehran's sociospatial stratifications: the city is divided into a northern and a southern region, with middle- and upper-class residents living almost exclusively in the northern part, whilst the poorest citizens in the south are kept out of the financial center through a highway system that is inaccessible to individuals without a car. There are two classes of people: those who have a car and those who have to take the bus. It is as if the different social classes that Banietemad has portrayed in her films—from *Nargess's* lower class to *The May Lady's* or *Khun Bāzi's* (Mainline, 2006) upper middle class—all meet along the routes and axes of Abbas's manual labor, which is comparable to that of Hossein (Hossein Emadeddin), also a (pizza) delivery man, in Jafar Panahi's *Talā-ye Sorkh* (*Crimson Gold*, 2003).[2]

We experience Tehran as a "fait social total" (Marcel Mauss): an operational space and a continuum of material reality, both driven by business and trade routes, circulation and bottlenecks, infrastructures and working conditions. The whole is structured by the tracks of the train that divide the city, by partition walls that obstruct the view and segment the image space, and by a series of contrasts between skyscrapers downtown and factories in the south, classical music (in the elevator) and the noise of machines (on construction sites), vertical and horizontal movements (elevator, motorcycle; see Atwood 2016: 78). There is a certain material attachment of the camera, a tactile relatedness between the street views, the architecture, and the character's movements, and not so much with visual situations of contemplation. Highly dynamic, impulsive, and confrontative scenes can give way to moments of contemplation—for example, when Abbas takes the elevator to the business world and has the chance to gain an elevated glimpse of the city—but this occurs only in rare moments.

Let me unfold some of the crucial strategies applied by Banietemad in order to avoid the symbolic game of hide-and-seek, which, in a way, is always (co-)governed by the regulations of censorship. Her main strategy is a hypertrophic tackling of the materiality, social reality, and everyday instances of censorship mechanisms. Whilst other directors try to abstract and distract from the semiotics and the material reality of *hijab*, Banietemad does not camouflage its reality but straightforwardly points to it, exposes it, and draws the spectator's attention to it right at the beginning of the film: after the mandatory text introduction, "In the Name of God," the first shot of *Under the Skin of the City* shows actress Golab Adineh out of focus in the video display of the state TV crew. She is asked to fix her scarf in order to enter into focus and thus into her role as an exemplary factory worker on her way to vote. As we know, she will refuse to assume this role. This highly reflexive construction brings into tension not only conflicting realities, but also the conflicting censorship codes producing those realities. We see something that is not allowed to be seen on Iranian state TV (Sedā va Simā-ye Jomhūri-ye Eslāmi-ye Irān: literally, Voice and Vision of the Islamic Republic of Iran), but is permitted in Iranian cinema: a disordered, messy *hijab* in close-up. By displaying the differences between television and cinema regulations, the film vindicates Banietemad's decision to move from documentary to fiction.

Banietemad's films constantly point to the reality of filmmaking and the difficulties of trying to make documentary films. Indexicality, according to her, is always the outcome of a tension between what Siegfried Kracauer would call the "camera-reality" (Kracauer 1960: 28)—its formative tendencies, movements, framings, and so on—and the reality in front of the camera. It is a reality under construction, a reality of relations and tensions. A significant example of Banietemad's way of constantly pointing to the act of filming and the act of producing realities between document and fiction can be found in *The May Lady*: the diegetic filmmaker, Forugh Kia, and her crew film and interview children in southern Tehran. When asked by Forugh Kia, "What do you want to be when you grow up?," a boy answers her: "A pilot!" At this very moment, a plane can be heard and the boy glimpses towards the plane in the off-screen space.

Due to the coincidence of sound and image, everything suddenly seems highly scripted and staged, as if Forugh Kia's intention was to produce an image that would be useful for propaganda purposes. Banietemad knows the "difficulties of making a documentary" (Atwood 2016: 33–60), and she likewise is aware of the ethnographic benefit of fictions based on "participant observation, interviews, and a lot of research" (Varzi 2014: 97). Truth lies in the blending of fact and fiction, not least because many aspects and routines of Iranian daily life are themselves scripted lies, the result of censorship (and tactics of subversion), and thus a form of fiction.

To return to *Under the Skin of the City*, Banietemad not only directly tackles the issue of the veil, but she also weaves a tightly knotted network of interrelated connections between textures, colors, and materials: for example, Tooba works in a factory producing white textiles, but white (of snow, wedding dresses, and so on) is also the dominating color towards the end of the film. In this regard, we could undoubtedly attempt a poetic reading of *Under the Skin of the City* that deciphers color symbolism and focuses on disparate melodramatic and expressionistic moments to be found in it, such as the pouring rain and darkness when Tooba's "pain and bewilderment overwhelm the film" (Mulvey 2001), or the artificial use of rear projection and the subjective points of hearing in order to audiovisualize Abba's increasingly hallucinatory perception.

This brings to mind André Bazin's analysis of (neo)realism as always resisting an interpretation that tries to impose an exclusive symbolic reading on individuals and situations (Bazin 2005: 42). The elements in Banietemad's films oscillate between the concrete, the metonymic, and the metaphoric (Mulvey 2001).

HISTORY OF THE PRESENT

As shown meticulously by Atwood, Banietemad's interest in economic disparities and conflicting realities crystalizes in her way of unfolding the cityscape in order to "unravel the myth of the reformist movement" (Atwood 2016: 75). The contrast between the promises of state propaganda and the disillusionment of social realities accompanies the films of Banietemad like a constant background beat, but it is especially in *Under the Skin of the City* that she tackles the inability of the revolutionary ideals and its reformist revisions to take account of the economic problems of society and of the lower classes in particular. Already, at the beginning of the film, after we have seen her in her role as an "exemplary factory worker," we discover an exhausted Tooba sitting in the bus and staring out of the window as election posters pass by and Khatami's voice can be heard: "And we shall broaden democracy and progress toward civil society. We will try to continually strengthen the dignity and stability of this nation. Our developments were the product of a great revolution and our problems . . ." The speech is interrupted several times by noises from the street—for example, a street fight between Basij and reform campaigners—slices of reality contrasting those that Khatami is trying to maintain and s(t)imulate in his speech. Noise and soundscape in Banietemad's urban ballads are always disturbers of the reality that we see, and vice versa. Both dimensions crisscross constantly. Beyond that, every social milieu is associated with specific ambient sounds like machine noises, elevator music, or the voice of reform from the beginning of the film.

It is not in Khatami's speech and his promises of reform that Banietemad tracks democratic movements or moments of solidarity and grassroot activities of a coming (or even already existing) civil society. It is in the streets and *Hayāt* (courtyards) of southern Tehran that *Under the Skin of the City* (Figure 2.3) unveils a solidarity that is, first and foremost, a kind of spatial solidarity, partly imposed on people by the impossibility of privacy. They simply do not have enough private space and thus have to hover between indoor and outdoor, *biruni* (outdoor) and *andaruni* (indoor). We are used to the dynamic interplay between censorship and its subversion, and we also know that outdoor shots (or in-the-car shots) in Iranian cinema are a tactic to avoid the imposed distortions of domestic scenes, yet Banietemad's films do not normally use exterior shots as a mere loophole to circumvent the non-realistic indoor artificiality dictated by censorship. Outdoor scenes set in the streets or in the courtyards confront us with the fact that privacy, intimacy, and interiority in the poor districts of south Tehran are continuously related and exposed to public life. One could call upon Bayat to speak of "cities inside out," "where a large number of urban subalterns" are "compelled, by necessity, to resort to the outdoor subsistence economy to survive and to public spaces to perform social and cultural rituals such as funerals" (Bayat 2017: 22). There is a continual coming and going in *Under the Skin of the City*: people arrive in order to leave and enter in order to go out, they alternate between inside and outside, stopping and going, pacing

Figure 2.3 *Under the Skin of the City* (2001)

up and down, and moving in circles. "C'est la bal(l)ade urbaine," Gilles Deleuze would say (as in films by Cassavetes and Scorsese; Deleuze 1986: 209). The central courtyards become spaces of an externalized intimacy, mediating contact zones where neighborly perspectives stumble onto each other and keep one another in check, but also produce moments of solidarity and resistance against domestic violence.

As Seyedkeyvan Mirmohammadi points out in his paper "Realism Without a Ceiling: The Hidden Idleness and the Violence of the Street," street scenes in films before the Revolution were "male-dominated" whilst a lot of street scenes in post-revolutionary films—and, one could add, especially those by Banietemad— seem to be female-dominated. We experience a certain "feminization of the city and the streets" (Mirmohammadi 2017: n.p.) and a vision of society beginning with the youth and their grassroots movements in the south of the city.

To conclude, I will ask once again with Tooba: *In film-hā ro be ki neshun midin?* Who do you show these films to anyway? Benedetto Croce's assertion that "true history is always contemporary history" (quoted in Ferro 1988: 25) is not at all out of date. Beginning in December 2017 and continuing into 2018, millions in Iran have taken to the streets, not only with anti-government but also with anti-system protests. I quote Hamid Mohseni, who wrote an article about the recent uprisings:

> The 2009 uprising was led by the urban, educated middle class . . . Now, it is totally another social group revolting in the street: it is mostly the (young) lower classes, the (precarious) labourers, the non-represented, but also students (which are part of every big uprising in Iran)—and, very importantly, one of the strongest movement in Iran for decades, progressive women in the front. (Mohseni 2018)

Banietemad's films show us those progressive women at the front. Integrating "film into the world that surrounds it" (Ferro 1988: 30), as Ferro demands in his plea for film as counter-history and counter-analysis of society, would also mean to imagine Tooba, the Mother Courage of Tehran, and (some of) her children joining in those street protests of 2017 and 2018. What makes Rakhshan Banietemad's films so indispensable and anthropologically rich is not only the fact that they "paint such accurate pictures of life in Iran at the time that they're made" (Varzi 2014: 98)—but also that they tell the history of our present.[3]

NOTES

1. Since the fictional film crew intervenes only at the beginning and the end of the film, never interacting with the audience, I would like to assign to it a semi-diegetic status, hovering between *hors-champ* (diegetic off) and *hors-cadre* (non-diegetic off): "The film

crew never formally exits the film's narrative, and the viewer is left to wonder whether the crew has been incorporated into the film's diegetic space or if the film crew acts as a bridge between the film's narrative and the film's self-conscious documentary world" (Atwood 2016: 70).
2. I would like to thank my colleague, Hossein Hemen Heidari (Basel), for drawing my attention to this association.
3. This chapter is the product of a research project on "Trauma- and Memoryscapes in Iranian Cinema," carried out at the Seminar for Media Studies in Basel (Chair for Media Aesthetics, 2016–19), funded by the Swiss National Science Foundation (SNF).

CHAPTER 3

Tales and the Cinematic *Divan* of Rakhshan Banietemad

Michelle Langford

Rakhshan Banietemad's *Ghesseh-hā* (*Tales*, 2014) consists of a collection of eight loosely interconnected vignettes that are structured to form a network narrative of sorts in which various actors reprise characters from the director's previous films. Banietemad gently folds the tales of distinct characters into one another, allowing them to quietly overlap and intersect, if only fleetingly. *Tales* provides a rich tapestry of experiences that speak to some of the most pressing concerns of contemporary Iranian society, including runaway girls, domestic abuse, prostitution, drug addiction, worker's rights, intergenerational conflict, and infidelity, but amidst these struggles the film also proposes the idea that it might still be possible to find love. By revisiting the lives of familiar characters from some of her earlier films, including *Khārej az Mahdudeh* (*Off Limits*, 1988), *Nargess* (1992), *Rusari Ābi* (*The Blue-veiled*, 1995), *Zir-e Pust-e Shahr* (*Under the Skin of the City*, 2001), *Gilāneh* (*Gilane*, 2005), and *Khun Bāzi* (*Mainline*, 2006) not only does Banietemad bring us up to date with some of her most memorable characters, but she also implicitly prompts viewers to ask what has changed in the intervening time. This is a question that applies to both the fictional diegetic world that is represented, and to the world beyond the frame of the camera. Viewers are encouraged to imagine how the vicissitudes of Iranian society and politics may have affected the lives of these characters. In *Tales*, we see characters that are weighed down not only by the mistakes and the misfortunes of the past, but also by the limited opportunities for social mobility and advancement available to them. However, whilst social conditions might not have improved for these characters, as Banietemad has herself remarked, "what is very important is they have changed to become better people" (quoted in Elphick 2015).

The eight vignettes are encased within a larger frame narrative about a documentary filmmaker (Habib Rezaei), whose struggle to make a film about social conditions in Iran bookends *Tales* and is also woven through several episodes. This premise allows his story to become intertwined with those of the other characters as he faces off against bureaucratic red tape and censorship that wish to prevent him from revealing the conditions under which these characters subsist. Through the figure of the documentary filmmaker, Banietemad effectively speaks indirectly of her own struggles as a maker of both documentary and fictional films attempting to bring the stories of ordinary Iranians to the screen. The presence of the filmmaker accords *Tales* a self-reflexive dimension that blurs the distinction between reality and fiction and marks some of the limitations of the documentary mode. Banietemad is mostly known for her gritty social realism, evident in her fictional films like *Under the Skin of the City*, *Gilane*, and *Mainline*; however, *Tales* reminds us that her film style has in fact developed over the course of her career, from the witty, almost surreal, social satire of *Off Limits* to the more melodramatic style of *Narges* and *The Blue-veiled*. In its incorporation of the tale of the documentary filmmaker, *Tales* also encourages us to think of her documentary and fictional projects as an extension of one another. At the same time, as I demonstrate later in this chapter, *Tales* also evidences traces of a kind of poetic cinema that has subtly developed as her career progressed, becoming most prominent in Bānu-ye Ordibehesht (*The May Lady*, 1998), another film that forges a deep connection between fiction and documentary cinema. She does this by presenting the vignettes not as complete narratives, but as brief, unfinished, and sometimes enigmatic glimpses into a moment of her characters' lives.

The Persian title of the film, *Ghesseh-hā*, and its formation out of short vignettes, remind us of the importance of the short story genre in the history of Persian literature. As J. T. P. de Bruijn (2012) notes, "The use of tales and anecdotes as parables is a particularly noteworthy feature of Persian literature"—although, like the European fairy-tale, the form has traditionally been used for didactic purposes. Short story collections have also appeared across the expansive history of Persian literature: from Sa'di's famous prose work, the *Golestān* (1258), to Gholam Hossein Saedi's '*Azādārān-e Bayal* (*The Mourners of Bayal*, 1964), a collection of eight interconnected short stories that Entezari (2011) refers to using the Arabic term "*Qeṣṣa*", although the Persian term "*dāstān*" is more commonly used. Banietemad's film differs from this literary tendency; whilst a moral lesson might be interpreted from the vignettes, they are not invested with an overtly didactic intention. Therefore, whilst *Tales* certainly seems to reference this literary genre in its title and structure, we may also think of the film as a kind of cinematic *divan*. In the Persian tradition, a *divan* is the collected works of a poet. Whilst each poem may constitute a work in its own right, when they are gathered into a collection, the reader is able to find resonances and common themes and to trace the development of an author's style. In a similar way, *Tales* collects together characters and stories from across Banietemad's rich and distinguished cinematic career. The film's use of intertextuality prompts us to reflect upon themes and stylistic characteristics that resonate and develop across her career in much the same way as is enabled by the collection of an author's works into a *divan*. With this in mind, I shall begin this chapter by discussing how the style and structure of the film help Banietemad to explore some of these key themes before I turn to look at how she blurs the distinction between documentary and fiction. I will then examine more closely the final two vignettes, in which the more poetic qualities of the film are brought to the fore, rendering love not as melodramatic excess, but as a heartfelt and ambivalent expression of the human condition reminiscent of earlier poetic treatments of love in Persian literature.

FRAGILE CONNECTIONS AND PRECARIOUS AFFINITIES: *TALES* AS NETWORK NARRATIVE

The decision to string together a series of short films in the making of *Tales* was a practical one on the part of Banietemad that enabled her to bypass the pre-production approval process managed by the Ministry of Culture and Islamic Guidance that is normally required for feature films (Armatage and Khosroshahi 2017: 142). However, the choice of a "thread structure", or what David Bordwell (2008) calls a "network narrative," is one of *Tales*' most powerful features and enables us to consider it a kind of *divan*. Network narratives, sometimes also called "mosaic" films, can be constructed through a range of different techniques. In the case of *Tales*, Banietemad has chosen to connect her stories through chance encounters and haphazard convergence. She does this by staging each one in a particular location, such as a taxi, the corridor of a government department, a women's shelter, and a bus full of disgruntled workers. Such locations provide opportunities for characters that have no other connection to each other to plausibly intersect, and since attention to realism is an important concern of Banietemad's filmmaking more generally, plausibility matters a great deal. According to Bordwell (2008: 194), a typical feature of "network narratives in any medium is the fundamental tension between realism . . . and artifice." Finding a balance between realism and artifice has always been a central feature of Banietemad's filmmaking. In works like *The Blue-veiled* or *Nargess*, Banietemad balances the representational verisimilitude of the social setting and characters with the structural artifices of melodrama, particularly through the use of non-diegetic music to punctuate emotion and the sudden-reversal-of-fortune motif in which characters that appear to be finally getting their lives on track are suddenly plunged once again into misery. In her later films, she moved away from some of these melodramatic techniques—for example, using non-diegetic music only sparsely, if at all—but her approach to realism continued to depend on a carefully structured plot and the development of significant thematic motifs. In a network narrative like *Tales*, there is a risk that the artifices necessary to allow characters to intersect might undermine any intended representational realism and render the logic of the narrative implausible.

Banietemad mitigates such potential implausibility not only because of her choice of locations but also because the extent of the interactions between characters does not lead to any major plot twists or reversals of fortune. For Banietemad, the haphazard overlapping of stories helps to reinforce a central motif in the film: the idea that life goes on, despite the pressures from society, politics, or families. This is the case, even where characters already know each other. Take, for example, the first tale, which centers around the story of Abbas (Mohammad Reza Forutan), one of the characters from *Under the Skin of the City*. After having fled in fear of his life at the end of the earlier film, he has returned to Tehran and is now working as a taxi driver. His first passenger is the documentary filmmaker. Through their conversation, we learn more about what has happened to Abbas in the intervening years—for example, he is now married with a small daughter, but times are tough and so both he and his wife work long hours and rely on his mother, Tooba, to look after their child. He delivers his story much like a monologue, the filmmaker serving as an impassive observer, although to Abbas's regret, the filmmaker never actually films him. Once he alights, Abbas picks up a new passenger, a young woman with a small child. The child is running a fever, but the viewer is left in no doubt about how the woman earns a living, as the encounter begins with her propositioning Abbas in coded language, offering to go "wherever you decide." Clearly offended, Abbas immediately asks the woman to get out, but eventually agrees to drop her a little further down the road.

As he drives, Abbas glances at the woman in his rear-view mirror and a flash of recognition passes across his face. This prompts him to tell the story of two girls, Masoumeh and Mahboubeh (Abbas's sister), who had been fast friends until Masoumeh had run away from home after her brother cut off her long ponytail and severely beat her. Interestingly, he tells the story as though it were a fable, speaking of the girls in the third person, despite the fact that it is the very same Masoumeh who sits in the rear passenger seat of the taxi, nursing her sick child. Viewers familiar with *Under the Skin of the City* might recognize Mehraveh Sharifinia, who reprises her role as Masoumeh, replete with her character's distinctive blue nail polish, and might also be dismayed to learn that her situation in life has not improved since we last saw her. She appears to be an unmarried mother and has resorted to sex work to survive. Whilst she does not openly acknowledge Abbas, her expression of shame confirms that she is the Masoumeh of whom Abbas speaks. We are given little more than a brief glimpse into Masoumeh's life before she leaves just as abruptly as she entered.

Masoumeh's departure reinforces Banietemad's light touch method for structuring the film through chance and contingency, and also demonstrates how far her cinema has moved from the melodramatic mode. Rather than building the encounter to a climax or crescendo that might trigger the unfolding of new narrative events, as we might expect in melodrama, here Banietemad simply lets Masoumeh slip away. Framing and the use of off-screen sound in particular help to fill the moment with heartfelt pathos. After Abbas has finished his impassioned story, he stops the taxi opposite a pharmacy, and finally turns to gaze directly at Masoumeh, who hides her face behind her hand in shame. A series of lingering shot-reverse-shots of the characters reinforces both recognition and distance, as they are never framed together in the same shot. Without explanation, Abbas goes across to the pharmacy to buy medicine for the child's fever. At this point, Banietemad cuts back to a close-up of Masoumeh, holding the shot for several seconds so that we can witness her pain and her shame as tears stream down her cheeks and she muffles her sobs, clinging closely to her small child. In the following shot, we see the pharmacy framed by the driver's side window, and after a few seconds, we hear the sound of a car door opening and closing. Another moment later, Abbas emerges from the pharmacy carrying a toy monkey and a bag of medicine. As he approaches the car, his posture tells us all we need to know—Masoumeh has fled—and as he slouches against the side of the cab, the toy monkey dangles poignantly before us.

As in many of her films, Banietemad chooses to conceal some key moments of the narrative from view. Hamid Naficy has discussed how Banietemad's cinema has long been structured through dialectics of veiling and unveiling, and the use of visual barriers in the composition of her mise-en-scène. Whilst such compositional choices are sometimes the result of censorship, as Naficy points out, the "reciprocity of veiling and unveiling [actual and metaphorical] necessitates that the obstructions that seem to *conceal* certain things from view also *reveal* something else, namely the director's intention" (Naficy 2000: 568). Arguably, Banietemad allows Masoumeh to slip away into the night without any progression in her story precisely because her dire situation cannot easily be resolved through a simple narrative turn or the kind gesture of a distant acquaintance. Rather than using the structural device of the chance encounter as a potential moment of rescue, as we might expect from melodrama, Masoumeh instead disappears once again to join the ranks of others who engage in sex work in order to survive. Abbas's fable-like narration of Masoumeh's story further adds to the impression that her story is just one of many in which a girl flees violence at home, becomes homeless, and resorts to prostitution (Sharifi et al. 2017). In an interview, Banietemad has highlighted the fact that her characters are based on an amalgamation of people she has observed in real life (Armatage and Khosroshahi 2017: 147). Girls like Masoumeh have immense difficulty being reintegrated into society (Sciolino 2000: 3), and the visual treatment of Masoumeh's departure from the story strongly reinforces this sad fact. Whilst the film may not offer up a solution for Masoumeh, a later vignette, set in a women's shelter, will draw attention to the kinds of sparse but committed services helping women in Masoumeh's situation, even if Masoumeh herself might have slipped through the net. There, we will be reintroduced to another character, Sara from *Mainline*, who appears to have turned her life around. But more on her story shortly.

Abbas's vignette lasts a few minutes longer as we cut to a new location outside his mother Tooba's home, where she has been minding Abbas's daughter, Sarvenaz. Here, Abbas functions as a thread to reintroduce us to Tooba, a character who first appeared as a quasi-documentary subject in *The May Lady* and became the central female protagonist in *Under the Skin of the City*. Her presence across the three films strengthens the effect of the film's *divan*-like structure. The brief encounter between Abbas and Tooba highlights the deep and continuing love she has for her son, despite the fact that his mistakes have cost the family their home. Once again, Banietemad uses her characteristic technique of concealment through framing. Throughout the scene, the camera remains positioned on the outside of the home, looking in through a partially opened door, allowing us to catch only the briefest glimpse into her private life. The positioning of the camera reveals Banietemad's intention to shine a light on social conditions rather than to delve into a domestic melodrama.

Tooba becomes the thread that connects the first tale with the second. A match cut takes us from Tooba's closed door to a blurred image of the corridor of a government office, which is gradually brought into focus as Tooba enters frame left, cloaked in a black *chador*. If the taxi of the opening tale provides plausible opportunities for chance encounters between characters, the generic government office corridor, which is a staple location of contemporary Iranian cinema—used memorably in the closing shot of Asghar Farhadi's *Jodāeiye Nāder az Simin* (*A Separation*, 2011)—is a space in which "fragile connections" and "precarious affinities" enable diverse characters to brush past one another ever so fleetingly (Bordwell 2008: 198). This vignette briefly reintroduces the documentary filmmaker from the first story as he seeks permission to interview some of the welfare center's clients. He is trying to negotiate with a bureaucrat who only has his own self-aggrandizement in mind, offering to let the filmmaker interview him but refusing permission to interview any clients. The character of the bureaucrat, played by Hassan Majooni, is new, but his character is a familiar one: a government managerial type, whose narcissistic attitude prevents him from ever really caring about his job or the people he is charged with helping. We came across many such characters in Banietemad's debut feature *Off Limits*, and this tale reintroduces us to the central character from that film, one Mohammad Javad Halimi (Mehdi Hashemi). It is Tooba who brings us to Halimi, approaching him to ask if he would write a letter for her. This small detail not only reminds us that, in *Under the Skin of the City*, Tooba had been trying to overcome her illiteracy, helped by her younger son, Ali (Ebrahim Sheibani), but it also adds another layer of intertextuality through the evocation of an absent character. Although Ali does not appear in *Tales*, we will later learn that he has been in jail for two years for taking part in a protest. Given that the film was made in 2011, we might read this as a subtle allusion to the 2009 post-election demonstrations against the voting in of Mahmoud Ahmadinejad for a second term. In Halimi, Tooba has found someone very well versed in Iranian bureaucracy, knowing immediately to whom she should address her complaint. Through this simple exchange, Tooba passes the narrative thread to Halimi, who suddenly sees an opportunity to push into the administrator's office to put forward his own complaint. As in *Off Limits*, Halimi's appearance in *Tales* allows Banietemad to weave a little comical satire into the film.

Repetition to the point of absurdity had been the major structural device of *Off Limits*, in which Halimi, attempting to bring a house burglar to justice, accidentally discovers that his new home lies in an area that has been excluded from any of the city's zoning maps. As a result, he roams from one gendarmerie office and police station to another, only to be told that they are unable to hear his complaint because of this peculiar zoning issue. His home lies in an effective no man's land. Throughout *Off Limits*, Halimi repeats his introduction and complaint almost word for word at each new location, a key comic device of the film. In *Tales*, Banietemad uses a similar strategy of repetition, only this time it is compressed into a much shorter timeframe. Halimi has come seeking compensation after undergoing an emergency operation. His medical emergency had occurred on a bank holiday and he was inadvertently taken to a hospital that is not covered by his health insurance. Furthermore, Halimi complains of the indignity of being required to submit to another examination of his private parts before the insurance company will reassess his claim. Perceptive viewers might see echoes of the absurd zoning issue he faced in *Off Limits*. In this case, he finds himself both spatially and temporally "off limits"—and this time, it is much more personal. Further intertextual layers are provided by the familiar mise-en-scène of the generic government office and the way that Halimi is made to stand far away from the bureaucrat's desk, as he did in the earlier film. Banietemad's approach seems to echo not only her own earlier film, but also a similar encounter between an old man and a bureaucrat in Sohrab Shahid Saless's 1974 film, *Tabiate bijān* (*Still Life*). Even more significant are the constant interruptions Halimi is made to endure from the indifferent bureaucrat's ringing mobile phones (one for his wife and one for his mistress). Just as there could be no happy ending for Masoumeh, Halimi is eventually thrown out of the office with no resolution to his issue: "You're attending to your multiple wives instead of doing your job!" shouts Halimi as he is dragged away by a security guard. At this moment, Halimi brushes past Tooba once more, her letter remaining incomplete. In the next shot, Halimi is riding the subway, and it is there that the next brief tale will take place.

As we can see from my description of these first two vignettes, Banietemad employs the structural device of the chance encounter, but rather than these encounters contributing to narrative progression, they merely show us brief snapshots of characters caught in a kind of eternal loop. Each character seems to inhabit the kind of no man's land evoked by *Off Limits*. This pattern of linking the tales together via a connecting character continues throughout the film. In the third vignette, Halimi unwittingly leads us to observe a brother and sister plotting to extort their father and introduces themes of generational conflict, marital discontent, and economic stress caused by the increasing cost of living and high rates of unemployment. The scene plays out in one of the shiny new carriages recently added to Tehran's metro system to alleviate growing congestion. This is one of the few signs of material progress shown in the film. We are introduced here to Doctor Gabiri (Shahrokh Foroutanian), who becomes the conduit to the next tale, which takes place in a women's shelter. Viewers might remember Doctor Gabiri from *Gilane*. An amputee from the Iran–Iraq War, he came to tend Gilāneh's (Fatemeh Motamed-Aria) son Ismael (Bahram Radan), who had been severely crippled in the war. In *Tales*, we learn, via a message left for Gabiri on the shelter's answering machine, that Ismael is on his deathbed. The intertextuality intensifies further in this vignette as we become briefly reacquainted with Sara (Baran Kosari), the central protagonist of *Mainline*, and Nargess (Atefeh Razavi), the title character of Banietemad's 1992 film. The documentary filmmaker also makes a brief appearance as he attempts, unsuccessfully, to find subjects who will agree to be filmed, and we are also introduced to a handful of new characters.

As with the other settings used in *Tales*, the women's shelter provides a plausible space for several characters from previous films to congregate and briefly interact. More than anything, however, this setting reminds us of Banietemad's ongoing commitment to a variety of social themes such as drug addiction, HIV, domestic violence, and the need for women's empowerment. Bordwell (2008: 191) has suggested that network narratives tap into "our social intelligence," demanding "that we trace out a web of personal relations among characters." Here, however, the relations are not necessarily personal, for we are asked to use our social intelligence to see the relationships between various social issues. At the women's shelter, we meet several women whose lives have been affected by one or more of these issues, including Samireh, a woman with HIV who has made numerous suicide attempts and is now waiting for her daughter's blood test results, presumably to see if she, too, has contracted HIV. But it is Nargess that becomes the focal point of this vignette. When we first meet Nargess, she is barely recognizable. She wears a veil across her mouth and nose, attempting to cover her horribly disfigured face, scarred almost beyond recognition. Gone are her youthful courage and assertiveness: now she appears nervous, weary, and hunched over from the weight of her situation. As the vignette unfolds, a man—her husband—comes knocking on the glass door of the shelter, demanding to speak with Nargess. His arrival prompts her to explain to the shelter manager that she ran away from him three months ago after he had failed in multiple attempts to overcome his drug habit and that he regularly beats her in front of her stepchildren. We also learn that she had married him after the father of her own children had died. It seems that much water has passed under the bridge since the tragic ending of *Nargess*, which saw her attempt to extricate herself from another toxic relationship. Whilst this conversation takes place in a storage room of the women's shelter, we hear her husband's incessant knocking intruding from the off-screen space. This raises the tension of the scene and reminds us of the many unseen forces that affect these characters' lives. As his knocking becomes more demanding, Nargess becomes increasingly agitated, prompting her to explain her situation further. Eventually, she admits that she had lied about how her face was scarred. It was not an accident, after all; her husband had attacked her with boiling water.

Throughout this sequence, Banietemad once again uses cinematic techniques to reveal her intentions. The frosted glass doorway of the shelter functions as a thin veil barely able to shield those inside from the threats of the outside world. This reinforces the idea that the shelter can protect women only in limited ways. The fragility of the barrier reminds us that such institutions are few and far between and have the capacity to affect the lives of relatively few women. The sequence uses several long takes, which alternate between shots of Nargess in the storeroom being comforted by two women and shots of the shelter doorway taken from inside the foyer. We never see Nargess's husband clearly, the frosted glass and lighting rendering him as little more than a silhouette behind the screen. This enables him to function as an emblem of many other men like him who, through attitude or situation, have become drug-addicted and violent towards women. Despite this, Banietemad portrays him as much more than simply a violent bully. For example, one of the women from the shelter is able to calm him momentarily, and his violent potential does not escalate when she confronts him with the horrible injuries he has inflicted upon Nargess. Instead, he sobs pathetically, begging Nargess repeatedly to come back to him. During the final shot of the tale, the camera gradually pulls in to form an intimate two-shot of the couple standing virtually side by side, separated only by the thin layer of frosted glass: Nargess inside, her husband outside as he repeats his apology again and again with the voice of a broken man. The camera lingers for a few seconds after Nargess walks off screen, suggesting, perhaps, that this time she will not accept his apology. The sound of a telephone ringing merges with his sobs, forming a sound bridge to the next tale.

In keeping with the thread structure, Nargess links us to this very brief vignette, which takes place in a welfare office. As the telephone continues to ring, the image cuts to an abstract shot. The frame is dominated by a woman in a black *chador*, which sharply cuts diagonally across the frame. The shot holds for a few moments before a figure emerges out of the blackness as she turns to face us. It is Nargess. As the camera pulls out, we see that Tooba is also there, waiting in line to apply for a small loan. Seemingly caught up in her own world, Nargess pushes to the front of the line, leaving Tooba somewhat disgruntled. When the woman at the desk notices Nargess's horrific injuries, she perpetuates the same lie that she had originally told at the women's shelter: that she had been burned in a gas explosion. Banietemad uses this brief encounter to reinforce a kind of precarious affinity between Nargess and Tooba. Viewers familiar with *Under the Skin of the City* might remember that Tooba's own daughter, Hamideh (Homeira Riazi), has also suffered domestic abuse. In the first tale, Abbas even asks Tooba if Hamideh has "argued with her husband" again, code, perhaps, indicating that the abuse is ongoing and that, like Nargess, Hamideh is caught up within a cycle of abuse and apology that renders her unable to change her situation. These precarious affinities add more layers to the intertextuality of the film. This brief vignette serves as a transition to a new story that will once again place Tooba in the spotlight.

WHO DO YOU SHOW THESE FILMS TO ANYWAY?

Before I move on to discuss Tooba's role in the film more fully, I will briefly turn to consider the place of the documentary filmmaker, who takes an active role in the sixth vignette alongside Tooba. As mentioned above, the tale of the filmmaker opens and closes the film. His presence not only reminds us of Banietemad's long parallel career in documentary filmmaking, but also asks us to consider the intersectional relationship between documentary and fictional filmmaking across her work more broadly. In this sense, both documentary and fictional work is effectively gathered together within this *divan*. Even before we meet the filmmaker, *Tales* is inscribed with his way of seeing in the very opening shot of the film. The image fades in from a black title screen to reveal shaky footage of Tehran by night flashing past in a continuous traveling shot. Later he will tell Abbas, "This is the way I observe". The noticeably grainy image is framed by the viewfinder of a digital video camera: timecode runs in the bottom right corner, crosshairs mark the center of the frame. We hear Abbas telling his story in voiceover, but for the moment, neither the filmmaker nor the subject can be identified. After about one minute, Abbas asks if the filmmaker would like him to slow down to get a better shot. The filmmaker declines. The shot is broken only when Abbas asks the filmmaker if he has a light, and we cut to the film proper, a mid-shot of the filmmaker seated in the rear passenger seat of the taxi, removing his glasses. Throughout this opening sequence, the film intermittently cuts back and forth between the high-resolution images of the film proper and the grainy footage from the documentary camera, which continues to capture fleeting images of the streets of Tehran from the window of the taxi. Viewers might notice that the streets are eerily quiet, seemingly deserted. We might even be a little bewildered when the filmmaker remarks that "this city is too crowded," a statement that seems to contradict the view of Tehran captured by his camera. This disconnect between word and image is telling, suggesting that it is difficult for a documentary filmmaker to ever capture the "real" Iran. As the film unfolds, we will see the filmmaker come up against various barriers. First, he is forbidden from interviewing clients in the government welfare office; then he is told by the manager of the women's shelter that it is too risky for the women to be interviewed, reminding us of the ethical complexities of documentary filmmaking, especially in a heavily controlled place like Iran. It is not until he meets Tooba that he finds his ideal documentary subject in the sixth vignette, which unfolds almost entirely through the viewfinder of his camera in three long takes joined by almost invisible edits.

Tooba is a seasoned "documentary" subject, functioning as a conduit between documentary and fictional modes of filmmaking. As mentioned earlier, Tooba first appeared in *The May Lady*, a film about a female documentary filmmaker, Forugh Kia, who is attempting to find an exemplary mother to feature in a documentary film. One day, Forugh meets Tooba by chance at the jail where both women's sons are held. Their encounter prompts Forugh to review interview footage of Tooba that she had shot sometime earlier. Interestingly, the timeline of that footage post-dates the narrative timeframe of *Under the Skin of the City*, a film that Banietemad had drafted in 1985 but was unable to produce until three years after the completion of *The May Lady* (Armatage and Khosroshahi 2017: 149). The film was eventually set against the backdrop of the 1997 presidential election that brought the reformist candidate, Mohammad Khatami, to power; however, as Atwood (2016: 77) points out, it was filmed in 2000 amidst rising disillusionment about the evident lack of reform. In the "documentary" footage seen in *The May Lady*, Tooba describes much of the narrative arc of *Under the Skin of the City*, except that the fate of Tooba's two sons seems to differ across the two films. The impassioned story that Tooba tells to Forugh Kia, addressing the camera directly as a "documentary" subject, might in a sense be understood as "source material" for *Under the Skin of the City*. This points to the capacity for fictional filmmaking to provide a commentary on social reality. Tooba's appearance as a (fictional) documentary subject in *The May Lady* invests her character's story with a kind of "truth" value carried over into the opening shots of *Under the Skin of the City*, which begins and ends with Tooba being interviewed by television crews. Blake Atwood (2016: 84) has argued that, between these two instances of filming, Tooba's political identity has developed considerably.

Like *Tales*, *Under the Skin of the City* makes us aware of the act of filming in the very opening shot, which shows a small video monitor that frames Tooba as she prepares to be interviewed. As she begins to speak, the camera pans left, revealing Tooba in the distance with several other women seated beside her. In front of her is a camera and a crew of two men. With an election looming, Tooba is being asked what working women expect of elected officials. Her response seems somewhat rehearsed: "They should have a strong faith in God," she begins. She stumbles over these words, as though she has tried to remember them by heart, and we hear several of the women around her echoing her words exactly, suggesting that the interview may be somewhat contrived. Eventually, Tooba becomes impatient, feeling as though she cannot express herself well enough and rises to leave. At the very end of the film, Tooba once again faces off against a camera. It is election day, and a camera crew has stopped to interview people outside a polling station. This time, Tooba is much more confident, speaking fluently and with conviction, proudly displaying her ink-stained finger. She has found her voice. In the midst of her impassioned speech, a male voice from off screen interrupts her, explaining that there has been a technical issue, and asks if she can begin again. At this, Tooba reacts angrily: "Just forget about it! . . . I lost my house, my son ran away, and people are filming all the time!"; she gestures "camera" as in a game of charades. "I wish someone would come and film what's going on right here! Right here!"; she gestures towards her heart. Suddenly, she looks directly down the lens of the camera, exclaiming, "Who do you show these films to anyway?," and it is with these poignant words that the film ends.[1]

Tooba's experience as a documentary subject and her now mature political consciousness are brought to bear upon the sixth vignette of *Tales* as her story converges with that of the documentary filmmaker. The vignette takes place on a minibus conveying disgruntled workers to confront the new owner of the factory where they have worked for many years and to demand their unpaid wages. The documentary filmmaker has joined them, having finally found some subjects who are willing to be filmed. As the vignette begins, the mostly male contingent of workers gathered in the bus are preparing to leave when one of them notices that Tooba is on her way. At this point the documentarian begins filming and we cut to his grainy video footage, inscribed with the markings of his viewfinder. We see Tooba in the distance, a tiny black figure struggling to cross several lanes of traffic on a busy highway. She has been delayed, not least because Nargess cut the queue in front of her in the previous tale, but also because she suffered a terrible coughing fit, the consequence of long-term exposure to dust in the textile factory where she works (indeed, such coughing fits have punctuated many of her previous film appearances). In keeping with the intertextual nature of *Tales*, this shot might even remind viewers of Nargess running along the highway at the end of *Nargess*, black *chador* billowing behind her.

The sequence is filmed in long takes with tight framing and jerky hand-held camera movements to produce the strong illusion of documentary authenticity. Initially, Tooba has only a marginal presence in the scene, with Reza (Farhad Aslani), the natural leader of the group, speaking directly to camera, dominating as the camera pans from face to face so that the workers may share their frustrations. The men emotionally complain that they are unable to pay rent and feed their families. One cannot help but think of how gender expectations in a patriarchal society might exacerbate their sense of humiliation and helplessness. Eventually, after the camera has provided an inclusive platform for most of the passengers to share their stories, a voice prompts Tooba to speak. It is now that she seems to channel her performance for the film crew at the end of *Under the Skin of the City*, saying dismissively, "Haven't they filmed us before?", and even miming "camera" as she did in the earlier film. The men encourage her, saying, "It might work this time!" At this, Tooba launches into a fluent monologue, not only touching on how certain co-workers have been affected by the shutdown, but also complaining of the increase in prices for basic goods and services, the rise in drug use among young people, and more personal issues, such as her son Ali's arrest. Throughout her tirade, various members of the group plead with her to avoid touching on political issues, the camera deviating momentarily from Tooba before finally returning to her in a tight close-up. She looks directly at the camera and asks once again, "Who do you show these films to anyway?", before once again collapsing in a fit of coughing.

In this scene, Tooba becomes a conduit for Banietemad to remind viewers of the social context in which the film is set, including the economic situation and sense of hopelessness among young people, many of whom, including her son Ali, spilled into the streets to protest in 2009. However, by the end of the vignette, we are reminded of the conditions that prevent such stories from being properly documented and disseminated. As the bus nears its destination, it is met by police and a tense altercation ensues. True to form, Tooba stands up to the police, demanding that she be allowed to alight from the bus. As the struggle continues, one of the policemen suddenly notices the camera and reaches up to block the lens with his hand. We hear a "beep," suggesting that the recording has been stopped, and the film suddenly cuts to black, abruptly ending the vignette. It is not until the final minutes of the film that we learn what happened. Accompanied by gentle non-diegetic piano music, the camera, in a wide shot, pans across a busy tangle of interconnecting roads at dusk. The camera movement brings the documentary filmmaker into view as he walks away from the camera along one of the roads. He is speaking on his mobile phone, narrating the events that transpired after the camera stopped recording. We learn that, whilst his camera was returned to him, it seems that his footage has been confiscated. "I'm used to it," he laments, "of course I'm still working," he reassures his listener, and optimistically exclaims that "no movie has ever stayed hidden, it will be screened somewhere, somehow, whether we're there or not." Through the figure of the documentary filmmaker, Banietemad reminds viewers of the broad impact that censorship has on filmmaking in Iran, which includes not only censorship from above, emblematized here by the seizure of the footage, but also the kinds of self-censorship employed by documentary subjects, afraid of the possible consequences of crossing poorly demarcated red lines. This ending seems to anticipate the fate of *Tales*, which was completed in 2011 but not screened in Iran until 2014, when it finally premiered at the Fajr Film Festival. Even then, its limited general release was held back for another year.

I WISH SOMEONE WOULD COME AND FILM WHAT'S GOING ON RIGHT HERE!

For the last two vignettes, Banietemad turns to explore the theme of love and relationships. These are the longest tales of the film and they unfold through a more purposeful narrative logic, with a clear dramatic arc that enables them to function as short films in their own right. In keeping with the threaded *divan* structure of the film, we are brought up to date with the lives of characters from previous films. However, unlike in the previous vignettes, Banietemad moves beyond straightforward representational realism to invest these tales with a poetic intensity that is reminiscent of the treatment of love in Persian poetry, which forms a tension against the narrative surface. This poeticism helps to make the social themes more personal and more moving whilst avoiding the heightened dramatics typical of the melodramatic mode. In doing so, they seem to respond to Tooba's request to film what is going on in the hearts of her characters, and this is arguably one advantage of fictional filmmaking over the documentary mode.

The tale of Reza and Nobar brings us into the home of two characters from Banietemad's 1995 film, *The Blue-veiled*. We first met Nobar (Fatemeh Mottamedarya) in this film as a young woman who worked in a tomato sauce factory. Rasul, the proprietor of the factory and an elderly widower, falls in love with her at first sight. However, his newfound love for this much younger woman from a lower-class family is met with stern disapproval from his daughters and their husbands, who do everything in their power to ostracize Nobar.

Nevertheless, the couple secretly enter into a temporary marriage (*sigheh*) and Rasul provides a small home for Nobar where the couple can meet in private.

In Reza and Nobar's vignette in *Tales*, many years have passed since the events depicted in *The Blue-veiled*, and it is Reza who provides the connective thread from the previous story. The scene takes place in the small apartment and courtyard inhabited by Reza, his wife Nobar, and their two young children. The story begins when a lawyer comes to deliver a letter addressed to Nobar. It is from Rasul, who has penned it on his deathbed. Nobar is not yet home, so the lawyer leaves the letter with Reza. We soon learn that Reza is illiterate and is unable to read the letter, but we are easily able to discern the distress caused by its arrival through Reza's body language. Perceptive viewers might recognize Reza from his fleeting role in *The Blue-veiled* and they also might remember that he had admired Nobar from afar. The arrival of the letter and mention of Rasul seem to dredge up old emotions, for Reza immediately concludes that it can only be a love letter from his former rival, and he imagines that the couple must have been corresponding behind his back for the last ten years. Once Nobar arrives home, he confronts her with this accusation, which she denies. Over the course of the sequence, we learn more about the characters' backstories and the contents of the letter are gradually revealed.

Reza forces Nobar to read the letter to him, which she does haltingly, seemingly fearful of each sentence. Although there is no indication of disloyalty on Nobar's part, the letter contains affectionate words, which visibly strike arrows through poor Reza's heart and render Nobar incapable of reading further. Finally, Reza has his young son finish reading the letter and we learn that Rasul has bequeathed to Nobar a small house in honor of her love and affection. Throughout the sequence, Reza's emotions oscillate between anger and heartache, which are expressed beautifully through Farhad Aslani's powerfully embodied performance. As the sequence draws to a climax, we sense that this is just one of many challenges this couple has faced over the years, and we may wonder if and how they might reconcile after this most recent challenge.

The intensely emotional tenor of the sequence might cause viewers to yearn for the couple to embrace, but of course, this is not possible. It is this kind of moment that proves the most difficult for Iranian filmmakers, who must navigate the complex and haphazardly applied censorship guidelines regarding interaction between men and women. Many Iranian filmmakers might simply pan away from the couple as they move towards an implied embrace, allowing the moment to carry on in off-screen space and in the minds of the spectators. They even might accompany this modest aversion of the camera's gaze with melodramatic music to help viewers fill in the gap.

Banietemad, however, has found an infinitely more touching solution. In the penultimate shot, we watch as Reza moves from the washbasin, where, moments earlier, he had tried to cool his head and dampen his emotions under the running tap. From there, he moves slowly towards the camera and leans his weight against a metal staircase. The camera slowly pans right and draws in closer, isolating Reza in the frame as he takes a seat on the step, directly facing the camera. His movements and the duration of the shot are painfully drawn out, conveying the depth of his emotion. Moments later, Nobar enters the shot, tentatively approaching Reza. She gingerly reaches behind him with her left arm as though to embrace him. With her right hand, she delicately fondles a crease in his shirt, tilting her head in towards his shoulder. Her delicate movements bring the couple almost, but not quite, into an intimate embrace. The final shot, however, reveals a new perspective; a high-angle shot from behind shows that Nobar's arm rests not on Reza's back, but on the step. In this shot, however, the configuration of bodies reinforces the impression that Nobar might indeed be resting her head on Reza's shoulder. With this combination of two shots, Banietemad has effectively produced the impression of an on-screen embrace whilst at the same time ensuring there is sufficient evidence to prove that the embrace never actually happened (Figure 3.1).

In many ways, this vignette is evidence that Iranian cinema's relationship with intimacy and love is beginning to come of age. Thanks to filmmakers like Rakhshan Banietemad, who are willing to push the representation of intimacy to the very limits of censorship, viewers can finally experience the much-anticipated and long-withheld embrace of husband and wife. With this fictional story, Banietemad has effectively responded to Tooba's challenge to film "in here."

It is moments like these, which are achieved without the addition of non-diegetic music to artificially orchestrate the emotional charge of the scene, that are the hallmark of Banietemad's mature filmic style and help to lend her films a high degree of verisimilitude. At the same time, however, touching sequences like this that are so carefully and tenderly filmed also seem to allude obliquely to the treatment of love in classical Persian literature and poetry. The most obvious element is the love triangle, a common device of love stories the world over, and a mainstay of Persian literature, where it is invariably combined with the theme of

Figure 3.1 On-screen embrace in *Tales* (2014)

ambivalent, unrequited, or unattainable love. The story of Khosrow and Shirin, immortalized by the twelfth-century poet Nezami Ganjavi, is perhaps the best-known example. In that tale, King Khosrow falls in love with Shirin, an Armenian princess whose beauty has also captured the heart of Farhad, a talented sculptor and master of geometry. In order to keep Farhad out of the way, Khosrow assigns Farhad to build a road through a remote area. Throughout much of the story, neither man is able to possess Shirin, resulting in much delay and disappointment, particularly when Khosrow is pressured into a political marriage with Maryam, the daughter of the Emperor of Byzantium. Although the stories diverge in some significant ways, we can see some echoes in the love triangle from *The Blue-veiled* that forms the backstory for this vignette in *Tales*. The power differential between the two men in *The Blue-veiled* echoes that between Khosrow and Farhad. Rasul, the factory owner, is able to use his economic power and higher social standing to steal Nobar's affections away from Reza, a young employee at the factory. Typically, however, other forces—in this case Rasul's daughters—get in the way, forcing Rasul to relinquish his young lover.

Like Khosrow and Shirin, only many years later would Reza and Nobar finally unite in marriage. Importantly, however, this vignette in *Tales* does not depict a simple "happy ever after" scenario. The male rivalry for Nobar's affections is reanimated by the arrival of Rasul's letter, which, although written on his deathbed, still has the power to evoke strong emotions in Nobar and Reza. Reza is once again struck by love's painful arrows. In the Persian poetic tradition, wherever there is love, pain and suffering are never far away.

This theme of the long-suffering lovers is picked up yet again in the very last vignette of *Tales*. In this tale, we are reintroduced to Sara, the central protagonist of *Mainline*, played by Banietemad's daughter, Baran Kosari. As the film opens, she is preparing for her marriage to her sweetheart, played by Iranian heartthrob Bahram Radan. As in the tale of Nobar and Reza described above, in *Mainline* Banietemad finds a clever way to bring a sense of love and intimacy to the screen whilst still working within censorship regulations. Sara's fiancé has sent a package from Toronto, where he waits for Sara to join him. The package contains a wedding dress and a video tape. On the television screen, we initially see Radan waltzing intimately with a woman, who is soon revealed to be a life-size dummy wearing a wedding dress. This joyous scene of impending marriage, however, soon turns to sadness as Sara relapses into a heroin addiction that she has struggled with for many years.

Whilst the theme of love in *Mainline* is not literally filtered through the proverbial love triangle of classical Persian literature, it is possible to perceive echoes of it within the film. In its animation of a desire, even stronger than that for her fiancé, Sara's drug addiction is emblematically presented as a rival lover that precipitates the failure of the love marriage. This is emphasized by her single-minded devotion to obtaining her next heroin fix. However, the more she desires it and the more she attains her desire, the more she is hurt by it. In classical Persian love poetry, the qualities of love are commonly personified by various objects, including wine, animals, birds, and flowers, as well as other natural phenomena. In *Mainline*, something slightly different is going on. Rather than the drug being personified to express a moral lesson, it is presented in the guise of a rival lover that serves to keep the "true" lovers apart. This emphasizes the great impact that drug addiction is having on Iran's youth, preventing them from leading productive, fulfilling lives such as that promised by Sara's impending nuptials at the beginning of the film.

The scourge of Sara's drug addiction comes back to haunt her in *Tales*. Sara has, as Banietemad suggests, become a better person. Having managed to beat her drug habit, she now volunteers at the women's shelter, helping female victims of domestic abuse and drug addiction. In the final vignette, she is assisting Samireh, who we met briefly in the tale at the women's shelter. Samireh has attempted suicide, suggesting perhaps that the blood tests she was awaiting in the earlier story have revealed that her daughter too has contracted HIV. Hamed (Peyman Moaadi) drives his taxi van for the shelter—one of his many part-time jobs—and comes to collect Sara and Samireh from the hospital. Coincidentally, in keeping with the thread structure, it is Nobar, an orderly at the hospital, who brings Samireh to Hamed's van. During this vignette, the relative privacy of the van provides the ideal conditions for an intimate conversation to take place between Sara and Hamed, a conversation that eventually turns to the topic of love. Before reaching this point, however, Hamed and Sara argue, each criticizing the other for not making the most of their lives. Sara teases Hamed for being expelled from university, where he had been studying engineering, for engaging in political protests—another likely reference to the events of 2009. In turn, Hamed accuses Sara of failing to move on from her drug addiction, even though she is now clean. Hamed confronts Sara: "Didn't you stop using so you could get on with your life? . . . I don't think you have quit yet. You still have some way to go." Throughout this heated session of truth-telling, the camera cuts rhythmically back and forth between Hamed and Sara, who is seated in the middle row of seats behind Hamed and in front of Samireh. Sara's gaze remains unfocused and occasionally she absent-mindedly twists a wisp of hair around her finger, as though her mind is somewhere else. This small detail adds a subtle but affective charge to the sequence.

Gradually, the heated argument begins to subside, but not before Sara challenges Hamed to get to the point. Finally, she interrupts him mid-sentence, asking, "Do you like me?" A moment of silence falls as the camera cuts back to Hamed, who has apparently not heard Sara's question. She repeats it. A longer period of silence ensues. Finally, Hamed responds: "What kind of question is that?" Sara interrupts him mid-sentence, repeating her question for a third time, this time demanding that he answer "yes or no." The dialogue in this part of the sequence slows down dramatically and is punctuated by longer periods of silence, which allows the impression of intimacy between the couple to grow even stronger. The pace of the editing matches this, cutting back and forth between one-shots of Sara and Hamed, broken only occasionally by a wider shot from the front of the van showing all three characters together in the frame and reminding us of the barely conscious Samireh in the back seat. During the shot-reverse-shot sequences, Banietemad produces a series of indirect gazes between Sara and Hamed. Intermittently we see Hamed look towards the rear-view mirror, through which we imagine he can see Sara. Sara in turn occasionally glances forward into the same mirror, where viewers can easily imagine their gazes meeting. This creates indirect optics of intimacy, which, when combined with the pace of editing and the momentary silences, produces a kind of cine-poetic cadence that allows viewers to feel the intimacy of the sequence not through the characters' physical intimacy but via cinematic techniques. The indirect gaze that has become a staple of post-revolutionary Iranian cinema, as one strategy among many to negotiate censorship, has been invested with a new purpose, producing an intimate connection rather than a cautious separation.

Repetition is also central to investing the sequence with a poetic dimension. Sara's earlier repetition of her question "do you like me?" becomes the first of several verbal refrains, which take on even greater significance towards the end of the sequence. Although Hamed has not yet responded to Sara's earlier question, he decides instead to answer it with a question of his own. Initially, he avoids asking directly. Instead, he says allusively, "Well, what do you think? (*Shoma chi?*)" Sara responds: "What do I think? (*man chi?*)" He tries to explain, but she interrupts again: "'what do you think?' isn't a question." He responds: "Well, I am asking. What about you? Do you . . . have feelings for me?" As he finally articulates his question, Hamed glances towards the rear-view mirror, once again making virtual eye contact with Sara. The camera cuts back to Sara, her gaze lifted so that it can meet Hamed's in the mirror. She pauses for a few seconds before giving her answer: "No! (*na!*)" This "no" cuts like the poetic thorn of a beautiful rose, and yet once again she responds "no", practically cutting Hamed off before he can finish his sentence. Banietemad chooses not to cut back to Sara as she utters "no" for a second time. Rather, her voice cuts across the image so that we may focus on Hamed's reaction as he pauses for a few seconds, not knowing what to say before posing a more direct question: "So, you have no feelings for me?" At this, the image cuts back to Sara as she repeats "no" for the third time. Whilst this might seem like a deployment of ritual courtesy (*ta'arof*) in which a refusal might be given three times before final acceptance, this is not quite the case here. The rhythm of the editing and the repetition of the dialogue reinforce the impression that a kind of poetic utterance has been building throughout the sequence. Their voices become calm and measured, allowing much of the earlier passionate negative energy to dissipate, rendering the exchange much more intimate and "touching." Although they use ordinary speech rather than the more formal language most commonly employed in Persian poetry, the scene attains a lyrical, or rather, cine-poetic quality through the rhythm of the editing and pacing of the dialogue.

Sara's three-time expression of "no" is quickly followed by yet another repetitive exchange. She enquires: "Is it finished?" (*tamoomeh?*). Hamed responds: "I don't know, is it finished?" (*ne midoonam, tamoomeh?*). Sara responds decisively: "Finished!" (*tamoomeh!*). Whilst, on the surface, this scene appears to be quite conventionally driven by colloquial dialogue, the poeticism that is rendered though vocal cadence—the alternation of sound and silence, pace, rhythm, repetition, framing, editing, and eye-line looks—serves to open up the sequence to a lyrical dimension that displaces narrative progression.

In response to Sara thrice answering "no" to his previous question, Hamed asks her whether the problem lies with him. The proceeding dialogue takes the form of yet another exchange based on repetition:

HAMED
I need an answer. Yes or no. Am I the problem? Or are you?
SARA
What's the difference?
HAMED
The difference is important for me.
SARA (repeats)
What's the difference?
HAMED
It makes a difference, answer my question. If the problem is me, then I have nothing to say. It's finished! (*tamoom*).

(After a pause)

SARA
Suppose I'm the problem?
HAMED
If you're the problem, it's okay. (*halleh*)
SARA
What's okay? (*chi halleh*)
HAMED
It's okay, I said. (*halleh dige*)
SARA
What's okay? (*chi halleh*)
SARA (She responds quickly almost cutting him off)

Suppose I am the problem.
HAMED
If you are the problem . . . then it's okay. (*halleh*)
SARA
What's okay? (*Chi halleh*)
HAMED
I've thought about this issue before. I've been grappling with it myself, to see if something is possible between you and me.

Once again, the use of repetition, vocal cadence, and pauses in the dialogue lend the exchange a poetic quality. In Persian, the repetition of the word *halleh* functions as a poetic refrain, albeit one that is decidedly quotidian. The remainder of the dialogue, which is delivered haltingly by Hamed line by line with long pauses in between, continues this suggestion of a lyrical exchange. He reveals that he knows that Sara is HIV-positive, a lasting legacy of her years of drug addiction, and a reminder of her former "lover" that now threatens to come between her and Hamed. With the revelation of this information, the pair fall into silence until Hamed once again gazes into the rear-view mirror, saying affectionately, "Sara *khanum* . . ."[2] He pauses, waving his hand to catch her attention. A cut back to Sara shows her slowly raising her gaze to meet his. As the shot cuts back to Hamed, still gazing towards Sara in the mirror, he pronounces the word *halleh* ever so gently once more, this time as a question, "is it okay?" The image holds for a few seconds more before fading to black as melancholy piano music plays on the soundtrack. That the vignette ends on the question "Is it okay?," followed by silence, leaves the fate of this couple undecided and the legacy of Sara's previous affair with heroin continuing to cast a shadow over her future. The question hangs poignantly, awaiting *her* answer.

Both of these vignettes use performance, dialogue, cinematography, and editing in unique ways to open up the film image—and with it, the theme of love—to a cine-poetic dimension that exceeds the narrative drive of the story. This suspension of the narrative works to further reinforce the importance of the poetic possibilities of film and the affective dimensions of love. Importantly, both sequences leave the question of the couple's union in a state of suspension, just as the fates of the other characters in the previous tales also remain open, unable to be contained by a single narrative.

CONCLUSION

Tales represented a welcome return to feature filmmaking for Banietemad after a significant hiatus of approximately five years. As Banietemad has explained, "after *Mainline* and under the Ahmadinejad government, I boycotted filmmaking . . . I didn't want to make films under such conditions" (Armatage and Khosroshahi 2017: 152). As mentioned above, the idea of making a feature film out of short films enabled her to circumvent the production approval process overseen by the Ministry of Culture and Islamic Guidance; however, it also gave her a unique opportunity to collect her œuvre into an intertextual cinematic *divan*. Whilst the film has been woven together from many parts, it is a whole and impressive contribution to Banietemad's œuvre that allows us to see many resonances across her fictional and documentary films. Indeed, the opportunities for intertextuality and modulation of filmic styles strengthen the film's commitment to exploring themes that have always been at the forefront of her fictional and documentary film practice. It also highlights some of the limits of documentary filmmaking in which the "camera is not able to record the 'real'" (Banietemad, quoted in Armatage and Khosroshahi 2017: 152) and the opportunities that fictional filmmaking offers for exploring deeper, more heartfelt stories. Whilst Banietemad stops short of claiming that her films can bring about social change, she refuses, like her characters, to surrender to conditions that might attempt to control or restrain her from making an impact. Reflecting the philosophical attitude of the documentary filmmaker at the end of *Tales*, she has stated:

> In the face of painful issues, resistances and struggle bring hope. For me as a filmmaker, hope for a better future comes through raising awareness through my films. My work keeps alive my aspiration to deal with the traumatic struggles that inspire and motivate life. (in Armatage and Khosroshahi 2017: 154)

As a cinematic *divan*, *Tales* is a fitting testament to this aspiration and to her life's work so far.

NOTES

1. *To Whom Do You Show These Films?* is also the title of a documentary film about housing that Banietemad made in 1993.
2. *Khanum* (literally, "lady" or "miss") is employed here as a sign of Hamed's respect for Sara.

CHAPTER 4

The Artistic and Political Implications of the Meta-cinematic in Rakhshan Banietemad's Films

Zahra Khosroshahi

INTRODUCTION

The first image that appears in Rakhshan Banietemad's latest feature film, *Ghesseh-hā* (*Tales*, 2014) is mediated by the fictional camera lens of an unnamed documentary filmmaker (Habib Rezaei). In this opening sequence, shot through the window of a taxi at night, he is recording the city of Tehran (Figure 4.1). He tells the taxi driver, Abbas (Mohammad Reza Forutan), "this is how I see." With the camera representing his point of view, the audience is offered a strong opening statement on the role that filmmaking will play in *Tales*; to film something is to see it, to make it visible. The meta-cinematic opening of *Tales* evolves into a theme and commentary on filmic technique that runs like a thread through the film. In this chapter, I argue that Banietemad employs this method as a way to comment on social and political issues in Iran. The film remains self-reflexive throughout, using its own medium as a way to engage with the wider context of its production and also the practice of filmmaking in the country. The film's ending is also significant: the documentary filmmaker, whose camera has by this point been confiscated, again stands in for his camera. Speaking on the phone in the film's final shot, he says: "Of course I'll keep shooting. Listen, no film will ever stay in the closet." The lines he utters in the closing moments of the film are significant in the Iranian context, commenting directly on the conditions surrounding filmmaking in Iran and the resistance displayed by directors like Banietemad in the face of restrictions and censorship. By bookending one of her most significant films with such strong statements about the importance of filmmaking, Banietemad has invited us to treat *Tales* almost as a manifesto for her practice.

Figure 4.1 The opening shot of *Tales*: through the viewfinder of a camera operated by a fictional documentary filmmaker

Banietemad's use of meta-cinematic techniques and scenes is a tool she has employed in other films as well. In her earlier works, *Bānu-ye Ordibehesht* (*The May Lady*, 1998) and *Zir-e Pust-e Shahr* (*Under the Skin of the City*, 2001), the director established her camerawork as a method for commenting directly on the form. Through a close textual analysis of her films, I will argue that, for Banietemad, "the medium is the message" (McLuhan 2013: 13) and that self-reflexive deployment of the camera enables and visualizes a significant part of the director's vision for cinema. The aim of this chapter is to explore in detail Banietemad's investigation of filmic form and cinematic language. Looking at the characters Forugh (Minoo Farshchi) from *The May Lady*, Tooba (Golab Adineh) from *Under the Skin of the City*, and the unnamed documentary filmmaker in *Tales*, I will examine the different ways in which these films use and respond to the role of the camera and filmmaking in Iran. I will demonstrate how, whilst the meta has always been a theme in her films, there is a strategy of progression and culmination which reaches a bold and political climax in *Tales*.

As such, this chapter will explore the centrality of the recurring theme of the meta-cinematic and the film-within-the-film as an artistic and political tool— one that is prominent and interlinked in Banietemad's body of work. I argue that, through the meta-cinematic, Banietemad comments directly on the very idea of cinema; the films allude to their own form, and this is especially significant in the way they challenge the censorship laws of the country. The chapter is also invested in what the camera reveals and where the visualization and use of the camera as a theme and technique lead us. Not only does the double-camera function as a vivid reminder of the cinematic form, but it also inevitably tells stories. These stories, enabled by the camera, are often concerned with gender, class, social, and state politics. In a country with censorship laws and strict guidelines, the hyper-visibility of the camera functions as a political statement. The significance of Banietemad's constant use of the meta-cinematic is at once artistic and political, which, as I argue, highlights the importance of the director's filmmaking practice and contribution to Iranian cinema.

In her book *Narcissistic Narrative: The Metafictional Paradox*, Linda Hutcheon looks at metafiction as "fiction about fiction—that is, commentary on its own narrative and/or linguistic identity" (Hutcheon 2013: 1). She uses the term "narcissistic" pointedly, "the figurative adjective chosen here as a way to designate this textual self-awareness" (ibid.). I will use Hutcheon's definition in this chapter as I explore the concept of meta and the film's commentary on its own filmic identity and narrative. As this chapter will explore, Banietemad's reliance on the meta-cinematic is not insignificant or limited, as it is a tool employed in other films as well. In addition, Banietemad's use of the meta-cinematic aligns her work with that of other important filmmakers in the Iranian canon. Abbas Kiarostami, one of Iran's most celebrated directors, has left behind a body of work that is highly reflective of the cinematic practice. Jafar Panahi is another prominent example, whose work offers a bold and political commentary on the state of cinema in Iran. His award-winning film, *This is Not a Film* (2011), responded directly to his arrest. He went on to make films such as *Taxi Tehran* (2015) and *3 Faces* (2018), which document not only his filmmaking, but also the culture of cinema in Iran. Though not devoid of politics, Kiarostami employs in his fictional narrative a meta-cinematic theme. Panahi's documentary style, on the other hand, is a bold political statement and a direct response to his arrest and the state of his country.

Banietemad uses meta-cinematic devices as a means of commenting on political and social issues through storytelling and narrative cinema. As this chapter will explore, this dates back to *The May Lady*, then appears again in *Under the Skin of the City*, and in *Tales*. But Banietemad's investment in cinema as a platform for social and political commentary dates even further back. A prominent example of this is Tooba's character, who not only appears in various narrative films but whose construction is inspired by Banietemad's documentary cinema. Documentary filmmaking is central to Banietemad's filmic career, impacting her style in later works as well. Most importantly, the entrenchment of the realist style and the meta theme in her films is significant because it reflects Banietemad's vision for the cinematic form:

> Cinema isn't my job; cinema is my life. Not that I am fascinated by cinema per se. Rather, cinema is a tool that visualizes and brings to the screen my concerns for my society and my country. Art for the sake

of art has no meaning to me. Art is a vehicle for raising awareness and producing knowledge, especially in societies like Iran. (Armatage and Khosroshahi 2017: 155)

In interviews, Banietemad has spoken of the important role of cinema as a social tool, and by drawing attention to the work that the camera can do in her films, Banietemad is explicitly advocating for the medium. The recurring theme of the meta and Banietemad's direct confrontation with issues and taboo topics in Iran reveal the director's vision behind her filmmaking.

According to Saeed Zeydabadi-Nejad, "social films" explore the country's post-revolutionary social and political issues through its cinema: "These issues range from social justice to the place of the clergy in the post-revolution society" (Zeydabadi-Nejad 2011: 55). Social films are crucially important to Iranian cinema because of the country's shifting politics. In addition to their explicit engagement with social issues, Banietemad's works stand out largely because of the way in which they merge the world of fiction and documentary (Sadr 2002: 471). Hamidreza Sadr writes of Banietemad that "she was one of the few documentary filmmakers who gradually moved into feature filmmaking. As a result, her films are often sympathetic portraits of actual people, and are frequently praised for their forceful and engaging approach to Iran's contemporary problems" (ibid.: 470). He continues by stating that the "importance of her films lies largely on the fact that they weave a path between fiction and documentary, between the imagined and the actual" (ibid.). This we see in many of Banietemad's films, where she blurs the line between fiction and documentary, film and reality. She achieves this through a realist and minimalist approach to filmmaking, with unexpected cuts, hand-held cameras, and a deep understanding of contemporary issues in the country. What this achieves is a cinema that is not only reflective of its time, but also dynamically responsive to its current issues. Films such as *The May Lady*, *Under the Skin of the City*, and *Tales* feature not only the film-within-the-film theme, but also Banietemad's dedication to a cinema that actively engages with contemporary social issues in Iran.

FORUGH IN *THE MAY LADY*

The May Lady's protagonist, Forugh, is a single mother, a filmmaker, and a lover, and her life balances and negotiates these roles. In the narrative, Forugh is assigned a new film project to find the "exemplary mother." Subsequently, she assumes the role of the filmmaker within the film, and the view through her camera becomes a central feature. The meta-cinematic theme not only drives the plot forward, it also offers a platform on which both Banietemad and Forugh explore the limitations of womanhood and motherhood. The film-within-the-film technique offers access into the lives of many mothers and their understandings of this contested role. In this film, the meta-cinematic is used as a way to develop Forugh's character, as well as to go beyond the surface to explore and complicate the theme of motherhood.

The May Lady is invested in the subject of motherhood through two lenses, one belonging to Banietemad and one to Forugh. The representation of motherhood in cinema, especially world cinema, is limited, as mothers in films are often "relegated to silence, absence, and marginality" (Kaplan 1988: 172). *The May Lady* contests this idea by explicitly including image upon image of mothers and their struggles. More importantly, the meta-cinematic in *The May Lady* comments on the importance of filmmaking in the telling of such stories, challenging misrepresentations of women and mothers in society. The lens through which we witness these stories and experiences is crucial because it alludes to filmmakers both real and fictional. Banietemad chooses when to highlight the difference between her lens and Forugh's, and when to merge them into a single perspective or frame. This allows Banietemad two key positions; firstly, when she highlights the fictionality of Forugh's work, she documents the work of a female filmmaker; secondly, she chooses when to associate her eye with Forugh's, thereby seeming to endorse the work or the message. Wayne Booth posits that "even with all the multiplicity of voices, every successful film does have what might legitimately be called an 'implied author,' or if you prefer, an 'implied center' that is, a creative voice uniting all of the choices" (Booth 2002: 125). In the case of *The May Lady*, the notion of the "implied author" is even more complex and layered. There is the director within the film (Forugh), the implied director (whose perspective is set back in the space of the "real" person making decisions behind the camera), and then the real director (Banietemad) whose actual decisions are introducing the sense that there is a "real director" present off screen. A key example of this blurring of fictional and real filmmakers occurs when one of Forugh's interviewees says, "A woman is not only a mother; she is a human as well." On the screen, Forugh's camera and Banietemad's lens—at first distinctive—merge into one here. Whilst, through Forugh's film project, we are always made aware of the self-reflexivity of the camera and the two distinct filmmakers, this merging displays a sense of harmony, or Booth's "implied center."

This notion of an "implied center" is made even more visible through the meta-cinematic technique. This becomes important because the various authorial voices/lenses that are present both behind the camera and within appear to endorse the same message. This is shown through *The May Lady*'s investment in interviews with various mothers, which become a large portion of the film. Through Forugh's camera, Banietemad sheds light on marginalized voices. The interviews draw attention to the way filmmaking operates, including the mundane technicalities of production. We see Forugh carrying out these routine requirements, setting up her camera and preparing her interviewee. In one instance, before she is ready to shoot, she asks her participant: "who do you think is an exemplary mother?" In this scene, as Forugh sets up, the scene conveys a realist tone where performance is blurred. Forugh's interview has not yet started, but it has for the viewer of Banietemad's film, and both Forugh and her subject are unguarded because the fictional camera is not yet rolling. In fact, the woman who is being interviewed even participates in this discourse, asking, "I have a question. Are you now filming me?" This alludes to the very performance of filmmaking, an explicitly meta-cinematic moment in *The May Lady*. The next shot is of Forugh's back as she engages in the performance of filmmaking. Then, the scene cuts to a close-up of the woman, from a perspective that we presume is how Forugh has framed the shot, as she explains her stance on motherhood. Once again, the two cameras merge and become one. The film's narrative and the documentary within the film become inseparable as one entity, and the subject becomes the focal point. Whilst initially we are made aware of the two cameras, the camera and the filmmaker both disappear into the background as the woman speaks, with only a close-up of this woman left on the screen.

The May Lady constantly engages and even negotiates with its own form and style, and uses Forugh's camera as a way to delve deeper into the stories of these mothers. Forugh's camera takes her to prison and to various corners of Tehran. The editing process that the film visualizes is perhaps one of the most significant. As Forugh compiles these clips and images of mothers on the screen, she also shows the process of filmmaking and the diverse range of stories and experiences of motherhood in Iran. For example, Forugh's footage brings to the screen images of mothers whose sons have never returned from war, as well as mothers who must now care for their children who have returned broken. Throughout, the film consistently remains fully aware of its own medium, using the film-within-the-film technique as a way to further explore the cultural, social, and political tensions surrounding motherhood in Iran. Whilst Banietemad is invested in the personal narrative of Forugh and her struggle, the film, through the meta-cinematic, extends and lends itself to other stories too, offering a more diverse and nuanced exploration of motherhood in Iran.

TOOBA IN *UNDER THE SKIN OF THE CITY*

Banietemad's films create a sense of continuity and progression, often revisiting characters and storylines from previous works, which provides a valuable temporal frame of reference for understanding social, political, and cinematic developments in Iran during a period of rapid and wide-ranging change. This is especially true of one of Banietemad's most iconic characters, Tooba, whose cinematic journey is intricately linked to the social and political conditions of Iran's film industry, as well as to the director's filmmaking practices. The role was developed by Banietemad in 1985 with actor Golab Adineh in mind for Tooba's first appearance in *Under the Skin of the City*. As a result of censorship laws, the film did not receive approval for sixteen years, finally screening in 2001 (Armatage and Khosroshahi 2017: 150). By this time, Tooba had already appeared, through Forugh's camera lens, on the Iranian screen in *The May Lady* in 1999. In *Under the Skin of the City*, Tooba takes center-stage, and she appears again in *Tales* years later in 2014.

Tooba's cinematic significance is complex— due in part to her journey to the screen and in part to her characterization as an illiterate, working-class mother who, despite reflecting the gender and class politics of her society, always embodies defiance. But the most important function of the character is the manner in which Tooba serves as a visual reminder of Banietemad's filmmaking practice and her devotion to cinema. Tooba's centrality within the director's films draws us to the recurring theme of the meta-cinematic, constantly asking questions about cinema itself. Tooba's most iconic line, "who do you show these films to anyway?", repeated in all three films almost like a catchphrase, comments on and questions the role of filmmaking in Iran, as well as the role of the camera for the director.

Tooba's role in *Under the Skin of the City* is also important in the ways in which it has shaped aspects of Banietemad's film career. Whilst Tooba is a fictional character developed over the years, her construction is inspired by Banietemad's documentary *To Whom Do You Show These Films?* (1993). In an interview, the filmmaker discusses the origins of Tooba and her famous line:

> The sentence which Tooba says in the film, the first time I heard this exact sentence was 24 years ago. I was making a documentary and a character called Mehri asked me: "Who do you show these films to anyway?" This sentence had so much meaning that it stuck with me. I used it time and time again in many films that I made since then. I think the reason I use it is as a reminder to authorities to know what people are feeling and be aware of their sentiments. (Talu 2015)

Tooba in many ways encapsulates Banietemad's filmmaking practices, and her origins, which date back to 1985, pay tribute to Mehri. As outlined by Banietemad herself, this sentence has "so much meaning", drawing our attention to the power dynamics at play in Iran, questioning the role and even importance of cinema. Tooba's skepticism of the camera, I argue, functions almost as a cry for help, where "who will watch these films?" seems to also say: "Will we be heard? Will we be seen? Is anyone, anywhere paying attention to the plight of the people?" There is undoubtedly an element of exasperation here, almost as if Banietemad is speaking through her character. This mood is picked up again in *Tales*, where Tooba once again faces the camera. This time when she says, "who will watch this anyway?", she continues with a smirk, "and if they do, so what?" Here, Tooba comments not only on a film industry that practices censorship and control, but also on the political circumstances of the country. She explicitly questions the filmic form, and its power (or lack of power) to create meaningful change. This sentiment and this skepticism, however, are confronted and even challenged by the end of the film in *Tales* when the documentary filmmaker has his camera back. Here, his fight to tell stories through the camera becomes a symbol of hope.

Under the Skin of the City engages with the theme of the meta-cinematic in various ways and, though Tooba's famous line is explicit, the film also has self-reflexive moments that are much more implicit yet still invested in the social and state politics of Iran. The film begins and ends with Tooba, marking her as central. Opening with a close-up shot, the film frames her face whilst officials interview her about the role of women laborers in the forthcoming election, which inevitably has political implications. The first image that appears on the screen is of a small Sony television, through which we first encounter Tooba. The image is at first blurred, and as it becomes more focused, the officials signal to Tooba to cover her hair. Here, following state orders, she adjusts her headscarf, fixing its edges and covering the exposed hair. In addition to the double screen, the scarf adds its own visual frame, marking Tooba as even more central in this opening scene. Here, I argue, the scene alludes to the petty politics of Iran regarding veiling, which is far more concerned with women's dress than with their workers' rights. The scene serves as a significant moment that invites us to think about veiling and its connection to the state, as well as the screen, directly confronting the issue of obligatory veiling. Banietemad, through the framing of Tooba's body, comments on the arbitrariness of the situation. She has found a clever visual device to note how much more strictly the headscarf is enforced on screen than in real life: a reminder that appearance matters more when it is captured in a format that can be shared, spread, and consumed.

By framing Tooba, this opening scene marks her as visually central to the film, foreshadowing her importance to the narrative from the very start. All the while, *Under the Skin of the City* is invested in the meta-cinematic—the frame-within-the-frame—to highlight the significance of filmmaking practice in Iran. The initial scene that centralizes Tooba comes full circle in the film's ending, but with different implications. In some ways, the film closes in the same way it begins, with Tooba as its focal point, the camera facing her directly. She is participating in the election, yet another politicized moment in the film, but this time Tooba is much more prepared for her appearance on camera.

There is no stuttering, her hair pokes out of her headscarf exposed, and her message is loud and clear: "Just forget it, I lost my house, my son ran away, and people are filming all the time. I wish someone would come and film what's happening here." Tooba points to her heart, and the film ends with her iconic question: "Who do you show these films to anyway?" As A. O. Scott concludes in his review, "there is a great deal of palpable political sentiment in this film: a quiet disgust at the way Tooba and her co-workers are exploited; a simmering contempt at the deeply ingrained habits of male domination" (Scott 2013: n.p.). But Scott also comments on the significance of Tooba's role in *Under the Skin of the City*: "the distraught mother facing the camera at the end is a figure not of pity, but of defiance" (ibid.). Tooba is now a passionate and articulate spokeswoman for change and resistance, and in a sense, Banietemad has found a way to film what is in Tooba's heart.

Throughout the film, Tooba's role remains intricately tied to the camera. She is at the heart of Banietemad's film; her defiance is part of the grander narrative (and one that is even further developed years later in *Tales*). But the treatment of the camera-within-the-film is also hugely significant, giving Tooba the cinematic space to develop, and to find her political voice. In its final moments, the film once again relies on the meta-cinematic not only to centralize Tooba and her struggle, but also to question the role of filmmaking. As shown thus far, in *The May Lady* the camera-within-the-film is used to bring to the fore cultural attitudes and perceptions of motherhood in Iranian society. Forugh's camera functions as a tool to offer a myriad of stories about women's experiences as mothers in a post-war Iran, all the while drawing attention to women's filmmaking. In *Under the Skin of the City*, Banietemad continues to use a second camera and frame to highlight social and gender issues in Iran, but she comments more explicitly on the act of filmmaking and, using Tooba's line, on the power and limitations of films. By the time we reach *Tales* in 2014, the self-reflexivity of Banietemad's cinema, and its back-and-forth dialogue with itself, has reached its climax. *Tales*, through its production context, structure, and narrative, embodies the very notion of meta. The film is a self-reflexive account not only of the filmic form, but of Banietemad's entire career.

THE DOCUMENTARY FILMMAKER IN *TALES*

Banietemad's latest narrative film, *Tales*, connects her previous works together through a series of shorts compiled into a feature-length film. In it, characters from her earlier films make an appearance, and through this revisiting and rewriting they are once again made relevant. With these seven short stories, *Tales* explores cultural taboos such as prostitution and drug addiction. It engages with gender issues, as well as social and state politics. Out of the stories of its characters pour the struggles of a society in pain. The background of the film and the characters' severe economic situations cannot be overlooked. During the production of *Tales*, Iran was under harsh economic sanctions and politically isolated from the rest of the world, and in this film, Banietemad explores and problematizes both the internal and the external political climates that impact ordinary Iranians. Through its portmanteau format, as well as its title, *Tales* invites its viewers to consider the power of storytelling. And yet there is even more at stake here. From its first shot to its final moment, *Tales* is fully invested in the practice of filmmaking.

It is the interconnectedness of these "tales" that makes the film's narrative structure especially unique. As one story ends, the next begins, offering a sense of continuity; in other words, we follow a peripheral character's journey from one story to another, making the film seamless and continuous. The characters, whilst connected to one another through the same cinematic space, have their own independent stories. The narrative structure of *Tales* is certainly reflective of Banietemad's artistic style. However, this format is also a result of its political context. The fate of the film industry underwent a drastic change in 2005 with Mahmoud Ahmadinejad in power. Zeydabadi-Nejad states that, in that year, "the newly appointed culture minister, Hossein Saffar-Harandi, announced that from then on distribution and exhibition of films which promoted feminism and secularism were prohibited" (Zeydabadi-Nejad 2011: 53). During this period, many films were banned. Importantly, then, the seven short stories in *Tales* come together as a result and consequence of the political restrictions in filmmaking at the time. These stories were meant to function as independent films because it is much easier to avoid censorship when making short films. After President Hasan Rouhani won the election in 2013, Banietemad decided to produce a feature-length film out of these shorter stories, connecting them together. In his review of *Tales*, Jay Weissberg writes:

> The film was ostensibly conceived as a series of shorts, making it possible to get a license under the Ahmadinejad regime, but with the current government she's been able to string together these stories of crushed hopes, addiction, abuse, and love. (Weissberg 2014: n.p.)

As a result, the narrative form and structure of *Tales* oscillate between various timelines. With this, the film takes us back to early post-revolutionary films by Banietemad. Her iconic and memorable films, such as *Nargess* (1992), *Rusari Ābi* (*The Blue-veiled*, 1995), *Under the Skin of the City*, *Gilāneh* (*Gilane*, 2005), and *Khun Bāzi* (*Mainline*, 2006), come to life in 2014 in her feature film *Tales*. The film lives through these various periods, and by returning to its past stories and characters, it also responds to its present. Through this, *Tales* flirts with the notion of time, producing a sense of nostalgia. Mostly, by inviting us to travel back in time, to rediscover and rewatch these lives and these characters, the film implicitly challenges the social conditions, legal institutions, and cultural attitudes of Iran's past and present. *Tales* not only draws our attention to the political atmosphere of Iran in relation to cinema, but also, through its form and style, pays tribute to Banietemad's artistic contributions to the country's cinema for over three decades. As such, *Tales* merges together art and activism—the political landscape of Iran informs the film, but also, the cinematic platform is Banietemad's confrontation with her country's contemporary politics.

As argued so far, the political and social context of Iran influence, and even necessitate, the structure of *Tales*. The film's indulgence of the meta-cinematic, however, is further complicated and layered, played out also at the filmic and textual level. Like *The May Lady* and *Under the Skin of the City*, *Tales* features a camera-within-the-film, and it does so as a way to comment on larger political issues and the status of filmmaking in Iran. The most telling of these moments is the bus scene that connects Tooba, Reza (Farhad Aslani), and their fellow workers in a confined space, as they make their way to a protest. What is significant here is the presence of the hand-held camera documenting the worker's outrage. The factory has shut down, and the owner has run off with the money. In this overly crowded bus, the workers have united to fight for their rights. The audience has access to these characters and their complaints through this hand-held camera that functions as the eye of the viewer. This small bus also creates a divide between the workers and the authorities.

In this scene, Banietemad once again plays with genre boundaries: the minimalist approach to filmmaking that is evident here adds to its realist style. Also, within the film, the filmmaker documents a "real" event—mimicking documentary filmmaking within the film. The story-within-the-story, whilst merely fictional, has an important function outside of the narrative. By touching upon a tangible issue that speaks directly about the economic situation of the country, the film comments on the impact of sanctions and the stifling internal politics of Iran. Whilst this fictional feature film relies on a realist style to confront everyday struggles, its reliance on the visible camera is also extremely meaningful. The audience's access to this scene is through the camera (Figure 4.2) that creates a double frame, displaying all the details (the battery charge, the time of recording, and so on) and reminding us that recording is in process. With this, Banietemad turns a once-realist film into one that is highly self-aware and meta-cinematic. Richard Tapper discusses how "many Iranian directors play with this poetically, by filming the making of the film, and by using documentary conventions and cinematic styles, minimal scripting, real people and real locations" (Tapper 2002: 15). This approach to filmmaking reaches its climax in this classic film-within-the-film bus scene, blurring the lines between fiction, realism, and documentary, and in the process drawing our attention to its filmic medium.

Figure 4.2 The bus scene through the hand-held camera of the filmmaker, showing the workers in *Tales*

Through its engagement with the mundane and everyday struggles, *Tales* offers a realist approach to cinema, both at the level of content and at the level of cinematic style. The audience joins Abbas's journey as he drives his taxi through the streets of Tehran. In its first ten minutes, the film deals with issues of filmmaking in Iran, the economic chaos that the country is experiencing, and prostitution—all filmed from a moving car. According to Negar Mottahedeh, realism is not "only about representational strategies embedded in specific notions of indexicality, iconicity, and the narrative's overall relation to a certain truth. Realism rests on narrative continuity" (Mottahedeh 2008: 162). *Tales* embodies and relies on narrative continuity as it connects various stories and characters to one another. An important question to consider is how the film achieves this through its visual means. It is my contention that the presence and visibility of the camera, and thus the act of filmmaking, have a lot to do with the film's portrayal and exposure of the country's social issues. Whilst many films may engage with the idea of the meta-cinematic, what marks *Tales* as different is the clash between filming and the authorities, which the film embodies through its production context and also through its narrative.

Tales visualizes the confiscation of the documentary-maker's camera, explicitly commenting on the conditions of filmmaking in Iran. As the workers, along with Tooba, attempt to get off the bus so that they can speak about their issues, the authorities keep accusing them of provoking hostility. Tooba refuses to give up, and the camera remains focused on her as she forcefully tries to open the bus door to get out. In this heated moment, as everything is captured through the lens of the camera, one of the authorities sees that filming is taking place and begins to scream, "camera!" He starts to cover his face, feeling threatened. At this moment, the camera-within-the-film stops recording, and the scene changes to the next story. In addition to Tooba's persistent fight, this scene has shown the fear and insecurities of authorities when filmed on camera. Most importantly, the camera shutting down in the middle of the "story" suggests its confiscation. In its final scene, the cameraman states on the phone that he has his camera back and that he will continue making films. He reminds the audience that no story will stay in the closet, and I suggest that we view *Tales* as that exactly—stories that are finally dusted off and compiled into a film. Its power lies in its awareness of the filmic medium and the many restrictions it faces and fights against.

The critical reception of *Tales* is also important to its deep and nuanced engagement with its social context. The way in which the film was made and received in Iran, along with its depiction of the political climate, make this an important contemporary work coming out of present-day Iran. As mentioned already, the film grapples with issues that are highly critical of the country's economic, social, and political situations. In our interview with the director, Kay Armatage and I asked Banietemad about the challenges she faced in making, producing, and screening *Tales*. It is worth looking at her response at length:

> *Tales* wasn't screened until four years after completion. It didn't receive the right to be screened under the presidency of Ahmadinejad [2005–13]. Even with permission to be screened, which came under Hassan Rouhani's presidency [2013 to the present], the immense pressure of opposing groups resulted in a two-year ban. Billboard ads for the film were forced to come down. The main cinemas that belonged to government institutions in Tehran and other cities boycotted the film and prevented its screening. They even blocked me from attending Q&A sessions and other events. At the end, without any publicity, and without any television or radio advertisement, and very few exhibiting slots, the film was screened. Despite all this, and without any advertisement, it took in ten billion Rials. (Armatage and Khosroshahi 2017: 153)

This encapsulates the complexities of Iran's film industry but also touches on the important role that cinema plays in Iran as a medium for change. As Banietemad speaks here about the constraints and challenges she faces in her filmmaking, it is difficult not to think back to Tooba's repeated question about viewership. And yet, the film's global success reminds us exactly about the importance of filmmaking.

The success of *Tales* goes beyond the boundaries of Iran. Screened all over the world, the film took home the award for Best Screenplay at the Venice

International Film Festival. The film's meta-cinematic theme has not gone unnoticed and yet, at times, it is under-appreciated. At the end of his review, Weissberg writes:

> Of course the documaker returns at the end, saying things like "no film ever stays in a drawer"—lines that pointedly refer back to Bani-Etemad as well as all filmmakers who push the boundaries of freedom of expression in censorious societies. The sentiment is important, yet did it really need to be so baldly stated, as if viewers weren't already aware of the character's purpose? More interesting is the conception of male–female relations, from the older couples in which women are long-suffering victims of impotent male rage to the younger generation, whose women display marked intellectual superiority and demand to be considered as equals. (Weissberg 2014: n.p.)

Weissberg rightly recognizes the generational difference in regard to gender relations that the film illuminates; however, whilst he recognizes the "sentiment" behind the meta-cinematic gestures of the film, he is critical of how "baldly" they are stated. Films in Iran undergo strict revisions to ensure they meet the guidelines of the Islamic Republic set out by the Ministry of Culture. It is impossible to ignore the role of the camera as an agent of social change in such films. Through *Tales*, Banietemad cleverly responds to the censorship politics of her country. In several moments, the film makes explicit and bold references to the issues of journalism and filmmaking in the country. In fact, the meta-cinematic elements of *Tales* become the very thread that connects these several stories together. The issue of censorship then becomes an integral part of the narrative and thematic structure of the film, commenting on larger issues of censorship and of freedom of expression that is often limited in a place like Iran. It is to this unique and timely social and political situation that *Tales* responds. Weissberg's commentary carries an assumption that these moments and "sentiments" are included only for the audience. I argue, in contrast, that filmmaking in Iran is often so politically charged that any stance against the censorship laws becomes a point of resistance.

Tales uses its own body—its own form—to convey various issues and to bring forth a complex representation of the social conditions in present-day Iran. And in doing so, Banietemad uses the camera as a central motif (and even a character in its own right) to comment on and problematize through filmmaking larger social and political issues. In this way, both within the storyline as a thematic technique, and outside of it as the practice of filmmaking, the camera becomes a powerful tool. Within the film, the camera functions to connect the separate "tales." The film's narrative structure relies on the intersection of seven different stories. In these narratives, Banietemad's most memorable characters once again return to the screen, reminding the audience of the historical and cultural significance of her previous films. These past stories and figures merge together, giving birth to a new story. Most importantly, however, Banietemad's characters embody a sense of nostalgia, showing how these figures have become iconic, yet, by revisiting these characters, they are rewritten, reinvigorated and redescribed in dialogue with Iran's present.

CONCLUSION

In its final scene, the filmmaker in *Tales* walks solo. He has his camera back after it had been confiscated by the authorities. Speaking on the phone, he says: "Of course I'll keep shooting. Listen, no film will ever stay in the closet. Some day, somehow, whether we're here or not, these films will be shown." And as these words are uttered, we are reminded yet again that we have just witnessed a story that has come into existence and "out of the closet" after years of censorship. The film's obsession—or, as Hutcheon puts it, "narcissism"—with its own form is not incidental. Storytelling is enabled by the camera, and so filming in *Tales* is a form of telling, exposure, and resistance. As shown in this chapter, Banietemad uses the meta-cinematic as an artistic tool to comment on social and political issues in Iran. The film-within-the-film theme becomes an important mode through which she critiques and challenges her society. These include issues around motherhood and the representation of women, as we have witnessed in *The May Lady*. In *Under the Skin of the City*, with Tooba's character and the double camera, Banietemad explores other dimensions of filmmaking, questioning the very idea of the practice. In *Tales*, Banietemad's commentary on film and filmmaking is even more heightened and political.

The cyclical return to the filmmaker in the final moments of *Tales* is crucial, reminding us again not only of the significance of the camera, but also the power of storytelling. So much of *Tales* is about filmmaking in Iran and is a tribute to Banietemad's past characters and even the camera itself. As illustrated in this chapter, the meta-cinematic theme plays in Banietemad's body of work throughout the years, as an artistic and cinematic style that provides social and political commentary. Most importantly, Banietemad's hyper-aware camera is always aligned with the vision she holds about filmmaking. In Iran, where the film industry and many of its artistic expressions are controlled through censorship laws, Banietemad's constant and explicit commentary on the filmic form is itself a highly political act.

PART III
Gender, Love, and Sexuality

CHAPTER 5

"Modes of Expression not Subject to the Law of Male Desire": Considering the Role of Voice-over and Enunciation in the Work of Rakhshan Banietemad

Rosa Holman

Cinematic sound has frequently been theorized as a subsidiary element, working to support the primacy of the image, but feminist film theory and women's cinema have often endeavored to foreground sound and privilege the voice. The narrative and aesthetic strategies for experimenting with this sound–image interplay are various and heterogeneous, but their purpose is intrinsically related to the recovery of women's identity and authority within film. Critics have often rightly expressed ambivalence about the application of "white feminist film theory" to non-Western national cinemas, arguing that its universalizing construction of "womanhood" and gender ignores the politics and particularities of location and socio-historical context. This chapter, however, seeks to affirm the place of 1980s feminist film theory on the voice in elucidating some of the strategies associated with the use of voice-over in the work of Rakhshan Banietemad. This theory's persistent emphasis on the voice as a site of resistance and enunciation proves highly relevant when discussing the intersection of gender and identity in Banietemad's œuvre. Arguably, the objectives of Banietemad's cinema frequently intersect with the aims of feminist film theory: that is, to reclaim discursive authority over the representation of women's identities and bodies to use the voice as a means of asserting knowledge, agency, and influence. The use of voice-over in Banietemad's films performs the complex role of both evoking the absent body and its forbidden desires, and deflecting the spectatorial processes of objectification and eroticization. It enacts a dialectical role, frequently enabling revelation, subversion, and forthright disclosure, and at other times remaining oblique, poetic, and dissimulating.

Applying feminist film theory need not deny a film its socio-political context or historical specificity. At no point should a monolithic and all-encompassing conceptual framework based in feminist film theory and practice be adopted as the only means of understanding Iranian women's cinema and the construction of gender and identity in Banietemad's film. Women's "voices" should always be conceptualized as heterogeneous entities, incorporating the "conflictual diversity of women's experiences, agendas and political visions" (Shohat 2001: 293). Theorizing women's "voicing" thus must always be married with historical background and cultural context. Feminist film theory needs to be persistently checked and, at points, countered by the "national and racial discourses, locally and globally inscribed within multiple oppressions and resistances" (ibid.: 294). This chapter is thus intent on retaining an emphasis on the politics of location and the importance of historical particularity whilst seeking to affirm the place of feminist film theory. In particular, it references the scholarship that emerged in the 1980s and focused primarily on the voice and its relevance in analyzing *Bānu-ye Ordibehesht* (*The May Lady*, 1998), *Our Times* (2002), and *Gilāneh* (*Gilane*, 2005). Feminist film scholarship remains pertinent to this body of Banietemad's work precisely because of the manner in which the voice is foregrounded. Often eschewing a physical on-screen presence, it is frequently the female protagonist's voice that attains prominence in the film. So feminist film scholarship, too, has continued to privilege the voice and sound, and in doing so, reformulate and revisit the notions of spectatorship, representation, gender, and power.

The voice in the context of Iranian cinema has particular cultural and social significance as a result of the Islamic modesty codes that were implemented by the post-revolutionary state. In an attempt to purify Iranian cinema and demarcate it as a product of the newly emerged Shi'ite state, *hijab* (modesty) became a central feature in the representation and regulation of women's bodies and subjectivity from 1982. In the new socio-political paradigm of post-revolutionary Islamic cinema, the act of looking upon non-veiled women was both sexualized and forbidden. As Negar Mottahedah notes, the "commandments for looking (*ahkam-e nigah kardan*)" enforced the presence of the veil as a compulsory aspect of women's participation in the cinema industry, working on the assumption that a "non-familial heterosexual male is always present in the audience" (Mottahedah 2008: 10). Confronted with modesty codes that restricted the realism of the film's diegesis, many directors adopted the voice as a new site of creative expression. Both Farzaneh Milani and Hamid Naficy have discussed the manner in which *hijab* had the paradoxical effect of strengthening and consolidating women's individual voices in all of their diversity and regional accents. As Milani wrote:

> Women are raising their voices, telling their tales. Even those that portray themselves as victims of society—conforming, enduring, suffering—are

gaining a significant victory in being able to plead their own cases and make their stories heard in their own words. They are survivors, the ultimate rebels, irrepressible, vocal and articulate. (Milani 1992: 234)

The voice in post-revolutionary Iranian cinema thus must also be considered as an instrument in the various campaigns for greater legal and personal freedoms. Ziba Mir-Hosseini makes the important point that an integral aspect of the drive for the expansion of women's rights in the 1990s was the socio-cultural revisioning of women's roles (2004: 214). The endorsement of women as "social beings" with a political role, as opposed to the prescribed familial and spousal functions, challenged some of the most fundamental precepts upheld by the Islamic Republic of Iran. Voicing in the context of Iranian women's cinema must be extrapolated, not just in terms of film theory and feminist scholarship, but via historical accounts that also situate the voice as a form of cultural and political visibility in post-revolutionary Iran.

The films of Rakhshan Banietemad also reflect this socio-cultural repositioning of women, where the voice is the site of personal, romantic, and sexual revelation, as well as the vehicle for enunciating and reimagining women's socio-political and familial role in Iran (Naficy 1994). The voice in Banietemad's films enacts a dialectical role, frequently confessional whilst at other times oblique and dissimulating. The voice in Banietemad's cinema is thus not subordinated by the visual image but often privileged. The foregrounding of the voice permits intimacy and personal revelation, as well as promoting ambiguity and poeticism. Veiling here is thus associated not only with both the presence of the sartorial veil and the representation and interpretation of the cinematic modesty codes, but also with the notion of veiled meanings and the use of poetic inference. The relationship between veiling and voicing in Iranian women's cinema is a complex one, connected as it is with both the process of disclosure and the masking of meaning. Veiling and voicing work dialectically, revealing and concealing, often simultaneously. Whilst the "voice" therefore must always be situated against the specific cultural codes dictating the representation of women in Iranian cinema, this chapter proposes that Banietemad makes use of the voice as a means of resisting and managing the prescriptions of Sharia *hijab*, and in doing so, reclaiming ownership over the representation of women's identities and bodies, and the expression of desire.

Hamid Naficy, in his discussion of Iranian cinema and subjectivity, writes in terms of an inner "core" and a public "shell" (1994: 131). The public shell is the familial, communal self that negotiates the social world, whilst the inner core is the secret, intimate, private self. In order for the two selves to function symbiotically and seamlessly, there needs to be a veil or a screen which protects the core self and keeps it concealed. The social strategies of "dissimulation, disavowal, aversion, indirection, evasiveness, cleverness, self-presentation and ritual courtesy" assist in maintaining this division between public and private subjectivities (ibid.). The veil is thus not only the sartorial *hijab* but also, according to Naficy, the social and cultural boundary that splits the self and necessitates a range of complex and subtle communication strategies. Language, like the self and the body, is also veiled and hermeneutic. The voice as an arbiter of language may be used to reveal and conceal intentions and desires depending on the use of informal/formal address, the degree of emotion portrayed in the tone and tenor, and the adoption of allegorical or poetic terms. It is important to understand, Naficy stresses, that these veiling practices are dynamic and dialectical in their application; *hijab* is as much about unveiling the body, the voice, and the core self as it is about obscuring the intimate aspects of experience and subjectivity—"that which covers is capable also of uncovering" (Naficy 2000: 561). Obviously, the references to the "core" in Naficy's schema may problematically imply an underlying unified and coherent subjectivity, with all its inherently universalizing and homogenizing overtones. But Naficy's discussion of the schism between the public and private personas is not interpreted here as a monolithic ontological model of subjectivity that reinstates a static and fixed subject position. Rather, it is understood as an exploration of the manner in which Iranian Islamic cultural mores have been received, interpreted, and applied, within both social and cinematic contexts. References here to the "shell" and the "core" are thus adopted as a way of delineating what behaviors and experiences are sanctioned as socially acceptable and appropriate, and what is deemed taboo, prohibited, and inviolable within the contexts, codes, and rituals of *hijab* in post-revolutionary Iran.

Naficy cites Rakhshan Banietemad's film, *The May Lady*, as a prime example of a post-revolutionary film that is both governed by and resistant to the prevailing modesty codes of the time (Naficy 2000: 561). *The May Lady* was Banietemad's sixth feature film and marked ten years of working as a director and screenwriter of social dramas. Films such as *Nargess* (1992) and *Rusari Ābi* (*The Blue-veiled*, 1995) established Banietemad as a respected and pioneering filmmaker within Iran. Her features continued to straddle the genres of melodrama and social realism, often self-reflexively gesturing to the processes of filmmaking, and documentary making in particular. *The May Lady* is thus characteristic of Banietemad's œuvre: the central character, Forugh Kia (Minoo Farshchi), is a documentary filmmaker and is a divorced, single mother to her adolescent son, Mani (Mani Kasraian). Forugh divides her time between filming and editing her documentary on the search for the ideal Iranian mother, nurturing the sometimes obstinate and jealous Mani, and conducting a relationship with an off-screen lover, Mr Rahbar. Banietemad employs a range of devices for evoking the absence of the veil. Not only do these strategies assist in retaining the reality aesthetic of the narrative, but they allow for a more complex portrayal of the schism between Forugh's public "shell" and what Naficy termed her private "core."

It is interesting to observe the manner in which Banietemad endows Forugh with what I call "substitute" veils as a means of gesturing to those experiences that may violate the codes of *hijab*. Some of these (such as in the scene where Forugh is seen preparing herself in the morning and wearing a towel loosely over her wet hair) serve the purpose of retaining a greater reality aesthetic and evoking the daily habits of veiling and unveiling. In other scenes, the function of the substitute veil is more subtle and complex; Forugh speaks intimately with Mr Rahbar on the telephone and yet neither character appears on screen. Mr Rahbar is visually absent throughout the entire film and can be heard only as a disembodied voice. In one particular scene, we hear the couple talking on the telephone. A semi-opaque curtain, literally dividing her apartment from the outside world, obscures Forugh. Instead, her presence is suggested solely by her voice and the shifting specter behind the billowing curtain. In another scene, Forugh's inner thoughts are externalized through a voice-over as Forugh is filmed in close-up, lying in bed. Her face is completely framed by a shadow that simultaneously acts as a veil (covering her hair and body) and suggests her unveiled state. These strategies have the advantage of both complying with and circumnavigating the cinematic modesty conventions; Forugh appears suitably covered and yet her body and her private desires are strikingly evoked. It is important that these substitute veils are semi-opaque; they are neither completely transparent, nor completely dense. They reside somewhere in between; they are porous, permeable, and flexible. They hint at exposure and yet they never fully disclose the body, nor the desires of the "core self." They neither fully reveal nor completely conceal their object. In fact, by not subscribing to notions of veiling and unveiling, Banietemad also rejects a whole body of regressive binaries associated with femininity: erotic/modest, active/passive, mother/whore. Forugh, as implied by Banietemad, refuses to conform to those narrow definitions associated with the polarities of veiled and unveiled. Instead Banietemad privileges allusion and intimation over strict representations of veiling or unveiling.

Just as the substitute veils allow us to glimpse Forugh's private desires, so too Banietemad uses the voice and voice-overs to evoke the intensity of Forugh's romantic relationship with Mr Rahbar. As Naficy has argued, the effect of disembodying Forugh's lover is that the voice itself is charged with heightened emotional affect, and ultimately the vocal exchanges work as a "substitute for . . . desire" (Naficy 2000: 572). It allows Forugh and Mr Rahbar to "become one vocally" and Banietemad to represent the intimacy of their relationship without compromising her adherence to the regulatory codes (ibid.: 573). The voice-over in *The May Lady* thus not only allows Banietemad to circumnavigate certain censorship restrictions, but also challenges the traditional conventions of representing women on screen.

Such strategies may also be associated with Kaja Silverman's framework when she discusses "dislodging the female voice from the female image" (1988: 166).

Theorists such as Mary Ann Doane (1987) and Silverman (1988) have argued that the voice-over, when the narrating character is also embodied within the diegesis of the film, might operate as a "feminized" and thus disempowered entity. Silverman believes that this is because a film's visual system often works against the authority of non-synchronized sound in an attempt to re-establish the primacy of the image. The female voice-over was frequently used in the films of the 1940s, particularly in the studio-created genre of the "women's film." Doane proposed that, in such films, the voice-over was adopted as a way of undermining the female protagonist, with the female narrative perspective being eventually exposed as deceptive, irrational, or incomplete (1987). But feminist film theory of the 1970s and 1980s also analyzed the manner in which the female voice-over breaks the unity of scopophilia and fetishism, and allows for more subversive, contradictory, or dialectical readings. In particular, Silverman suggests that women's experimental and avant-garde cinema situated the female subject beyond the objectifying gaze of the male spectator. In *The Acoustic Mirror: The Female Voice in Psychoanalysis and Cinema*, Silverman argues that the female voice-over and other acoustic strategies can work to disrupt the ingrained hermeneutic codes of dominant cinema. By "dislodging the female voice from the female image" (1988: 166), women are freed from representational conventions that limit female characters to immanence, sexuality, and passivity. This process of disembodiment can be achieved in several ways: through multiple female voice-overs, non-synchronized dialogue (or pronounced lip syncing), monologue, and musical lyrics. Silverman's intervention is very much informed by Jacques Lacan's theory of "lack" and Jacques-Alain Miller's notion of "suture." As Shohini Chaudhuri writes:

> Through every frame-line and cut, cinema threatens the viewer with castration, making them aware of their own irredeemable lack by gesturing to the greater authority of the hidden enunciator. At the same time, this wound is sutured over with a signifying chain that distracts the viewer by offering meaning and narrative. (2006: 49)

Chaudhuri explains that whereas suture is often understood as a visual mechanism (such as the shot/reverse-shot), for Silverman the rule of audio synchronization is also a means of maintaining the illusion of cinematic cohesion. The disembodied female voice-over is thus a strategy for breaking with the suturing mechanism of synchronization, allowing the female identity to exist within the symbolic order (the sphere associated with language and discursive authority). Silverman also uses Freud's "negative Oedipus Complex" as a way of theorizing the manner in which the female subject may regain symbolic power through identifying and desiring the mother. Silverman termed this drive the "homosexual–maternal fantasmatic." Whereas mainstream cinema works largely to limit women's voices to the function of an "acoustic mirror" (distracting male spectators from their lack/impotence), according to feminist film theory of the 1980s, women's avant-garde and experimental cinema constructs "alternate models of female subjectivity" (1988: 57).

Whilst Banietemad does not use multiple female voices in *The May Lady*, the intersection of Forugh's and Mr Rahbar's voices arguably achieves a similar effect. Bodies are effaced and desire is predominantly inscribed in the film through intonation, wordplay, and sound. The film opens with a monologue from Forugh in a voice-over, whilst a series of photographs featuring women are framed in close-up. The confluence of Forugh's voice with the varying images of women "problematizes . . . corporeal assignment" and again challenges the representation of the female character as a coherent, visual object (Silverman 1988: 165). Interestingly, the use of voice-over in *The May Lady* can be theorized as working on two levels: both evoking the intimacy and desire of the lovers and situating it beyond the gaze of the objectifying spectator and censor. By "dislodging" the body from the voice, the expression of desire and pleasure may be inscribed into the film via the medium of the lyrical voice-overs, which both exposes and obscures Forugh's subjectivity. The substitute veils enable the body to be simultaneously veiled and unveiled, and so too the poetic language of the voice-overs (detached as they are from a coherent visual subject) allows Forugh's desire to be voiced and unvoiced. This tension between exposure and obscuring points to a form of cinema that privileges intimation and inference over transparency and monolithic meanings.

When describing the work of ground-breaking poet and filmmaker Forugh Farrokhzad, to whom Banietemad's protagonist in *The May Lady* pays constant homage, Rahimieh and Brookshaw describe the artist's innovation as instituting "modes of expression not subject to the law of male desire" (2010: 4). So too does the representation of the most intimate aspects of women's subjectivity in Banietemad's work avoid fantasies of eroticism and purity, creating a discursive space beyond voyeurism and objectification, prescription and censorship. This chapter needs to be careful to avoid the descriptor "feminist" when discussing the ideological orientation of the films in question. Iranian women filmmakers have themselves been careful, and at other times adamant, to distance themselves from such a universalizing, hegemonizing, and Euro-centric idiom. Yet it has been productive to observe the manner in which the aims of feminist film theory do at times coalesce with the strategies employed by some Iranian women filmmakers. In creating films that centralize women's experiences, Banietemad eschews the regressive dichotomies and discourses associated with both modernist and traditionalist conceptions of femininity and women's socio-cultural status. Indeed, the intersection of filmmaking and activism has special relevance when examining the works of Iranian women filmmakers, despite the guarded and diplomatic manner in which they have to identify, or deflect, their political motivations. A study of Banietemad's cinema needs to acknowledge the risks and ingenuity of such filmmaking and the manner in which these cultural artefacts participate in a set of broader cultural and political discourses and debates.

Indeed, Banietemad's documentary *Our Times* (2002) plays with these very notions of filmmaking and activism. The film is set during the presidential campaign that took place during May and June 2001, beginning eighteen days prior to the election ballot. This first section of the documentary follows Banietemad's sixteen-year-old daughter, Baran Kosari, and her friends as they canvass for the re-election of President Khatami. Banietemad comments via voice-over that "they in fact recognised the election as a chance to speak out their needs and desires." The documentary then shifts to interviewing the various women who have put themselves forward as presidential candidates, with an extended section on one particular candidate, Arezoo Bayat, who is a single mother living with her young daughter, Zeinab, and her blind mother. As she is confronted with imminent eviction, the remainder of the film follows Arezoo and her difficulty in locating a new home.

Our Times is peppered with scenes of Banietemad shown driving her car through the streets of Tehran, narrating and reflecting on the events of the documentary via a voice-over commentary. Reminiscent of scenes in *The May Lady*, the camera is positioned behind Banietemad so that only her eyes are visible in the rear-view mirror. The reoccurrence of this scene, particularly during the first half of the documentary, reinstates Banietemad's authorial presence through her on-screen bodily presence via her voice-over. As Cecilia Sayad astutely observes, in the construction of the directorial presence in cinema: "The staging of authorship normally shifts between assertion and divestiture, palpability and disappearance, exposure and masking" (2013: xxiii). So, too, Banietemad's presence in *Our Times* recreates the dialectical tension between concealing and revealing, previously discussed as such a central feature of *The May Lady*. But in this case, it is Banietemad herself who oscillates between asserting her on-screen presence and then receding into the role of an off-screen observer. The scenes in which Banietemad appears in the car neatly encapsulate this paradox and form a kind of authorial signature throughout the film: as the director, she maintains her authority through both her voice-over and her bodily presence, but she also remains "masked," with spectators only glimpsing the director's eyes via the reflection in the rear view-mirror. Authorship is a central concern throughout Banietemad's œuvre, with the poetic voice-over and self-reflexivity adopted as means of inscribing the authorial presence into the cinematic narrative. In documentary films, authorship continues to be asserted through the use of the voice and an aesthetic of reflexivity, but it also emerges through the unique on-screen interaction between the director, their subject, and their audience.

Alexandra Juhasz argues, in her essay "No Woman is an Object: Realising the Feminist Collaborative Video" (2003), that documentaries that attempt to reveal socio-cultural injustice have the potential to reinstate the processes of oppression and marginalization. In discussing her role as the director of the film *Released* (2000), which is composed of five short videos exploring women's experiences in prison, Juhasz stresses the importance of eschewing victim narratives:

> Produced with the intention to reveal and heal injustice and pain, such performances serve primarily to cement the systems of domination, suffering, and pleasure that form the natural mechanics of both the original punishment and its depiction. In this way, the documentary exchange is also like the prison. Both systems weaken some and strengthen others, using technologies of vision and distance, all the while buttressing hegemonic power. In both the prison and the documentary, the one charged with vision wields power. Distance and difference, in both scenes, force or coerce silence and testimony in turn. Class, race, and gender relations structure these interactions and are thereby solidified. And, by maintaining the classic position of subject/object, the victim documentary also necessarily reestablishes the inside/outside binarism that is not merely metaphoric but definitive of imprisonment. (Juhasz 2003: 73)

The question is, then, by representing Arezoo as powerless to effect systematic change, has *Our Times* entered the hazardous terrain of the "victim documentary," in which socio-economic suffering is perpetuated through the filmmaking process? Juhasz and feminist scholarship of the documentary in general (Crow 2000; Juhasz 2003; Lesage 1984, Smaill 2012; Waldman and Walker 1999) have identified the need to reposition the viewer so that the spectator is provided with alternatives to the voyeuristic practices of objectification and victimization. It is useful to apply Juhasz's schema as a means of assessing Arezoo's representation in the film and the degree of authority and voice that Banietemad affords Arezoo in *Our Times*.

Interestingly, the scenes of Arezoo's increasingly desperate search for accommodation are interspersed with (an off-screen) Banietemad encouraging Arezoo to continue to reflect on her aspirations as a presidential candidate. "Tell me why you decided to become a candidate," Banietemad says to Arezoo, even as the single mother sits on a street corner between visiting real estate agents. Each time that Banietemad questions Arezoo in this manner, the subject becomes animated as she recounts how she would achieve greater housing opportunities for single mothers. The processes of hypothesizing and strategizing appear to energize the deflated Arezoo. As she confides to Banietemad, "In my dreams I saw myself amongst the people. I thought that if I really became President I would understand all people because I've been in every situation they have—poverty, uncomfortable living, addiction, and unemployment".

Later, sitting in the street, she continues: "I just wanted people to listen to what I had to say." In persisting with the thread regarding Arezoo's interest in politics and her own personal aspirations as a politician, not only does Banietemad provide her subject with a platform to practice oratory, but she and the implied audience of the documentary become the attentive listeners that Arezoo has so long desired. With women largely discounted from the formal political process through their disqualification by the Guardian Council, Banietemad develops an alternative public forum for women's political voices to be publicly heard. Between 2002 and 2004, *Our Times* was shown at film festivals in such diverse locales as Boston, Los Angeles, Taiwan, Seoul, and Locarno. As Banietemad explained in an interview at the time of the film's release, "I want to set a precedent, so that all the documentaries that are being made and that don't have a place to be shown can finally find an audience" (Proctor 2002). Her commitment to distributing and screening *Our Times* provides an avenue for women to be re-enfranchised with a political voice and an attentive, receptive audience.

Whilst Banietemad and Arezoo may be unable to overhaul the systematic patriarchal privilege of the Iranian government and its arbitrary and unjust exclusion of women, as an established and respected filmmaker, Banietemad is able to exercise agency in promoting the capability of women as political thinkers through the medium of the documentary. *Our Times*, as Hamid Naficy notes, is believed to be one of the first documentaries to have been distributed commercially under the Islamic Republic and was screened in "fourteen theatres nationwide" (2012b: 46). In her account of a "packed" screening at the Khanehy-e Honarmandan (Arts Forum) in Tehran, scholar and commentator Naghmeh Sohrabi (2002) writes that due to the popularity of Banietemad, all seats were taken in the regular hall and thus she and many others had to watch the film from a rehearsal room. Sohrabi describes *Our Times* "as an alternative form of protest" that gives "dignity" to her subjects.

Banietemad thus creates the opportunity for Arezoo's story to be heard not only via the international film festival circuit, but also, and more importantly, within her own country and by her fellow Iranians. The distribution of *Our Times* both within Iran and abroad, in which almost an hour of the film is dedicated solely to Arezoo's story, demonstrates Banietemad's commitment to finding an audience for her documentary subjects so that their stories can finally be "heard" by large and diverse audiences.

And it appears that Banietemad does afford the same degree of "dignity" to Arezoo in *Our Times* in encouraging her subject not only to recount her personal history, but also to discuss it within socio-political terms. Arezoo is thus portrayed as a woman negotiating highly difficult circumstances and capable of interpreting them in socio-political terms and theorizing solutions. The film finishes with a freeze-frame of Arezoo's face as she stands outside her workplace, having just been dismissed by her boss. Her expression is one of barely contained grief and exhaustion. Via a voice-over, Arezoo is given one final opportunity to speak:

> Mrs Bani-Etemad, I am Arezoo . . . On the last day of registration for the Presidential Candidacy when I went to register, I thought that people should hear what I had to say because my thoughts were similar to theirs and my life experience was similar to theirs. On the day of the elections, in the midst of moving house, I lost my birth certificate. I couldn't vote and the president was elected anyway. And you made a film. And I said some things. But there is still a great deal more I want to say. Maybe one day I will write it all down or maybe . . .

After Arezoo's distressing experiences of having lost her home, her employment, and her right to vote (and being filmed in the process), Banietemad ultimately privileges her subject's voice and her desire for an audience, with the final words of the documentary attesting to her continuing desire to speak out. Not only does Arezoo acknowledge that she "said some things," she admits to wanting to "say more." The "voice" of the documentary has shifted from that of Banietemad's authorial narrative to that of Arezoo's story, thus replacing Banietemad as the key orator. This final scene avoids victimizing or objectifying Arezoo's suffering and instead positions her as the authoritative, speaking subject. It does so through two strategies, the freeze-frame and the voice-over.

No longer viewed observationally from a distance or in an intimate close-up in which spectators witness her spontaneous displays of distress, Arezoo's power in the film's final moment emanates instead through the timbre of her voice, the conviction of her tone, and her emphasis on the fact that "people should hear what I have to say" and "there is a still a great deal more I want to say." The accent is almost entirely on the act of speaking itself, both acoustically through the medium of the voice-over and via Arezoo's recurrent use of the word "say" (*goft*). Indeed, her voice in this scene remains unwavering in its strength and assurance—inflected with the notes of experience and resilience. This chapter previously discussed the importance of Kaja Silverman's (1988) theorization of the female voice-over as disrupting the ingrained hermeneutic codes of dominant cinema by situating the female subject beyond the objectifying gaze of the spectator. So, too, in this scene, does Arezoo's representation via the freeze-frame and the voice-over place the emphasis on Arezoo's agency, capability, and socio-political judgment. The fact that her voice was presumably recorded in post-production also implies that Arezoo has at last been provided with the opportunity to speak in a more considered, reflective, and perhaps even rehearsed manner. Just like President Khatami, who in several scenes is shown speaking to large crowds, so too is Arezoo permitted the opportunity to speak outside of the urgency and distress surrounding her search for accommodation. Once again, Banietemad utilizes the voice-over as a means of affording her subjects an authoritative and galvanizing medium to articulate their identity, their desires, and their political hopes for the future. In exploring alternatives to the "victim narrative", Juhasz proposes that the voice be used as a means of conveying the "strain", "fatigue", and "wariness" of the subject's experience, but in tones that are "not fearful, are notably non-didactic, and are rarely pathetic" (2003: 90). As Juhasz writes:

> Instead these women present themselves as well-qualified judges of a systematic condition that they have experienced personally. So, in our video, the viewer or documentary is not set up to judge the victim. Rather, the victims judge the system(s). (2003: 90)

Certainly, Arezoo's voice at the conclusion of the film fulfills Juhasz's criteria for a non-victim narrative, in that the tenor of her voice denotes resilience and force despite the manner in which the political system has failed her. Juhasz stresses the importance of the voice in allowing the subject to tell her own story, whilst avoiding objectification and judgment by the viewer. In foregrounding Arezoo's voice in the final moments of *Our Times*, Banietemad effectively positions her participant as an authority on women's suffering, whilst not categorizing Arezoo as a victim herself. In addressing herself directly to Banietemad, "who made a film," whilst she as the social actor "said some things," the emphasis is placed on the reciprocal process of filmmaking. Whilst the practice of joint authorship or collaborative representation may not be fully realized here, in the final moments of the film the participant is privileged as the expert voice, capable of articulating suffering and envisaging socio-economic alternatives. Arezoo's final monologue also could be theorized as a gesture of consent, addressed to Banietemad, in which she provides the filmmaker with permission to construct the "film." In allowing Arezoo to complete the documentary in her own words, the social actor and the director enter into a dialogue in which they jointly inscribe women's experiences in Iran.

Significantly, the final words of Arezoo's monologue are: "Maybe one day I will write it all down or maybe . . ." The repetition of the term "maybe" infuses this scene with Banietemad's characteristic elements of ambiguity and indeterminacy. Whilst Arezoo's speech appears to reinstate her self-belief and the importance of her voice, there also remains an element of ambivalence: a recognition of the unknown, where even defiance and continued struggle do not guarantee freedom or better outcomes. In their discussion of the prevalence of the freeze-frame in Iranian cinema, Chaudhuri and Finn (2003) discuss the strategy as that which "suspends interpretation," allowing the image to remain open and ambiguous. Arezoo's frozen image, mirroring her final word, "maybe," also points to the territory of the unknown and unknowable: namely, Arezoo's future prospects, her employment, her ability to care for her daughter and disabled mother, and her own emotional welfare. Whilst it was argued that in a film such as *The May Lady* the dialectical impulses of concealing and revealing meant that the protagonist's identity was always "glimpsed" and remained ambiguous, in *Our Times* it is the material reality that is positioned as unknowable and incomprehensible. The protagonist can only hazard a guess at her future prospects, her personal determination and strength being persistently offset by the unpredictable and problematic nature of socio-political reality in post-revolutionary Iran.

Gilane represents yet another shift for the filmmaker in terms of the treatment of the voice and its dialectical relationship with the image (Figure 5.1). The film was a directorial and written collaboration with Mohsen Abdolvahab, who, like Banietemad, had a background in documentary filmmaking. The film is set in the village of Espili in the Gilan Province, northwest of Tehran. The year is 1988 and Iran is suffering through its eighth year of being at war with Iraq. Here in Espili, Gilāneh (Fatemah Motamed-Aria) anxiously watches over her adult children, Ismael (Bahram Radan) and Maygol (Baran Kosari). Like

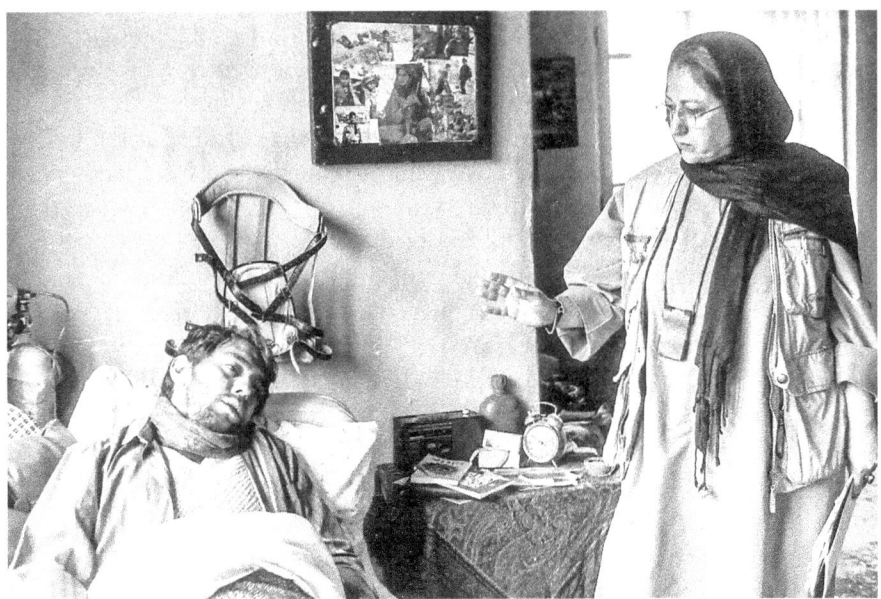

Figure 5.1 Banietemad on the set of *Gilane* (2005)

Gilāneh, whose husband was martyred in the current Iran–Iraq War (1980–8), both son and daughter have also become caught up in the conflict. Ismael is leaving for the war front yet again, whilst pregnant Maygol becomes increasingly distressed about the loss of contact with her Tehran-based husband, Rahman. She, like many other city-dwellers, has left town in order to seek refuge from the air attacks perpetrated by Iraq.

Gilāneh remains stoic and optimistic in the face of such hardships; excitedly anticipating the forthcoming birth of her first grandchild, Ismael's prospective wedding, and the building of her own family restaurant in the village. But Gilāneh's resolve is tested when Maygol decides to travel back to Tehran in search of her husband, and Gilāneh is forced to accompany her. En route, the mother and daughter encounter the displaced communities of the war, traumatized soldiers, and televised images of the dead. Staggering their way into Tehran, they discover the capital in ruins and Maygol's apartment abandoned, her husband presumably having left for the front.

Overcome by grief and anxiety, Gilāneh frequently attempts to bury and mask her distress with her *chador*. The labor-intensive process of wrapping and unwrapping their bodies in veils and blankets, as they attempt to ward off the cold en route to Tehran, takes up considerable screen time. The landscape of the film reproduces this process and, in doing so, reveals the inadequacy of the veil in protecting the human form against the suffering of the war. Builders try to cover the skeletal frame of the restaurant with flimsy tarpaulins that are no match for the deepening fog and freezing winds. Gilāneh's small house is surrounded by a washing line, on which sheets billow in the cold wind, drawing attention to the house's isolation and exposure. There is a sense that Banietemad and Abdolvahab are intent on revealing the "nation's wounds, rather than effacing them through the discourse of martyrology" (Langford 2012).

Michelle Langford (2012) discusses the manner in which various "post-revolutionary filmmakers reconfigured notions of *vatan* [homeland] in their cinematic engagement with the history of the Iran–Iraq war (1980–1988), its material and emotional aftermath and the "duty of care" required to "tend to the nation's wounds." During the eight-year conflict, the Iranian state maintained that soldiers had a *taklif-e shari* (religious duty) to participate in the conflict and defend the freedom of not only Iranian soil, but all Shi'ite Muslims (Nooraninejad 2018). Participation in the war became a religious obligation and thus a form of "sacred defense," in which martyrdom was encouraged and glorified. As part of its ideological program, the government instituted a War Films Bureau from 1983, which specifically supported productions that positively memorialized and justified the deaths of those who died as martyrs in the war. Gilāneh, however, exposes the inadequacy of such ideological discourse and its tragic implications. The distress of the various women impacted by the war, widowed or made permanent carers to disabled soldiers, is represented in the starkest way possible. The device of coupling the blank black screen (or "slug") with a voice-over is used three times during the film and acts as a mechanism for evoking the individually and collectively experienced trauma of the war. Significantly, in all three scenes the black screen is either proceeded or followed by the image of Gilāneh embracing her children and attempting to calm their suffering.

In the opening scene the black screen is accompanied by the sound of sirens, gunfire, and Maygol's voice whimpering in a nightmare. The screen remains black for twenty-five seconds before the visual of Gilāneh's and Maygol's bodies becomes evident, and we hear Gilāneh comforting her daughter in her bed: "Don't be afraid, you were dreaming!" In the second scene, Gilāneh is again embracing Maygol, this time in Tehran during the air raid, and as people are enveloped by smoke and chaos, Gilāneh is heard crying: "Relax, relax, my dear! God willing, my Delavar [grandson] will be born healthy. So will Ismael's children." The screen fades to black, but Gilāneh's voice continues as a sound-bridge, sobbing via voice-over: "Ismael! Ismael! Dear Ismael! Where are you sweetheart?!" Inter-titles then explain that fifteen years have elapsed; the year is now 2003 and the Gulf War is impacting the region. The screen returns to black and this time we hear the sound of rasping breath before the screen reveals Ismael convulsing and foaming in a paroxysm of post-traumatic distress. Gilāneh attempts to comfort him and her voice sings out in pain as she tries to hold him down but is instead thrown from his body.

Whereas the "veiled images" or "substitute veils" in *The May Lady* represented an "off-screen" and inferred desire, in *Gilane* the black screen may depict the unrepresentable horrors of the Iran–Iraq War in its final days before the ceasefire of 20 August 1988. I have discussed elsewhere the manner in which the blank black screen is adopted as a formal device to evoke those tragedies and traumas that defy visual signification (Holman 2016). In relation to Forugh Farrokhzad's documentary, *Khaneh siah ast* (*The House is Black*, 1962), and her employment of the blank screen and use of voice-over, I observed that such a device draws attention to the limits of visual reproduction and places an emphasis on the capability of the voice for evoking the experiences of embodied suffering (Holman 2016).

However, the black screen may also operate as the "ultimate cinematic shadow" or "curtain" that encloses a scene (Sadowski 2017). Whereas it was Forugh's subjectivity and her desire that were veiled and unveiled in *The May Lady*, it is the visual image itself that moves in and out of darkness in *Gilane*. The cinematic syntax of *Gilane* reflects this cyclical process of veiling–unveiling–veiling via the repetition of the black screen and the manner in which it cloaks or enfolds the scene and thus the spectator's access to the diegetic world of *Gilane*. As Langford (2012: n.p.) argues, "Gilāneh" refers to both the individual subjectivity of the war widow and the allegorical representation of "Mother Gilāneh" as an embodiment of the Iranian soil and the homeland itself. The black screen in the middle of the film thus acts as a "temporal ellipsis" that purposefully links the history of the Iran–Iraq War to the film's second act during the Gulf War. Langford, referencing Gilles Deleuze and Walter Benjamin, argues that the blank screen thus serves as a "cinematic rendering of time as simultaneity: past and present coalesce, the one folded into the other". In this sense, Gilāneh's invocation of Ismael's name demonstrates the manner in which trauma is like a palimpsest for the Iranian people: accumulating and ever-present. The scars of the Iran–Iraq War remain overlaid with the pain and isolation experienced during the "present" Gulf War.

However, it is the role of voice and sound that ensures that the blank screen is never devoid of meaning or signification in *Gilane*. The use of soundscapes imbues the dark images with both a highly individually and a collectively experienced sense of trauma. At the beginning of the film, Gilāneh is able to dismiss Maygol's experience as a "dream," which can be diffused by comforting words and soothing prayers. By the second act, Gilāneh is living a permanent nightmare. Now elderly, she finds herself caring for a physically and psychologically disabled Ismael. A small roadside hut catering for passing visitors has replaced the dream of the family-run restaurant, which Gilāneh personally attends between caring for her son. Due to Ismael's deteriorating condition, she desperately seeks out someone with access to a telephone that can call for a doctor. But despite her various attempts, she remains cut off and isolated, now an observer as the world moves on. When a neighbor passes on a horse and casually asks after Ismael, she does not answer, instead whispering to herself: "What do you want me to say?" All Gilāneh's hopes now rest with the arrival of Atefeh, another war widow, who she wishes will marry her son despite the age difference and the fact that she would essentially replace Gilāneh as a permanent carer in an isolated village. As the day continues, the prospect of Atefeh's arrival becomes increasingly unlikely. In the final scene of the film, the doctor, himself maimed by his service in the war, finally arrives with a sedative and medication for Ismael. He observes that Gilāneh looks "weak," to which she replies, "Better to be a dog, than a mother!" As he leaves, he implores her to take shelter: "Mother Gilāneh, go inside, it is bitter cold." But utterly exhausted and dispirited, Gilāneh appears to be unable to move. Instead, she is left alone, gazing upon the landscape, as her home is enveloped by a thick, cold fog.

The mist that blankets the house and appears to erase Gilāneh herself performs quite a different function from the black blank screen. Whereas the blank scene privileged the voice and used sound to frame the darkness with a highly specific cultural and located meaning, the white fog operates as a veil of silence enveloping its war victims and, allegorically, all oppressed Iranian people. In the final moments of the film, robbed of her former hopes and stoicism, Gilāneh is rendered voiceless and obscured. Gilāneh infers that silence may be the sole tool available to women in their confrontation with the ideological doctrine of militant Islam and the state program of martyrdom. In her chapter, "Silence as Female Resistance in Marguerite Duras's 'Nathalie Granger,'" E. Ann Kaplan discusses the "politics of silence, as a female strategy to counter the destructive male urge to articulate, analyze, dissect" (1988: 95). Kaplan argues that silence may enable the protagonist to resist the oppression of male-biased language and the symbolic order constructed through its discourse. But as Kaplan also notes, silence as a form of dissidence is a highly problematic strategy that may result in women being excluded from the processes of change and empowerment. "Silence seems at best a temporary, and desperate, strategy, a defense against domination, a holding operation, rather than a politics that looks toward women finding a viable place for themselves in culture" (ibid.: 103). Gilāneh's final retreat into silence and wordlessness represents the failure of martyrdom as an ideological and religious construct in Iran. Far from assisting her to support her son, the state has left her physically and psychologically broken, barely able to support herself or her charge. The Islamic Republic, as well as the international community, has abandoned "Mother Gilāneh"—and, by extension, all Iranian women and victims of the war. In *The May Lady*, Forugh was on a quest to find the "ideal mother" in her documentary project. Gilāneh, as a selfless, stoic, and ever-devout mother, embodies the very "ideal" promoted by the Islamic Republic. But as Gilāneh discovers, the service of motherhood continues into perpetuity and is relentless in its demands. The only way that Gilāneh foresees an escape from the prison of motherhood is by ostensibly replacing herself with yet another exhausted and grief-stricken war widow. To Gilāneh, this seems like a more plausible option than receiving any ongoing assistance from the state, for, in Gilāneh's eyes, it is the women who must shoulder the burden of the dead and disabled.

This chapter has been interested in examining the relationship between the acoustic voice and its relationship to the visual image in Banietemad's films. It makes the case that, just as the voice may attest to the presence of the director, the subjectivity of the character, or an allegorical representation of Iran itself, it may also conceal, complicate, and diffuse meaning. Voicing thus should never be understood as the simple process of revelation and disclosure. Instead, voicing in Banietemad's cinema is often predicated on the principles of poeticism, ambivalence, and allegory. One of the central arguments of this chapter has been that there exists a tension in Banietemad's films between revealing and concealing (or veiling and unveiling) women's history, experiences of homeland, and selfhood. The use of inference and "veiled" meanings often enables her to construct a more realistic and intimate women-centered narrative. Voicing, however, also refers to the innovative use of the voice-over in Banietemad's cinema and thus the indirect representational strategies central to the processes of inscribing identity.

Whilst Western feminist film theory of the 1970s and 1980s was centrally concerned with conceptualizing the role of spectatorship and the manner in which the practices of voyeurism and scopophilia objectified, eroticized, and victimized women on screen, Iranian women filmmakers have been confronted by a different set of challenges: namely, the formalization of the modesty codes instituted by the Islamic government. It would be specious to ignore the very specific, particular, and local contestations surrounding the representation of women in Iranian cinema and the manner in which identity, sexuality, and relationships are informed by a history of Persian poeticism, *hijab*, and the corresponding practices of "dissimulation," discretion, "performativity," and "indirection" (Naficy 2012b).

The voices in Banietemad's films are diverse, manifesting in the cinematic text via heterogeneous strategies, and sometimes not constituting a literal acoustic voice at all, but a silence, a fissure, an enigmatic gap. At other times, the voice is foregrounded as a literal vocal entity, expressed via the voice-over that privileges the importance of enunciating women's identities. This chapter has thus argued that the voice remains one of the most important constituents of Banietemad's œuvre, as both an aesthetic strategy and a means of reinstating socio-political visibility and influence. Here, voicing refers not only to the consolidation of artistic authority, but also to the opportunity to opine, analyze, and rehistoricize. The female voice in Banietemad's films is thus in perpetual flux, alternating between the roles of authoritative documentary-maker, political analyst, and distressed mother figure. Indeed, the common thread throughout the aforementioned films is the ongoing emphasis on motherhood and the protagonists' continued struggle to embody the qualities of the "ideal" mother. What becomes clear in these films is that such a maternal "model" is completely unattainable, and even those who seek to exemplify such purity and devotion will be punished in some way by the forces of ideological and cultural marginalization. Forugh, Arezoo, and Gilāneh are thus bound by their attempts to negotiate motherhood in an isolated landscape, reclaiming their identities through vocalization, enunciation, and the expression of their ongoing grief.

CHAPTER 6

Affective Listening, Sonic Intimacy, and the Power of Quiet Voices in Rakhshan Banietemad's *The May Lady*: Towards a Cinema of Empathy

Laudan Nooshin

INTRODUCTION

In one of the opening scenes of *Bānu-ye Ordibehesht* (*The May Lady*, 1998), the central protagonist, documentary filmmaker Forugh Kia, travels with her film crew from the affluent north of Tehran to the poorer south of the city. This affluence is marked in the establishing shots of modern apartment blocks and building sites, indexing the opening up of the economy in the 1990s, following more than a decade of austerity and war, all set against the imposing backdrop of the Alborz mountains to the north. But not everyone has benefited from economic recovery. As the car journeys south, it approaches a set of traffic lights and we see street children from the provinces dodging the traffic in an attempt to reach the occupants of temporarily stationary vehicles in order to sell their wares. One group crowds around Forugh's front passenger seat window, and she asks where they are from and why they are not in school, finally urging them to move out of the way for their own safety as the lights turn green. This short scene establishes Forugh as an empathetic presence, something that is reinforced in the course of the film, and which is most obviously marked through the act of listening, and in particular a kind of empathetic listening that will be explored in this chapter. As Forugh continues on her journey, the social divide (crudely conceived as between north and south) is marked both visually by the more traditional, low-lying mud and brick architecture, and sonically by the more open acoustic of spaces without high-rise architecture, and by the regular overhead sounds of airplanes, marking the area of Tehran close to the (until 2007) international Mehrabad airport. Forugh and her team arrive at the filming location and we see them filming a group of children, as Forugh asks them what they want to be when they grow up. This elicits a range of responses—teacher, engineer, lawyer, actor, filmmaker, and finally, as everyone's gaze is drawn by the camera to firstly the sounds and then the image of a plane overhead, pilot. The contrast between these aspirations and the enormous obstacles that stand in the way of these children achieving their ambitions is marked by a quality of attentive listening and empathy that sets the tone for the whole film. There is a great deal in this opening sequence that speaks to Banietemad's concern with social justice and inequality. In particular, the car journey and the sounds of the planes reinforce the contrast between Forugh with her social and physical mobility, and the children who are largely trapped in the cycle of poverty that successive governments have failed to tackle. This contrast is made even more stark in the scene that follows, as Forugh returns to her comfortable (north Tehran) apartment and has dinner with her teenage son, Mani, who she feels takes his many social privileges for granted.

This chapter explores the act of listening in *The May Lady* and attends both to what the characters in the film listen to, and to what that listening means. I am particularly interested in how the act of listening lays bare aspects of the materiality of sound that have, by and large, been under-theorized and often overlooked in the literature on Iranian cinema with its almost exclusive focus on the visual. Despite the centrality of sound to the post-1979 film aesthetic, most obviously in arthouse cinema, an almost fetishist preoccupation with the visual and other dimensions, such as political and social commentary, has largely obscured the role of sound and, by extension, the labor of sound engineers and sound designers. But what might an attention to sound reveal about the work of Banietemad, and in particular the kinds of messages that lie hidden within the sonic? This chapter will explore these questions with specific reference to a single case-study film, *The May Lady*, in which sound plays a strategically central role. I focus on three interrelated themes, outlined as follows. First and foremost, *The May Lady* is a film about *listening*, both physically and metaphorically, about who listens to whom and who has the authority to listen and to be listened to. Through Forugh's performative act of listening, the audience is invited to pay attention to the voices of the women from all walks of life that she interviews and films. Indeed, the structure of the film itself amplifies these through a kind of "double listening" as we listen to Forugh listening. Further, Forugh's authority and position as a respected professional are largely marked through the ways that her colleagues and others listen to her. However, *The May Lady* goes beyond the purely metaphorical deployment of female voice as a symbol of agency and actively foregrounds the intensely material and embodied sounds of women to an extent rarely heard before in Iranian cinema. Alongside the questions above, then, the chapter asks what kinds of subjectivity are engendered through the foregrounding of such voices. The tendency to fetishize the visual, both on the part of censors and among scholars, has left the empowering potential of sound largely unacknowledged. Drawing on a range of literature, on the voice in cinema and on voice as a site of female agency, I examine how the purely sonorous material qualities of the spoken voice, such as timbre, texture, and contour—often presented as being outside of referential meaning—in fact communicate a great deal to the listener "beyond words." In this way, *The May Lady* facilitates a new kind of filmic intimacy, affective subjectivity, and embodied listening rarely experienced before in Iranian cinema.

The final aspect of sound that I will consider is how, almost as voyeurs, the audience is invited to listen in on and share the sonic intimacies of Forugh's daily rituals. Since the film follows her in a largely linear way, we hear the world almost entirely from Forugh's perspective as we are enfolded in her listening experiences, which include the sounds of domestic work and exercising, as well as the liminal spaces that connect her public and private lives, such as the car and the stairwell of her apartment block. We are also admitted into the most intimate spaces, where, in the absence of sanctioned physical contact, Forugh's communications with her lover are entirely sonic, by way of love letters and telephone conversations. In particular, through the poetic letters, Banietemad aestheticizes strategies designed to circumvent restrictions on the visual portrayal of intimacy.

It is perhaps no coincidence that a film about listening should have been made at a time when the national discourse in Iran increasingly promoted notions of civil society, to which listening to others is central, and to the "dialogue among civilizations," which requires a listening sensibility between nations. Such discourses were particularly associated with the presidency of Mohammad Khatami (1997–2005), during which time Iran experienced a cultural flowering. *The May Lady* is thus very much of its time, capturing something of the national mood in the late 1990s.

LISTENING (AND FEELING) THROUGH THE LADY: TOWARDS A CINEMA OF EMPATHY

One of the many interesting aspects of *The May Lady* is the sheer number of voices and perspectives that are heard, primarily through Forugh's work as a documentary filmmaker and her encounter with voice after voice through interviewing, filming, editing, transcribing, and so on. Thus, the structure of the film allows for an amplification of these voices through what I term "double listening": the audience experiences the voices through Forugh's performative act of listening and we attend to them in ways that are shaped by her responses to what she hears. Due to the nature of the project for which Forugh has been commissioned (identifying and making a film about "exemplary mothers"), almost all of the voices are those of women, largely from disadvantaged sectors of society. Much has been written about the ways in which Banietemad's work blurs the boundaries between documentary and feature films, representing the two sides of her professional life, and *The May Lady* is no exception (indeed, there is a strong element of autobiography in the film). What is particularly striking is the sheer number of women we encounter, each with her own story. There can have been few, if any, Iranian films previously in which so much of the voicetrack is dominated by the sounds of women. Banietemad is known for "giving voice" to the disenfranchised through her films, but what the double listening arguably facilitates is a concentrated attention on these voices as they are put into a listening "frame," a frame that accords value to those being listened to. The message is that we may learn something from those whose voices barely register in the cacophony of national debate. This focus on listening also draws attention to the subtle power relations at play in terms of who has the authority to be listened to. We hear these voices because Forugh has selected them; our listening is contingent on her mediating role as gatekeeper. As an educated, middle-class professional, Forugh commands a level of authority and respect which is, in large part, marked through the ways that her colleagues and others listen to her. But her status is also precarious and provisional: the moment her voice is detached from that status, she is just the sound of another woman, as in the scene where she is making telephone calls to arrange interviews with government and other public figures. One office she calls immediately assumes that she is a secretary calling on behalf of a male filmmaker, as Forugh responds: "You mean any woman who calls you should be a secretary?" (39'28"). Whilst disembodiment can in some contexts be empowering, it can also work to fetishize, in this case the female voice as the only defining feature of the sound-producing body.

There has, of course, been considerable scholarly attention to notions of listening, most obviously in sound studies and associated areas, but also in many areas of music studies, including those related to film and media. From Pauline Oliveros's concept of "deep listening" to Anahid Kassabian's "ubiquitous listening" (2013) and Michel Chion's (1994) work on cinematic listening, there have been various attempts to identify and categorize different kinds of listening and types of listener. Tom Rice provides a useful overview of theoretical approaches to listening, including culturally and historically shaped modes of listening: cultural–historical, technological, sociological, and multisensory/corporeal (2015). Michelle Langford considers Chion's three modes of listening in the context of Abbas Kiarostami's film *Shirin* (2008), to which she adds a fourth, "a kind of affective listening in which we listen with our bodies and through which a range of sense perceptions are activated" (forthcoming). I would argue that something very similar is taking place in *The May Lady* where there is an intense identification of the viewer–listener with Forugh's "earpoint" as we become drawn into her sound world. This kind of listening shares much with that discussed by Winters in relation to representations of concert listening in films, where music creates "a shared subjectivity between film audience and character" (2014). We listen through Forugh but we also listen *together* with her as one body.

The fact that Forugh is ultimately unable to fulfill her brief in identifying an exemplary mother also sends another message: that there are many voices which need to be heard. The individual stories of suffering proliferate and consume Forugh, such that she becomes overwhelmed as she listens repeatedly, to the point of obsession. From the single mother married at sixteen and divorced at twenty-five, with three children; to the woman widowed in her twenties with three children, who has educated herself through night school and is now aiming to go to university; to the mother who lost one son to the Iran–Iraq War and who has for many years devoted her life to caring for the paraplegic son who was wounded in the same conflict; to the woman queuing every week to visit her son, in prison on charges of drug smuggling; and on and on. What is most striking from the first interview that we hear (19′21″) is the quality of listening, as Forugh sits at her living-room table in the privacy of her apartment, sifting through photographs of the women she has talked to, whilst listening to an interview with one Behjat Bordbar Azari. At first, we see her making notes; she then pauses and stops writing to listen more intently, placing one hand under her chin and the other against her head, then sighing as she brings her closed fists up to her mouth. It is significant that we first hear Behjat's disembodied voice before the film cuts to a flickering, low-quality video recording of her as the setting shifts to the more public space of Forugh's workplace editing room (the unbroken voice providing a smooth transition between the two spaces). The camera cuts between images of Forugh, deep in reflective listening with her hands under her chin, and the screen that she is watching. What is of interest here is not just how Forugh's intense performance of listening invites the audience to share the aural experience with her, but through the embodied listening conveyed through her body language, the invitation extends to a sharing of Forugh's emotional journey. What I want to argue here is that Forugh engages in a very particular kind of empathetic and affective listening, encountered repeatedly throughout the film: one that facilitates a new kind of filmic intimacy and embodied subjectivity that had rarely been experienced before in Iranian cinema and which might be termed a "cinema of empathy."

From the interview with Behjat, Forugh fast-forwards to the sounds of another on the editing machine, and within seconds we are transported to the "actual" interview on a terrace, in or close to the interviewee's home. Once again,

Figure 6.1 *The May Lady* (20′47″)

the unbroken voice-over of the interviewee provides the transition between "on-screen" and "live" presence, and again Forugh is placed as the immersed and empathetic listener, without the barrier of the camera. Now in direct dialogue with her interviewee, we see Forugh respond and smile (Figure 6.1).

There are some interesting class and ethnic issues at play. The interviewee starts by introducing herself as "Taghizadeh" in Azari, marking her as being from Iranian Azerbaijan, most likely a first- or second-generation migrant. Forugh asks her to continue the interview in Persian, but the opening serves to alert the audience to the sounds of ethnic otherness. Taghizadeh's *chador* clothing indicates her lower social class, but she is not so religiously fervent as to don a black *chador*. It turns out that Taghizadeh is a formidable woman who, despite social and financial hardship as a widow and single working mother, not only has managed to ensure the education of her three children, but has herself attended night school and is preparing to take university entrance exams. At this point, Forugh cannot resist exchanging a glance with Mani, who she had previously admonished for taking his (privileged middle-class) educational opportunities for granted. Education as a route out of poverty and dependence for women is a central theme in Banietemad's films, seen, for instance, in *Zir-e Pust-e Shahr* (*Under the Skin of the City*, 2001), where the illiterate protagonist Tooba is taught to read by her son.

It is interesting that in the course of these two interviews the film moves seamlessly from the privacy of Forugh's apartment, to the more semi-public space of the editing suite and out into the more public world (but still within the confines of Taghizadeh's home), marked by the "audience" of curious onlookers from an opposite window, who are presumably not privy to the sounds that the film audience hears. This movement marks the different degrees of privacy and publicness that are so integral to conceptions of space in Iran, and is also mirrored by the equally seamless move from audio only (in the apartment) to video recordings (in the editing room) and the final live interview. Significantly, what stays constant is sound, in the form of the narratives of the two women, which arguably serve to mediate the blurred boundaries between the "real" and the "documentary" aspects of the film.

One of the most emotionally charged early scenes in the film is a visit to a family which lost one son in the Iran–Iraq War (1980–8), the other returning paralyzed. Forugh and Mani approach the family's home via a narrow passage and are admitted into the room where Mohammad lies, tended to by his mother. Mani takes photographs whilst Forugh films and interviews the mother and other family members. The experience of listening to their story takes on heightened emotional weight as we see Forugh and Mani struggling with their tears. We hear the click of the camera over the voice of the mother telling her son how much she loves him. The on-screen image shifts from the room itself into Forugh's viewfinder; this is the first time that Forugh is shown behind the camera and is coincidentally one of the passages that feels most uncomfortably voyeuristic (Figure 6.2). The image then shifts to the editing

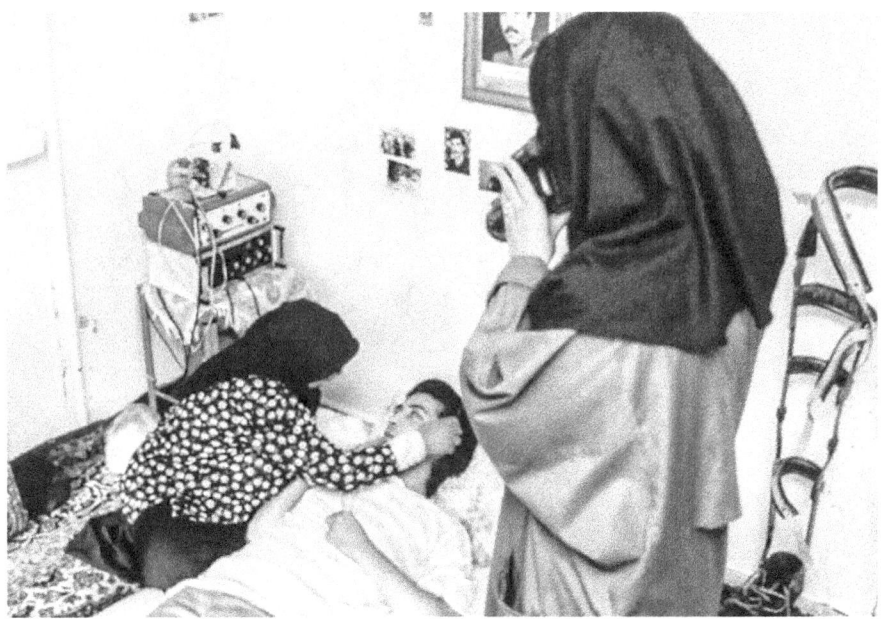

Figure 6.2 *The May Lady* (24′53″)

room as we hear the voice of Mohammad's physiotherapist; we observe the blurred screen from behind Forugh's head but are unable to see her reaction. Moving back to "viewfinder" mode, Mohammad's mother explains that her other son went to the front and was killed the following day. As she describes kissing her dead son's body, we see Mani listening and responding emotionally, the first time in the film that the audience listens through someone other than Forugh (Figure 6.3). Switching again to the editing room, a side-shot shows Forugh lost in thought; as the mother says, "May God never expose any mother to such a scene" (the death of her son) and starts to cry, we see Forugh respond by moving her hand up to her mouth.

There are messages within messages here. Just as we listen to Forugh listen, so Banietemad hopes that those in positions of power will take notice of the many whose lives were destroyed by the war, left to deal with their loss as best they can. Once again, class issues come to the fore, since it was largely young men from poorer, religious backgrounds who went to the front. This passage segues into a transition scene with Forugh in her car and the voice-over of another war-bereaved mother talking about receiving the news of her son's death, as the visuals transition to a cemetery and we see *chador*-clad women tending the graves of their loved ones. The camera pans across row after row of graves, with another voice describing being asked to identify her son, and we connect voice to body as the camera focuses on Forugh at the end of one of

Figure 6.3 *The May Lady* (25′53″)

the rows filming the mother. At the exact point of extreme traumatic memory, where the mother describes collapsing at the sight of her dead son, the film cuts to a grainy image of an intense close-up of her face through the viewfinder; as she wipes her tears with the corner of her *chador*, the camera cuts to Forugh with the camera to her eye, struggling to contain her own tears. As with the earlier scene, the cutting back and forth between the two women— Forugh responding empathetically to the intense emotion of the moment— allows the audience to listen both with and through Forugh and to enter her own subjectivity as a mother of a teenage son who, had he been born ten years earlier, might well have met a similar fate. Finally, Forugh crouches down and embraces the woman. Once again, her empathetic listening becomes a medium through which to project these largely marginalized voices and unheard stories onto the national consciousness.

Throughout the scenes described above, the audience experiences something akin to what Najmeh Moradiyan Rizi (writing about the film *Shirin*), describes as "the circulation of the female look" (2016: 51). Moradiyan Rizi draws on the work of Laura Mulvey, who outlines different cinematic "looks"— that of the camera, of the audience, and of the characters looking at each other (1989: 208)—to which Moradiyan Rizi adds the "'look at the viewer,' which is an imaginary look" (ibid., quoting Willemen 1986: 216). In *The May Lady*, the seamless and continual shifting from camera (viewfinder) viewpoint to Forugh's viewpoint, to the audience observing Forugh observing (or listening to) another woman's viewpoint, lends a multi-perspectval quality that resonates with the multiplicity of voices in the film. Discussing the notion of "voicing", Amanda Weidman argues that:

> Voicing emphasizes the strategic and politically charged nature of the way voices are constructed both in formal and everyday performances ... a speaker may be inhabiting others' voices and words and artfully orchestrating a multitude of voices to tell his story. (2015: 238)

In a similar way, Forugh inhabits the voices of others and becomes figured primarily as a "listening body": her central role is arguably to listen, and indeed, she practically becomes a technology of "listening in" like a stethoscope or a headphone. Interestingly, her lover (Dr Rahbar) is also positioned as a listening body but in a much more passive manner. The audience encounters him visually only once, briefly, through Forugh's eyes, as she watches him hesitantly from an upper level at her workplace. Our main encounter with Dr Rahbar is through the sound of his voice, again as received by Forugh: in telephone conversations or through love letters, as discussed below.

This section has offered just a few examples of Forugh's empathetic listening. What becomes evident is that this listening and Forugh's always attentive body language are bound up with the portrayal of her general character. Further, time and again, Forugh's act of listening is presented as an embodied act; thus, for the audience, sound serves to generate a physically experienced shared affect and embodied empathy with the characters on screen.

LISTENING TO THE LADIES: ACTIVATING THE FEMALE VOICE

Having considered the significance of Forugh's performative role as a listener in *The May Lady*, I now turn now to the sounds that Forugh (and, through her, the audience) listens to. As the film progresses, Forugh becomes increasingly weighed down by the stories she hears, gradually reaching a point of overload with one heart-wrenching narrative after another. This generates an ever-expanding bricolage of voices, which Forugh struggles to contain. Sonically, a large proportion of the film's voicetrack is given over to the sounds of the female voice; the only male voices heard regularly are those of Forugh's teenage son and his friends, and the disembodied voice of Dr Rahbar through telephone conversations or letters, plus very occasionally one of her co-workers, an interviewee, or some other brief encounter. The foregrounding of the female voice in *The May Lady* thus operates not just metaphorically as a well-worn index of agency, but in very tangible and material ways through a form of sonic saturation. This arguably facilitates a powerful means of projecting particular kinds of female subjectivity, which fly under the radar of those seeking to control such subjectivities for reasons discussed below. This section will consider both the sheer quantity of female vocal sound in *The May Lady* and the very particular qualities of voice and their significance. I argue that the proliferation and "excess" of female voices offer a sensorial experience that works alongside, but is subtly subversive in comparison with, other more overt projections of female agency.

There is a considerable literature exploring issues of voice, agency, and gender, including in relation to film (Doane 1980; Silverman 1988; Chion 1999; and Whittaker and Wright 2017). Whittaker and Wright offer a useful overview of the latter, addressing a number of issues that are relevant here, including the voice as a site of political agency, the material and embodied properties of voice, and questions of affect, including a chapter on the voice in Iranian cinema (Mottahedeh 2017). In Iran, there are particular sensitivities around the alleged power of the female voice, which has generated a set of official discourses and controls in the public domain which are also rooted in traditional social and cultural norms and expectations of gendered behavior. Whilst not unique to Iran, such discourses have, since the 1979 Revolution, focused particularly on solo female singing, which has been prohibited in public, other than to all-female audiences. Group singing is permitted but with certain and variable stipulations about the number of singers. Several commentators have noted that such controls, argued in the name of religious propriety, are in reality assertions of patriarchal power structures; restrictions on female singing are one of a number of controls, but has taken on particular significance due to the myriad ways in which it can and has been challenged, and also because of its symbolic silencing of women. The reasons given for prohibiting solo singing but allowing groups are revealing and pertinent to this discussion: group singing, it is claimed, cancels out the individually heard vibrations and nuances of the female voice, which are considered *haram* (religiously forbidden) due to their potential to arouse lustful thoughts and invoke bodily desire. Whilst there is, no doubt, some element of arbitrariness in these restrictions, evidenced also by inconsistencies and contradictions in restrictions elsewhere in the public domain, such discourses tap into deep-rooted anxieties about the power of the female voice that go well beyond Iran and which can be found in stories such as those about the Greek Sirens and other such femmes fatales who lure men to their doom. In other words, there is something about the timbral and other qualities of the sung voice at play in these widely circulating ideas about the power of the female voice. Indeed, it is interesting to note that restrictions on female singing in Iran do not extend to the spoken voice; on the contrary, it is quite normal to hear the spoken female voice in all arenas of public life, including on national media (there are many female television announcers and news presenters, for instance), and there are no restrictions on the voices of female actors. Only solo singing is marked as potentially dangerous and requiring control. In the absence of any official sanctions on the spoken voice, then, *The May Lady* operates within a perfectly legitimate framework and Banietemad is able to push this sonic dimension to its limits, such that the audience experiences an excess of female vocal sounds. This subtle and understated provocation reveals the myriad ways in which quiet voices can speak back to "larger structures of power" (Weidman 2015: 237).

I pause for a moment to consider what it means to attend "only to sound" in relation to human speech. Weidman has written about the ways in which dominant discourses have separated voice into its signification and the sound "itself," with the former privileged over the latter in discussions of meaning. She traces the history of such discourses and considers how the "binary set up in Western philosophical and linguistic thought between the signifying authorial voice and bodily, material vocality was closely articulated with a social project central to Euro-Western modernity" (2015: 234), most evident in the work of Enlightenment thinkers such as Rousseau and Locke, and later in structural linguistics, the result "privileging referenciality over other functions of language, creating an opposition between content and form and privileging the former" (ibid.:

234). This view "treats the sonic, material aspects of voice as secondary and as potentially disruptive to the sovereignty of the subject" (ibid.: 233). One possible response, Weidman suggests, is to "valorize the second term of the binary, the sounding, material voice." In other words, the significance of voice in *The May Lady* is as much about the materiality of sound—its timbre, texture, contour, and shapes—as the words themselves. This is what Roland Barthes refers to as "the voice within the voice", expressed primarily by what he termed the "grain" of the voice, originally in an essay of the same name, written in 1972 and published in *Image–Music–Text* (1977). Whilst the original essay focused on singing rather than speech, Barthes's oft-quoted (but much less often theorized) term is useful here for an understanding of what one hears "beyond (or before) the meaning of the words" (ibid.: 181), and for the attention it draws to the materiality of sound and the always already embodied quality of the vocal grain:

> . . . something which is directly the cantor's body, brought to your ears in one and the same movement from deep down in the cavities, the muscles, the membranes, the cartilages . . . Above all, this voice bears along *directly* the symbolic, over the intelligible . . . The "grain" is that: the materiality of the body speaking its mother tongue . . . The "grain" is the body in the voice as it sings, the hand as it writes, the limb as it performs. (ibid.: 181–2, 188)

The concept of vocal grain thus serves as a useful shorthand to indicate the quality of voice at the meeting point of timbre, texture, contour, vibrancy, and the many other things that contribute to the uniqueness of each voice. In attending to voice, then, we may miss a great deal if we focus solely on what is being said. As Whittaker and Wright (quoting Steven Shapiro) note, "the voice always stands *in between*: in between body and language, in between biology and culture, in between inside and outside, in between subject and Other, in between mere sound or noise and meaningful articulation" (2017: 4). There are two aspects to voice which are of particular interest here: the very real material aspects of sound and the embodied nature of the voices that we hear. As Langford observes of the film *Shirin*,

> . . . the acousmatic dimension of the film foregrounds not just women as spectators, but emphasize another veritable blind spot of Iranian cinema by foregrounding women's *bodies* among other bodies in ways that far exceed the allowable visual representation of women's bodies and their desires. (forthcoming)

So, too, in *The May Lady*, women and their bodies are centered through sound. And Banietemad is able to do this in large measure because the attention of the gatekeepers of Iranian cinema have been so focused on the visual and on what is being said that they have paid little attention to what the materiality, sound quality, and timbre of film sounds communicate to the listener.

As well as her central role as a listener, Forugh is also the most important voice in *The May Lady*. The film adopts a first-person narrative that follows Forugh chronologically from start to finish. Hers is the first voice that we hear, as a quasi-whisper as she writes poetry in the opening scene. Shot from behind, with the viewer peering over Forugh's shoulder, it is unclear whether the sound is a voice-over or diegetic whispering as she writes. Forugh's is also the final voice of the film as she picks up the telephone receiver and dials Dr Rahbar's number. Her "*Salaam. Man Forugham*" can be understood in Persian as a straightforward greeting—"Hello. This is Forugh"—or as an assertion of being—"Hello. I am Forugh." Naficy describes the symbolic significance of this moment:

> ... in which the lead character faces the camera and names the unnamed, herself, "I am Foruq," is the triumph of woman over women, of the individual over the collective, of modernity over pre-modernity. (2012b: 163)

A similar use of voice as a statement of personhood can be seen in the film *The King's Speech* (2010), as discussed by Weidman. When:

> ... the stuttering Bertie [British King George VI] declares "I have a voice!" we hear this as a profound moment of self-realization and self-assertion, not simply a declaration of fact. With such a declaration, Bertie activates a host of culturally salient associations between voice and individually, authorship, agency, authority, and power ... (2015: 232)

In the same way, Forugh's final words are a confident voicing of both individual and collective female agency, a fitting ending to the film. *The May Lady* makes extensive use of reflective voice-overs spoken by Forugh, including poetic love letters exchanged with her lover (see below); indeed, even where there is no voice-over, the structure of the film conveys a sense of first-person narration. Referencing the work of Alexander Fisher, Whittaker and Wright note the first-person voice-over can serve as a "political statement when afforded to those otherwise denied platforms from which to speak" (2017: 12). But I am also interested in how the actual *sounds* of Forugh's voice make such a statement. Weidman reminds us of the "always-constructed relationship between voices and bodies, particularly in media contexts" (2015: 236). Forugh's is not just any kind of voice, and it is important to ask what kind of voice she is given and why: what do the sonorous and material qualities of

Forugh's voice—its timbre, texture, contour, and so on—communicate to us "beyond words"?

One of the most striking features of Forugh's voice, that sets the tone right from the start, is its calm and quiet understated quality that contrasts with many earlier female protagonists in Iranian cinema; her voice is also pitched relatively low in the female vocal range. All of these arguably help to construct Forugh as a character who is well grounded, stable, and reliable, as well as contributing to her aura of authority and empathy, as already discussed. Such qualities are shared by many of the other female voices in this film, including those who have much reason to feel aggrieved at life and whose emotions of sorrow, anger, resignation, and so on take on a particular embodied sonic form through the process of voicing. But there are also voices that project something starkly different in their excess and overflow of emotion, particularly anger. We first encounter this during Forugh's visit to a prison, where she talks to and records family members, mainly women, who are waiting outside to visit their male relatives. For reasons that are likely related to the difficulties of filming actual prison visitors, the interviewees at this point are played by actors. This may not be immediately evident, but viewers familiar with Banietemad's work would recognize characters from her earlier films such as *Nargess* (1992) and the reference to Nobar from *Rusari Ābi* (*The Blue-veiled*, 1995); later, we encounter Tooba, who appears in *Under the Skin of the City* (2001) and *Ghesseh-hā* (*Tales*, 2014). This, together with the introduction of recognizable actresses such as Golab Adineh (Tooba) and Banietemad's daughter, Baran Kosari (here playing Senobar, Nobar's child sister), inserts a new element into the film at this point, reflecting strategies more generally characteristic of Banietemad's work: firstly, the blurring of boundaries between "fiction" and documentary/"reality"; and secondly, the reappearance of characters from earlier films. If recognizable actors are now "posing" as interviewees, does this reframe our understanding of the veracity of earlier voices? This scene starts from within Forugh's camera viewfinder and then moves outside the viewfinder frame to show Forugh talking with Senobar. What is noticeable about this scene, which self-consciously shifts the frame of representation along the reality–fiction spectrum, is that the women's voices *sound* different and contrast with those heard so far: these are openly angry and agitated, and reveal a level of desperation that was much more contained in earlier scenes. They are also noticeably higher in pitch. It is interesting, then, that this excess of emotion should be voiced by actors rather than "real" interviewees, although the audience may not necessarily distinguish between them (particularly audiences outside Iran). Presumably, Banietemad was able to exercise directorial authorship over their voices in a way that was not possible with non-actors. Perhaps the latter felt constrained by the camera and unable to express themselves fully. Unlike the scenes described earlier, the film audience does not see Forugh, since she is behind the camera, but hears her talking to the women with the same calm and empathetic grain of voice, now providing even more of a contrast with the voices heard through her and which arguably demand our attention because they have to fight for a space to be heard in a way that Forugh's, through her relative privilege, does not. Her ability to command attention affords her the capacity (and luxury) to retain her aura of patient calm. In this way, class and privilege are arguably etched into the sounds of her voice. As Forugh's internal conflict increases, so the voices she is in dialogue with become increasingly distraught and unstable, and marked by emotional outbursts. As she scrolls through film clips in the editing room, we observe and hear the increasingly desperate and overwrought voices: a woman grieving at a lost (married) daughter, with implications of domestic violence: "If the law had protected my daughter, she would be alive now." Another tries to gain access to her children: "I tried hard to see my kids for six years but couldn't. O God, you know how hard I tried. I went to the court, the welfare, everywhere." It is not clear whether this is "real" footage or played by actors. The emotional impact of these voices is made even more powerful by being framed—preceded by and interleaved with—interviews with three well-known public figures: writer Shahla Lahiji, (then) member of parliament Faezeh Hashemi Rafsanjani, and lawyer and human rights activist Mehrangiz Kar, the voice of the latter continuing over images of the law courts. These women all speak with a grain not unlike that of Forugh: calm, authoritative, in control of their destiny. The accumulation of voices and emotion is too much for Forugh at this point and she turns off the screen and stands in silence, exhausted, resting her head against her arm. She then turns the screen on again and starts to click through many images of women, but now, significantly, "silenced," with the volume muted. For thirty seconds, all we hear is Forugh clicking on images, focusing in on single faces, and then back to multiple images (Figure 6.4). This "crisis" scene directly precedes her decision to resign from the project.

There are two scenes in the film where Forugh's voice changes, taking on some of the same qualities as the women she has been listening to: in both, her voice loses some of its authority in the face of forces beyond her control, whether her absentee former partner (now abroad), who has made what she views as empty promises to her son, or the government official to whom she is obliged to plead after her son is arrested following a raid on a house party (Figure 6.5). Asking where Mani's father is, he points to Forugh as a divorcee and single parent as responsible for her son's allegedly "immoral" behavior (attending a party with music, members of the opposite sex, and most likely alcohol). These scenes present different faces of social and state patriarchy, against which Forugh's professional authority counts for little as she becomes defined solely through her gender and marital status. There is a marked change in Forugh's vocal tone in these scenes, particularly in the higher pitch and volume as she veers towards a loss of control, at the same time intensely aware that this would likely disempower her further.

Figure 6.4 *The May Lady* (43′48″)

Figure 6.5 *The May Lady* (53′20″)

Soon after the scene with the government official, Forugh encounters Tooba, a woman she had interviewed for an earlier project. This encounter lifts Forugh's spirits, despite the misfortunes that have befallen Tooba's family since they last met, and prompts her to look for the old photographs of Tooba and watch her interview footage, filmed in the textiles factory where

Tooba works. At the start of the interview, Tooba attempts to assume the serious manner that she believes is expected of her, but is unable to keep a straight face in front of the camera and dissolves into laughter, covering her face with her headscarf. This generates a mirroring and embodied response from Forugh (watching the recording on her television at home), not dissimilar from the empathetic responses described earlier. Tooba recomposes herself and offers short answers to the questions, as if reading from a script. Finally, as Tooba explains that her husband is unable to work any longer, Forugh asks how the family manages to make ends meet and Tooba responds with "life proceeds somehow," before being overwhelmed by the situation and breaking into laughter again. Tooba's is an interesting voice: it carries the same emotional weight as some of the earlier interviewees, but is marked by a candid and often irreverent straight-talking, as well as being imbued with an element of humor which seems to offer a glimmer of hope in the face of adversity (bearing in mind that Tooba is played by an actor and her voice could presumably be crafted by the filmmaker in a way that is less feasible with real interviewees). This optimism, however, is almost immediately set against a very different kind of voice. Fast-forwarding the video, Forugh plays later footage, shot in the factory after Tooba has discovered that her older son has sold the family home without her knowledge and that as a result they are now homeless. She shouts angrily at Forugh, gesturing and mimicking her filming, asking "What is it? Why do you keep filming me? My life is no good for a film." Tooba is shouting both from anger and in order to make herself heard over the noisy factory looms, another sonic indicator of the social difference between Forugh's privileged and quiet working environment and those of the mainly female workers shown in this scene. Tooba's words are finally drowned out by the factory clamor, symbolic of the voices that become silenced and which this film seeks to make audible; all we hear at the end is "Go after your own life" (Figure 6.6). As the camera shot alternates between the footage of Tooba and Forugh watching, we hear (through Forugh) the voice of a woman trying to hold her family together in the face of multiple social and personal pressures. The footage then shows Tooba and Forugh in the alleyway outside Tooba's home. She is apologetic for having taken out her anger on Forugh, and when Forugh urges her to tell her what has happened, we hear the story of a single family that encapsulates many of the social pressures faced by Iranians, including homelessness, unemployment, and addiction. Forugh listens, then turns off the video and sits in reflective silence, resting her face on her hands.

Whilst there is a great deal in this film that speaks to Iran's social divides, Banietemad also seeks to promote empathy and understanding across those divides. This becomes most evident in a passage towards the end of the film, the second time that Mani finds himself in custody, following an earlier scene where he storms out of the apartment (angry at the unexpected arrival of Dr Rahbar) and speeds off in the car, eventually driving through

Figure 6.6 *The May Lady* (1:00′37″)

a checkpoint of unofficial voluntary *basij* militia. Once again, Forugh has to plead for his release, but this time it is not a government official that she has to talk to, but Mr Sadegh, a young *basiji* and survivor of the Iran–Iraq War, who Mani punched when challenged at the checkpoint. This scene is visually and sonically marked as located in the poor neighborhoods of south Tehran, as Forugh first goes to the young man's home and is directed to find him at the local mosque. She waits outside in the shadows of the alleyway to the sounds of religious chanting broadcast from the mosque loudspeakers. Rather than adopt a confrontational vocal tone, as she did with the government official, Forugh instead advocates understanding and reconciliation between the two men, and by extension across social communities, and appeals (successfully) to Mr Sadegh's empathy by asking him to forgive her son so that he does not end up in jail "with thieves and smugglers" (Figure 6.7). Mr Sadegh's voice, in turn, is soft-spoken as he makes his case: "When your son was playing with toys, I was with my brother at the battlefield playing with bullets [i.e. safeguarding the nation]. Now I guard day and night the same streets your son speed drives." To this, Forugh responds by invoking common values and a shared youth: "You are talking of values that are shared by all. My son is a youth like you. Differences in your outlooks should not make you stand against each other." As in her exchanges with Tooba, Forugh here addresses the whole nation: a

Figure 6.7 *The May Lady* (1:18′45″)

small, quiet voice delivering the most powerful of messages. In the scene that follows, we see Mani, now released, waiting outside the courthouse, with Forugh watching from a distance as the two men shake hands.

This section has explored the significance of the female voice in *The May Lady*, both metaphorically and literally. Listeners experience a multiplicity of female perspectives and an excess of female vocal sound that together arguably generate a form of agentive subjectivity that was quite new to Iranian cinema at the time. An important aspect of the sonic materiality of *The May Lady* is conveyed through vocal "grain," which I argue plays an important role in constructing Forugh as an empathetic listener.

SONIC INTIMACIES

The discussion of this chapter has so far has focused primarily on voices in Forugh's professional life; in this final section, I turn to the sonic intimacies of her private life. Throughout the film, the audience is invited to experience aspects of Forugh's daily life and rituals, including the sounds of domestic labor such as cooking and cleaning. Early in the film, we see her return from work and start to prepare the evening meal. Sound becomes a truly visceral experience through the gushing faucet water as Forugh washes the carrots, the sharp click of the knife on the chopping board as she slices mushrooms and then scrapes them into a bowl, and the frying of onions and tomatoes. For much of this passage, Forugh's visual presence is reduced to her hands and there are no other sounds or verbal interaction. I suggest that this focus on domestic sound serves to frame Forugh (once again) as a listener, as well as drawing attention to her juggling of professional life and domestic responsibilities as a single parent. The film is punctuated by further scenes that foreground the sounds of the home and of domestic work, including the particularly satisfying swish of curtains as Forugh opens them in the morning, at the same time setting off a wind chime; the spraying of plants; and the bubbling of tea brewing and then being poured into small glasses. Domestic labor returns later in the film when we see and hear Forugh vacuuming and shaking out bedsheets whilst also making work telephone calls. As well as the sounds of domestic spaces, we hear Forugh's exercise routine as she jogs and walks in the hills around her home, each of these passages following on from a scene of reflective intimacy in which Forugh reads a love letter, writes in her journal, or talks with Dr Rahbar on the telephone. Though short, these exercise scenes are important in providing Forugh with a quiet space for reflection, a space that is largely devoid of sounds other than those generated by her own body. We hear her footfall on the path, crunching the fall leaves, and her panting as she stops and doubles over to catch her breath; the second jogging scene concludes with Forugh wiping sweat from her face with the end of her shawl and looking up to the sky, still breathing heavily, as she finally makes a decision about her future life. Arguably, the entire personal narrative "thread" of the film has been building up to this point.

It is notable that whilst Forugh's professional sound world is dominated by the voices of women, the more personal narrative involves much more engagement with male voices: most obviously her son and her lover, and more briefly with Mani's adolescent friends, the government official, Mr Sadegh, and her downstairs neighbor, plus the unsounded presence–absence of Mani's father. Like many of the women interviewees, the government official and Mr Sadegh are marked as being of a lower social class than Forugh, but they are also in positions of relative authority, and this can be heard in their vocal grain, which conveys a sense of power and entitlement, particularly that of the government official. There is also comparatively little male–male interaction in the film, other than between Mani and his friends, the scene at the mosque, and the reconciliation between Mani and Mr Sadegh that follows. By contrast with the male voices in Forugh's private life, there are relatively few women: the friend that she walks with and confides in, and one of Mani's friends, but no relatives or extended family, other than her mother-in-law, who she visits with Mani. These are all somewhat muted in comparison with the male voices in her life.

Like many Iranian arthouse directors (and for reasons that I have discussed elsewhere; Nooshin 2019: 38–41), Banietemad tends to avoid non-diegetic music in her films. In *The May Lady*, other devices are used by way of a substitute soundtrack, particularly in transitional scenes where music might have played a continuity role. Almost every transitional scene is accompanied by a voice-over of Forugh's reflective thoughts, extracts from letters, the voices of interviewees, or scenes and sounds of driving. Music, where it is heard, is always diegetic and always in domestic settings or spaces that link Forugh's public and private worlds, most notably the interior of her car and the stairwell of her apartment block. The first time we hear music is Mani's loud rock music spilling into the stairwell as Forugh returns home and encounters her downstairs neighbor throwing his wife out of the apartment. When Forugh tries to help, he tells her to mind her own business and suggests that she attends to her own son and gets him to turn his music down. Forugh hurries up the stairs and enters the apartment, as the music blares ever more loudly from Mani's bedroom. The significance of this scene goes beyond the case of a teenager annoying others with loud music; in the context of the Islamic state and government restrictions on popular music, rock music becomes a marker of middle-class privilege, as well as a site of danger, with the threat of neighbors reporting it to the police. Indeed, this is precisely what happens in the later scene, when Mani and his friends attend a party which is raided after complaints by a neighbor. Here, the "unsounded" party music is understood by the audience. The scene directly preceding this in the car as Forugh drives Mani and his friends to the party begins with the sounds of the teenagers singing the popular folk song *Mikhām Beram Kuh* ("I Want to Go to the Mountains") at the top of their voices. When Forugh asks them to quieten down, one of Mani's friends responds, "Guys, let's sing with soundproofing" and they start to (mock-)sing in whispers. This leads to a conversation about the right of young people to enjoy themselves, as part of which sound becomes a trigger to critique government discourses and restrictions. The friend complains, "When you're young, they object to whatever you do. The way you walk, your hairstyle, your dress . . . your glance," and another responds "We might as well die and be born as forty-year-olds." In all of these scenes, music becomes a signifier of a particular Western-oriented youth culture that the government had sought to contain and silence, and for which restrictions became more relaxed, particularly for locally produced pop music, in the late 1990s, around the time that *The May Lady* was released (Nooshin 2005). The reference to "sound proofing" speaks both to the fact that popular musicians have, since the Revolution, mainly worked underground and had to soundproof their music-making spaces, lest any sounds leak out, and to the symbolic silencing of young people. After Forugh drops Mani and his friends at the party, she goes to a café to work until it is time to collect them. This scene offers a parallel and contrasting musical experience to the implied party music, and is the only example of non-diegetic music in the entire film: indeed, the somewhat abrupt appearance of a heavily orchestrated Italian ballad (the song 'Caruso' by Lucio Dalla (1986), performed by Luciano Pavarotti) seems rather incongruous, given the marked absence of any non-diegetic music elsewhere in the film.

Perhaps the most striking and effective example of sonic intimacy in *The May Lady* is in the communication between Forugh and Dr Rahbar. In the face of censorship rules that prohibit physical and eye contact between male and female actors—rules that present particular challenges for portraying close relationships—Banietemad has, like other Iranian filmmakers, "found ways of indirectly suggesting moments of tenderness, intimacy and even eroticism through allusion, metaphor, allegory and other forms of suggestive imagery" (Langford forthcoming). In *The Blue-veiled*, for instance, she plays with such rules, using shadows creatively to suggest intimate contact between lovers. In *The May Lady*, almost like voyeurs, we are admitted into the most intimate spaces of Forugh's life, where her contact with her lover is entirely by way of telephone conversations and poetic love letters. It is as though Banietemad responds to the challenge of the state censors by taking the restrictions to an extreme and avoiding any simultaneous physical presence, and yet she still manages to create a sense of intense sensuality by shifting intimacy into another domain, the sonic. Forugh and Dr Rahbar never occupy the same physical space and, as noted earlier, the viewer only sees Dr Rahbar once, fleetingly, and from a distance. Instead, they are transformed into "acoustic bodies" (Langford forthcoming). In this context, the voice-over of poetic love letters and Forugh's own writings take on immense significance, with thinly veiled allusions to her namesake, Iran's foremost female poet, Forugh Farrokhzad (1934–67). Appearing regularly and at points in the film where we might have expected music, the voice-over arguably comes to function as an alternative soundtrack. In using poetic writing in this way, Banietemad draws on a centuries-old tradition of poetry as a vehicle for hidden messages, one that has found its way into Iranian cinema—unsurprisingly, given the centrality of poetry to Iranian culture. This intriguing aspect of *The May Lady* has attracted the attention of a number of scholars. Naficy (2012b: 161), for instance, notes the weaving together and shadowing of the two voices in ways that interestingly parallel some of the structures of Iranian classical music, particularly *āvāz* sections, where a solo instrument typically shadows (and embellishes) the vocal line at a short distance. The most extended example of this is where Forugh is first shown at home reading a newly arrived letter from Dr Rahbar (the passage begins at 44:50); the scene then shifts to her driving, to the continuing sound of his voice, to which hers joins, reciting the same words, her voice weaving in and out of his, usually slightly behind, sometimes slightly ahead, occasionally dropping out entirely; finally, Dr Rahbar's voice fades out and we hear Forugh repeat the final lines of the letter. In the context of Iran's censorship regime, and for audiences that can read its significance, the effect of two voices, one layered over the other, opens up possibilities of iconic eroticism that go well beyond what would be permitted by legal and social modesty rules, generating a suggestive sensuality that is arguably as powerful as any open display of intimate relations. The lovers may be prohibited from touching or looking directly at one another, but that does not stop them from becoming metaphorically bonded through sound; indeed, sound here arguably become fetishized as a symbol of physical love. Discussing Banietemad's poetic–filmic device, Naficy notes the "unequal" veiling rules by which censorship focuses almost exclusively on the visual. Interestingly, sound *per se* appears not to evoke the same sensitivities and level of anxiety as music, and therefore largely evades censorial scrutiny (2012b: 160–1). And yet, as noted, there is a not unproblematic and complex network of significance in the poetic voice-over in *The May Lady* whose subtlety makes it invisible/inaudible to the moral gatekeepers. Further, modesty rules that fetishize the visual ignore the very materiality of sound discussed earlier, thus missing the point that the sonic is as much a form of physical penetration as the visual gaze—arguably, more so. Banietemad thus cleverly makes of use of poetic prose to aestheticize a hidden transcript of subversion as she confronts the normative privileging of (patriarchal) vision. Langford's concept of the "aural gaze" (discussed in relation to *Shirin*) seems apposite here, as the audience is "encouraged to listen with the attentiveness of a fully embodied spectator, surrounded by a rare scene of female desire in post-revolutionary Iranian cinema" (forthcoming), and which would have been ever rarer when *The May Lady* was released (ten years before *Shirin*). Where the visual gaze is limited or prohibited, the lovers listen to one another: earthly love is made audible when it cannot be made visible. In this way, the all-enveloping poetic sounds arguably become an extension of the lovers' bodies, allowing for the expression of desire in ways that fly under the censorial radar.

As well a vehicle to communicate with Dr Rahbar, Forugh's voice-over provides a space for reflecting on her relationship with Mani and the central theme of the film: the tension between the codes of modesty and social expectations of her as a mother, and her desire to embark on a romantic relationship. It is interesting that, whilst Forugh's character is very much defined through her role as a listener, Mani is unwilling to listen to his mother, and she patiently waits until he is ready. Towards the end of the film, Forugh makes her decision to talk to Mani, explaining to her friend as they walk in the hills, "My son has to listen to my unspoken words." This is followed directly by a scene in which, having decorated the apartment with candles for her birthday, Mani leads Forugh into the living room, sits her at the table, and gives her a gift. She reciprocates by handing him her diary and photographs from his childhood, and then proceeds to articulate the "unspoken words" that she needs him to listen to. But it seems the words are too difficult to address to him directly: instead, we hear a voice-over of Forugh telling Mani about her marriage to his father in the heady days of the Revolution and what followed as their marriage fell apart. She describes her feelings of being defined by society almost exclusively through her (single) motherhood:

> Forugh remained somewhere else and fell into oblivion, a place where many other women in the same situation remain, leaving behind a part of themselves. No one bothered to consider that a woman isn't a human being in need of love. (1:14′31″)

Finally, Mani listens to his mother, as he looks at the photographs and weeps silently. But just as this listening is about to lead to understanding, the doorbell sounds and Mani storms out of the apartment at the (presumed) arrival of Dr Rahbar. Even after Forugh collects Mani from the courthouse (following his "pardon" by Mr Sadeghi), he resists her attempts to talk to him in the car. In the final scene, we see Forugh and Mani back home, sitting silently in the living room, with diegetic music playing in the background. The telephone rings and Mani deliberately turns up the volume to mask the sound. It seems he is not yet ready to become an empathetic listener, but Forugh's wry glance towards him indicates that she has hopes that he will. The scene cuts to her phoning Dr Rahbar and the closing declaration of personhood: "This is Forugh/I am Forugh."

CONCLUDING THOUGHTS

As I hope to have shown in this chapter, sound and listening play a strategic and significant role in *The May Lady*. I have argued that a key theme of the film centers around listening, about who listens to whom and who has the authority to listen and to be listened to. In particular, the female voice is foregrounded to an extent rarely experienced previously in Iranian cinema, as the audience listens to Forugh and, through her performative act, to voices and stories that would normally struggle to be heard. In particular, listening in *The May Lady* becomes a somatic experience, in which audiences engage with the very materiality of sound through their listening bodies. That materiality is experienced most directly through vocal "grain," and in the case of Forugh I argue that this is central to her construction as an empathetic character. In the final section, we entered Forugh's private sound world and explored the sonic intimacies of her personal life. In particular, the discussion considered the aestheticizing strategies by which Banietemad circumvents restrictions on the portrayal of sensuality and eroticism by capitalizing on the fetishization of the visual, which has left the immense power of the sonic largely unscrutinized. Sound thus becomes a playground for trying out new ideas away from the panopticism of the state: we hear this both in the proliferation and excess of female voices and in sound as a site of sensual pleasure. In all of the above, sound becomes a vehicle for creating (to quote again from Winters), "a shared subjectivity between film audience and character" (2014), which in turn generates a sense of filmic intimacy, affective subjectivity, and embodied listening. In this way, sound is implicated in creating a cinema of empathy, of which *The May Lady* is an outstanding example. Above all, the central message of the film is about listening as a first step towards personal and social reconciliation and change. Without that, nothing else can follow.

CHAPTER 7

The Blue-veiled: A Semiological Analysis of a Social Love Story

Asal Bagheri

This chapter presents a semiological analysis of *Rusari Ābi* (*The Blue-veiled*, 1995), directed by Rakhshan Banietemad. Within this framework, the particular focus will be on descriptions of love or familial relationships. To explain the importance of this pioneering film in the depiction of a heterosexual romantic relationship, it should be emphasized that the 1979 Islamic Revolution brought about many changes in society, one of which was the use of "private" and "public spaces." The implementation of the post-Revolution law required particular dress codes and specific rules of behavior between men and women, especially in "public spaces." When discussing art and the issue of public and private spaces, what the artist must broach is whether one is showing the distinction between the rules outside and inside of the house or expressing an opinion about it. As art is aimed at the public, it must follow the laws on public spaces, and cinema as an art form has to deal with this dilemma of "showing" or "expressing" (Bagheri 2017: 385).

Two major problems occur when romantic or familial relationships are shown on the screen. The first one is the fact that relations and gestures which exist in the Iranian society, but are forbidden by religion and country laws, cannot be shown on the screen. The second issue is that, even though some relations and gestures are permitted by religion and country laws, they are forbidden on the screen because of the non-symmetry of actors in relation to the characters they play.

Using a two-step semiological analysis, named "Semiology of Indices" (Houdebine 2009: 121–6), this chapter aims to show how Banietemad depicts love and/or familial relations in the censured post-Revolution Iranian cinema (Bagheri 2012). This semiotic is based on flexible structuring and indefinite objects, such as publicities, theaters, films, and so on. The first phase is the "systemic analysis," which consists of looking for a formal structure. The second phase, consisting of an analysis of content, will focus on meaning, effects, and signification processes. The interpretation of the corpus elements is made at the internal level of our object and also at the external level, when cultural, social, and encyclopedic references are mobilized to analyze the meaning. According to social, cultural, and historical rules, we will attempt to interpret the previously defined categories in our systemic analysis. The purpose is to observe what is hidden behind these cinematographic methods: the real meaning revealing paternal love, forbidden love, and sexual relations.

Indeed, the systemic analysis highlights what I have named the "iconic," "scenic," "sound," and "technical" strata within the scenes of the film. It also shows explicit elements, which reveal the existence of a degree of repetition on a formal scale. We can see there is a formal grammar respected when it comes to the expression of relationships between men and women in Banietemad's cinema in general. Illusions of closeness, love declarations, eroticism, sexual propositions, and relationships are suggested through various phrasal configurations of the indices, such as "glances," "abortive gestures," "turn-around scenes," "the child," "symbolic objects," "intermediate spaces," "off-screens," "direct transitions," "speech," and "music." These indices are the base of a hidden grammar which I previously applied in my PhD thesis (Bagheri 2012). *The Blue-veiled* is a pioneering example of how Iranian cinema chastely explores love, expressing its own "Iranian form" concerning relationships between men and women. This is achieved by constructing space in keeping with traditional Iranian domestic architecture, as noted by Khatereh Sheibani (2011: 15)—with space divided between *biruni* (the external for guests) and *andaruni* (the internal for family and privacy)—but also by using stylistic devices found in classical Persian poetry.

BANIETEMAD'S FILMMAKING

Before conducting an analysis of *The Blue-veiled*, it is important to discuss the place of this film in the director's career. Three distinct periods are to be observed in Banietemad's feature films with regard to analysis of male–female relationships. The first period sees a male focus with films like *Khārej Az Mahdudeh* (*Off Limits*, 1988), *Zard-e Ghanāri* (*Canary Yellow*, 1989), and Pul-e Khāreji (*Foreign Currency*, 1989). The second focuses on women in love, with *Nargess* (1992), *Rusari Ābi* (*The Blue-veiled*, 1995), and Bānu-ye Ordibehesht (*The May Lady*, 1998). The third period sees a focus on women without men, in *Zir-e Pust-e Shahr* (*Under the Skin of the City*, 2001), Gilāneh (*Gilane*, 2005, co-directed with Mohsen Abdol Wahab), and Khun Bāzi (*Mainline*, 2006, co-directed with Mohsen Abdol Wahab). Banietemad's most recent feature film,

Ghesseh-hā (*Tales*, 2014), is an episodic film which sees the continuity of plots from six of her previous films, and therefore transcends categorization.

Banietemad's first feature film, *Off Limits*, depicts the problem of housing and the lack of security in Iran. A simple state employee, whose house is robbed, cannot find justice, so he sets up a neighborhood vigilante group with the help of local people. Her second film, *Canary Yellow*, is about a shoe repairer in a small village who sells his business to buy a small plot of land, but he is cheated by the vendor. The same thing happens when he goes to the capital to buy a car, with the aim of making a living from it. Her third film, *Foreign Currency*, is set in the late 1980s. Its main subject is the smuggling of foreign currencies, particularly the US dollar. Banietemad depicts the bleak reality for state employees in Iran, living with low salaries, housing problems, rising rents, ineffective social insurance, and the need to have a second job. It is the story of an average person troubled by financial problems in an unhealthy society, where the dollar has the lead role and the last word.

With these three early features, Banietemad shows her intention to make films that depict social problems within her country, laying the foundations for what would become her characteristic style of filmmaking: social realism. Nevertheless, in the first years of the Revolution, cinema had no place for women on screen. Therefore, neither Banietemad nor any other female director was in a position to portray a female or feminist perspective any more than their male counterparts. Banietemad insists that she does not want to be identified as a feminist filmmaker, but rather as a filmmaker who happens to be a woman. However, from the second period of her filmmaking, debuting with *Nargess*, Banietemad has continued to highlight the plight of women in her work. As noted by Saeed Aghighi (2016: 40–5), one of the characteristics of Banietemad's films from this period is the "love triangle," which places in opposition different kinds of relationship: Afagh and Adel (illegitimate relationship) and Nargess and Adel (legitimate relationship) in *Nargess*; Reza and Nobar (unrequited love) and Rasul and Nobar (reciprocal love) in *The Blue-veiled*; Mani and Forugh (son–mother love) and Dr Rahbar and Forugh (illegitimate love) in *The May Lady*.

Nargess is the first film after the Revolution that is based on a social taboo. Banietemad depicts a love triangle, despite the prohibitions. A young thief is in a relationship with an older widowed woman, also a thief. The young man falls in love with another woman, who is "pure and innocent," and asks his mistress to play the role of his mother and go and ask for the girl's hand in marriage. This film has played a revolutionary role in Iranian cinema, as it was the first since the Revolution to portray a negative image of a poor woman. Prior to this film, women had always played pious roles. From that moment, Banietemad continued to portray a real image of Iranian women in her films and many others have followed her. Women in Iranian films played the roles of mothers and workers but also prostitutes, thieves, and mistresses (Bagheri 2017: 387).

After *Nargess*, Banietemad made *The Blue-veiled*, a social romantic story which this chapter will discuss later in more detail. Banietemad's next film, Bānu-ye Ordibehesht (*The May Lady*, 1998), is a drama which battles with the sentimental myth of family life in Iran. Forugh Kia, an intellectual documentary filmmaker, is divorced and raising her teenage son alone. She has a lover, but her son cannot accept her relationship with this man. The lover is never shown on the screen and is present in the film only with his voice. Banietemad, in this way, outmaneuvered the censors. At the same time, she focuses all the attention of her film on the female character. Another important aspect of the film is that it highlights the life of an intellectual woman with a high social position, which was very rare in Iranian cinema at that time (Bagheri 2017: 388).

In 2001, the third period of Banietemad's filmmaking began with *Under the Skin of the City*. Like all of her films, the three made in this period concentrate on social issues in Iran. Women are no longer depicted in unconventional love relationships, as was the case in previous films, but they become single or badly accompanied mothers, assuming all the responsibilities for their family. *Under the Skin of the City*, like *The May Lady*, was produced after the first election of Mohammad Khatami (President of Iran from 1997 to 2005), with Banietemad referring directly to social and political changes taking place in the country. The film is set during the last weeks before the election of 1998, and follows the daily life of a working-class family in Tehran. Many social issues are depicted, from poverty, drug addiction, and runaway teenagers, to class issues, unemployment, and women's labor. As with most of her films, the ending is uncertain; however, the spectator is allowed to retain some hope for the future of the film's heroines.

Banietemad's next two feature films are *Gilāneh*, which concentrates on post-war social problems, and *Mainline*, which realistically portrays the phenomenon of drug addiction among middle-class Iranian girls: In *Gilāneh*, the directors depict a woman who sacrifices her life for her son, who has returned from the Iran–Iraq War sick and disabled. *Mainline* is a road movie about a young, middle-class girl who lives with her mother and wants to be treated for her drug abuse. It is the first film in Iranian cinema history to have dealt with the problems of a middle-class girl's drug addiction. The directors portray two strong women trying to escape their grim reality (Bagheri 2017: 390).

THE BLUE-VEILED: A TURNING POINT

With these brief insights into some of Banietemad's feature films, one can understand her evolution as a social realist director across three decades;

nevertheless, her style is also romantic. As Aghighi asserts: "The superiority of emotional action over realism has found its most important place in *The Blue-veiled*" (2016: 66).

The Blue-veiled touches on a taboo subject. It is a "love at first sight" story between a wealthy old widower, Rasul (meaning "prophet" in Persian), and his employee, Nobar (meaning "firstling"), a young, poor girl living beside a brick furnace in a no man's land neighborhood, called paradoxically Ne'mat Ābād (meaning "district of luxury or blessings"). The film challenges the barriers of age and class. At the end of the film, Nobar and Rasul, the two protagonists, decide to live together, despite their uncertain future. According to Hamid Naficy, this is symbolized in the film's closing scene, which "shows the lovers walking toward each other on a road, when suddenly a passing freight train splits the frame, separating the two. Spectators are left to surmise whether the two will have a joint future" (Naficy 2012b: 159).

Like all of Banietemad's films, *The Blue-veiled* is a plea for justice and equality. For this reason, the self-esteem and dignity of Nobar in this film are exemplary. But *The Blue-veiled* also marks a turning point in the director's career. This is the only film in which the man (the lover) is depicted as a "good" and ideal partner. In her next film, *The May Lady*, the lover seems to be ideal, but he is invisible. Another marked divergence between *The Blue-veiled* and her other films is the depiction of Rasul's daughters as dependent on their husbands, without a role in society and making wrong decisions. After this film, we do not see this kind of woman in Banietemad's work; rather, female characters like Nobar—poor, dignified, with social and familial responsibilities—become a leitmotif.

THE BLUE-VEILED: SEMIOLOGICAL ANALYSIS

One of the most fascinating aspects of *The Blue-veiled* is the way in which Banietemad navigates censorship restrictions concerning on-screen depictions of heterosexual love relationships. Banietemad was one of the first directors to introduce a new cinematic language to portray loving relationships. This implicit cinematic language was central to my PhD research, which applied Anne-Marie Houdebine's semiotic framework (2009: 121–6) to the analysis of male–female relationships in post-revolutionary Iranian cinema. These analytical and cinematic techniques are outlined in Table 7.1. In the following paragraphs, these principles will be applied in considering certain scenes from *The Blue-veiled*, explaining how this formal grammar is used by Banietemad to present illusions of closeness, eroticism, love, and sexual relationships.

Table 7.1 From "Les Relations homme/femme dans le cinéma iranien postrévolutionnaire" (Bagheri 2012)

Strata	Categories	Variables		
Iconic	Gesture	Glances		
		Abortive gestures		
		Turn-around scenes		
	Connector	Children as animate "objects"		
		Inanimate objects		
		Symbolic objects		
Scenic	Space	Outside		
		Inside		
		In-between spaces	Car	
			Courtyard	
			Others	
Sound	Additives	Linguistic		
		Music		
		Direct transition		
Technique		Off-screen		

ICONIC STRATUM: GESTURE

The iconic stratum considers acting and objects on the film set. I have devised two categories—gestures and connectors—with each divided into three subcategories. Gestures as a part of acting can replace language. Even in real life, our gestures can at times convey more meaning than our words. In cinema, many things can be communicated using gestures, without vocal articulation. The science which studies gesture is known as kinesics. According to Jeanne Martinet, kinesics is designated as the branch of semiology which deals with "gestures as signs constituting systems used for communication alone or in conjunction with language" (Martinet 1974: 137–9). Ray L. Birdwhistell further defines anthropological kinesics as the study of bodily activity, structured for and by non-verbal communication and transmitted through the visual channel. It is therefore necessary to understand the gesture in a very broad sense, including, for example, the smile conceived as a social act (Birdwhistell 1968: 9–26). For our purposes, three major gestures are significant: glances, abortive gestures, and turn-around scenes.

Figure 7.1 Exchanging glances in *The Blue-veiled*

Glances

In *The Blue-veiled*, glances play a very important role (Figure 7.1). They tell us the story of the characters. The film is a "love at the first sight" story, both symbolically and literally. The two main characters exchange looks frequently throughout the film. The first signs of attraction between Nobar and Rasul are shown by the "game of glances." He notices her at first, and he keeps looking at her, whereas she looks at him and then looks down, suggesting she is intimidated. However, when she thinks that her boss is not looking at her, she looks at him intently. For more than half of the film, we observe this kind of "eye game." The last time the two characters are together, Nobar looks at Rasul directly and she is determined. They are together and their relationship has progressed. This is no longer a "seduction game"; we observe a woman who knows what she wants from her lover. The evolution of their game of glances echoes the shift in their relationship, from an employee–manager relationship to a secret illegitimate relationship, and finally into an assumed legitimate love relationship.

The first time they talk to each other in the office, Rasul is sitting behind his desk and Nobar is standing, thus emphasizing the obvious difference in their social class. The more the film progresses, the more the ideal egalitarian world of the director manifests. In the marriage scene, discussed later, the camera follows the woman's body movement to the man, and whilst the camera remains static, she leaves the scene with him. She is the one who comes to get him. Implicitly, we can deduce that it is she who invites him to take the plunge—to make love. In this evolution, we can see how the director deconstructs segregation linked to gender and social classes. This procedure is replicated in another key scene, when Rasul goes to Nobar's house at night to declare his love. He knocks at the door and Nobar's hand emerges to take Rasul's suitcase from his hand. Music is playing and the scene is without speech. This is a very symbolic moment, showing that she no longer feels inferior. In taking the suitcase, she is ready to receive his love.

Abortive gestures

Body movements are essential in *The Blue-veiled*. A common ruse of Iranian directors to show that contact between a women and men consists of not fulfilling the character's gestures. This unfinished movement of the body portrays an illusion of proximity, with these half-gestures occupying the screen and the spectators' mind.

In *The Blue-veiled*, the father–daughter relationship is dotted with abortive gestures (Figure 7.2). In several scenes, when one of the daughters comes to see her father, this illusion of proximity is created through a configuration of aborted gesture, accompanied by an animated, inanimate, or symbolic object. For example, one of Rasul's daughters arrives in the courtyard of the paternal house. In greeting her father, twice she leans towards him, but finally steps back before passing the child in her arms to her father. On another occasion, her father is seated in a chair in the courtyard. She leans towards him, as if she might kiss him, but instead places her hand on the back of the chair. In these two scenes, proximity emanating from outstanding actions highlights an illusion of intimacy—one which is not permitted on screen.

Turn-around scenes

Another ruse of the director is to create gestures which occupy the screen. One of the most important occupying gestures is what I have termed "turn-around" scenes. The void that can be created by lack of contact in a farewell scene is furnished by the turn-around scene, consisting of a character turning

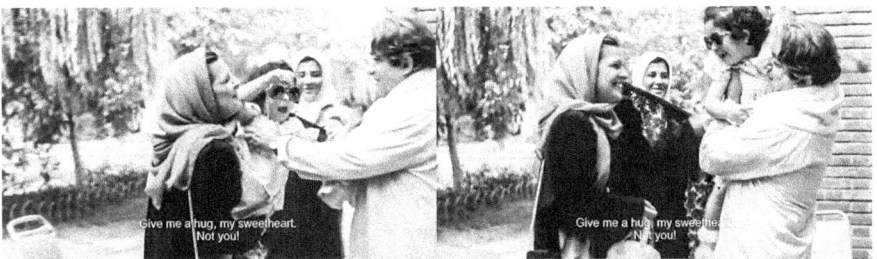

Figure 7.2 Abortive gestures in *The Blue-veiled*

around, as if pretending to leave. In one scene, Nobar and Rasul are in the car. She wants to say goodbye to her lover; they talk and are sad to leave each other. Nobar opens the door but she turns around to say something. This gesture is a substitute for kissing goodbye. When she gets out of the car in front of her home, she turns around a second time, following him with her eyes.

ICONIC STRATUM: CONNECTORS

Just as body gestures and movement can replace physical contact, so too objects in the film set can be used to imply intimacy. Indeed, in order to connect two protagonists, Banietemad uses a range of animate, inanimate and symbolic "objects." The reason for using these objects, beyond the demands of the script, is to explain, implicitly or explicitly, the lack of physical contact between a woman and man.

Children as animate "objects"

Children are used in Iranian cinema to connect adults in two ways: the child as a substitution for the adult; and/or the child as a contact neutralizer. Like many other Iranian filmmakers, one of Banietemad's tactics to bypass censorship regarding physical contact between men and women is the use of children in her films (Figure 7.3). In *The Blue-veiled*, for example, contact with a child—Nobar's little sister, Senobar—is used throughout to convey the love

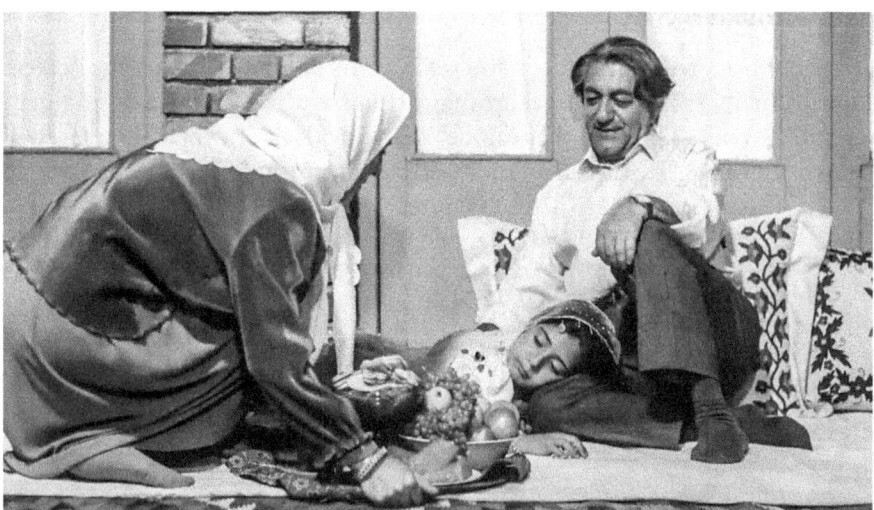

Figure 7.3 Children as animate "objects" in *The Blue-veiled*

story between Nobar and Rasul. From the beginning, their relationship is shown through the relationship each has with the child. The first speech contact is between Rasul and Senobar. Then, when Rasul wants to talk to Nobar, he calls the child and talks to her, but Nobar is the one who answers. When he wants to give Nobar something, it is the little girl who takes it. Later in the film, Rasul approaches the two girls to talk to Nobar; he takes Senobar in his arms and caresses her, as if he is caressing Nobar. After their marriage (a temporary marriage, according to Shi'ite law), he is in Nobar's courtyard and he caresses the little girl's hair as she sleeps on his legs, whilst the woman bends down to put the basket of fruit in front of them. The movement of the leaning female body and the colorful fruit, coupled with Rasul's monologue about Nobar's beauty resembling that of a tomato, as he caresses the child, suggests an erotic scene. Thus, the evolution of the physical and sentimental contact between Nobar and Rasul is depicted through the evolution of his relationship with the child. In another scene, Rasul approaches Nobar, accompanied by her younger brother; Nobar is happy and she takes her brother in her arms. In this scene, the child represents the contact between Nobar and Rasul, yet at the same time destigmatizes this contact.

Banietemad also uses this subterfuge to demonstrate the affectionate relation between Rasul and his daughters, including the aforementioned scene in the courtyard, where the daughter passes her child to her father. The spectator can imagine that the father and daughter are about to kiss or hug, yet the configuration of an abortive gesture means that the child neutralizes the implied contact. When I asked the director about the codes she employs to show the father–daughter relationship, she confirmed that nothing is accidental and this was all planned. With regard to using mise-en-scène as a means to circumvent censorship, she adds: "when there are prohibitions on showing certain relationships, the staging plays a paramount role, because it's up to you to put people in a situation in which their respective relationships, and your objective as a director, are shown properly" (Banietemad 2010).

Inanimate objects

As Banietemad explains, the objects and props used on the set become even more important in censured cinema. In several arrival or departure scenes in *The Blue-veiled*, an object has been placed between Rasul and his daughters. Forugh, one of the daughters, arrives with a saucepan in her hands; her father is watering the garden with a garden hose and then he wipes his hands with a towel on his shoulder. Thus, three objects block the contact between them. The same thing happens in another arrival scene: Rasul comes out of the bathroom with a towel in his hands, or the daughter puts her hands on the back of her father's chair, instead of putting them directly on his shoulders. These objects afford the director the possibility of avoiding contact in the film, whilst staying close to the reality of life.

The same subterfuge is used to indicate physical contact between Nobar and Rasul. When Rasul hands Nobar his coat, his suitcase, or a piece of bread, for a brief moment, they lay their hands on the object at the same time. There is also a telling scene in which Rasul touches the shoes of Nobar, whose bare feet are seen beside them. These scenes allow us to surmise his desire for her. Intimate contact is substituted by suggestion, as one can imagine her feet in the place of the shoes. Nobar's nude feet can also be considered symbolic objects in the film.

Symbols

According to Ferdinand de Saussure, a symbol is a "locked" sign in a given era or culture (Saussure 2005 [1916]: 101). In *The Blue-veiled*, symbols are immanent, as a sign, an index, an object becomes symbolic within the narration of the film itself. Bare feet, for example, are used as a sexual symbol. Feet are the only part of the female body, besides the face and hands, that can be shown nude on the screen. Therefore, the nudity of the feet in two scenes implies an erotic nature and is extremely meaningful in the diegesis.

Being able to film the body in multiple ways is an asset for the Iranian filmmaker. One tactic is to do so in a fragmented way. The body is not shown to the spectator in its overall form: a stray hand, a bare foot prompts the spectator to imaginatively reconstruct the unity of the body. When Rasul places Nobar's shoes on the floor, a camera shows the movement of Nobar's naked feet, with the intimate encounter substituted by body language. Indeed, body language is crucial in this scene. Nobar is standing on a step and Rasul is sitting down beside her feet, arranging her shoes. He is both symbolically and literally at her feet, in a weak and inferior position, weeping and declaring his love, his future dependent on Nobar's response.

In another key scene, to show their physical and sentimental union, the director films the lower part of their bodies, again focusing on the feet. Nobar's white skirt (marriage dress) and nude feet are depicted alongside Rasul's elegant shoes and trousers, as the pair cross a small pool of water. According to a metonymic procedure, the nude body is replaced by her bare feet in the water, which allows for the imagining of a sensual and erotic scene. This scene, which is the exposition of their temporary marriage, is full of various indices suggesting a sexual relationship. At first, before the union of feet in the water, the moon is gradually revealed. The music is rhythmic, suggesting a happy event. The shot is cut. Then, the camera is static, when feet are passing in the water and go off screen. The shot is again cut. Outside, we see little lights at night. The wedding night is depicted as implicitly as possible. Banietemad confirmed the implicit message of this scene by insisting that censorship requires this kind of symbolism. Because she cannot show the sexual act in this category of society, she must remain modest.

TECHNIQUE STRATUM

As I have explained, the position of the camera in the marriage scene, and how the shots are juxtaposed, help to develop the director's intended symbolism. Indeed, these procedures are part of the technique stratum, which takes into account cinematographic technical elements. Two cinematographic procedures are used extensively in this film to suggest physical contact between a woman and a man: the off-screen and the direct transition.

The off-screen

In its extension, the image is limited by the frame. The shot is the portion of the imaginary in three-dimensional space contained inside the frame. According to André Gaudreault and François Jost (1990: 85), the off-screen or "out of the shot" refers to the elements that are imaginatively attached to the frame (Figure 7.4). As André Bazin describes, the shot functions as an open window to the world. Cinema leads us to think that the shot is a fragment of space, cut out and organized according to a point of view. What remains outside the camera is the off-screen. The latter, a term introduced by Bazin, is defined

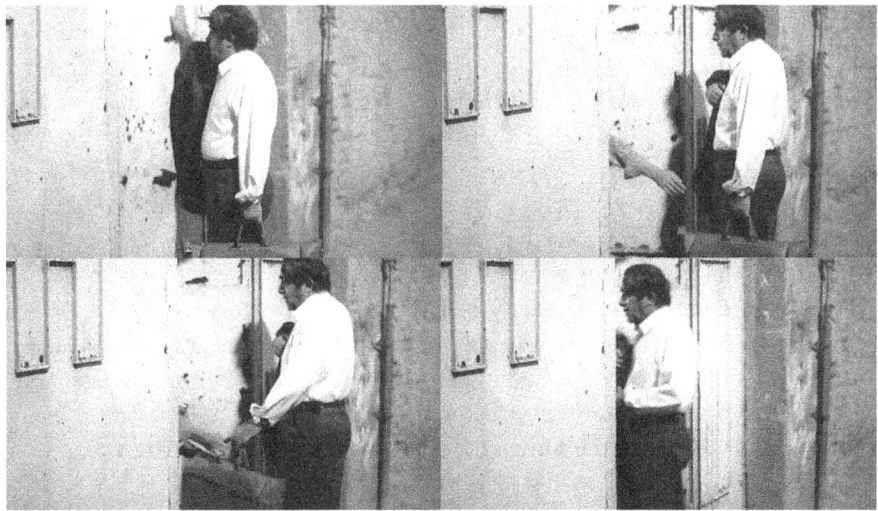

Figure 7.4 The off-screen in *The Blue-veiled*

as the set of elements which, not being included in the shot, are nevertheless imaginatively attached to it. Bazin explains his idea:

> The limits of the screen are not, as the technical vocabulary sometimes suggests, the frame of the picture. The latter is a cache which can only expose part of reality. The frame polarizes space inwards, everything that the screen shows us is on the contrary supposed to extend indefinitely into the universe. The frame is centripetal, the screen centrifugal. (Bazin 2005: 12)

Using the off-screen to give the possibility of imagining without seeing is a common process in Iranian cinema. Indeed, the off-screen alone, or in combination with other indices, gives rise to several meaning effects, such as sexual relations, which cannot be displayed due to the censorship rules. That is why action off screen is used to let the audience imagine or mentally visualize scenes of romantic physical contact.

As mentioned above, when the camera remains static on the water and the two lovers leave the scene, the off-screen is used in two ways: the upper part of their bodies is out of shot, suggesting a closeness—for example, holding hands—that the spectator can imagine; and their love union is suggested far away from the camera frame. Another example of this procedure is when Nobar takes the suitcase, Rasul enters her house, and the door closes. What is happening behind the door is left to the audience's imagination.

Direct transition

Editing is the principle that governs the organization of visual and sound film elements, or the assembly of such elements, by juxtaposing them, chaining them, and/or by regulating the duration. However, editing is not limited to cutting and gluing scenes. It is the result of the imagination of the director, who imposes his or her style and creates a particular vision of the world. The importance of editing is explained by Eisenstein:

> Two fragments of films whatsoever, placed together, inevitably combine into a new concept, a new quality, born from their juxtaposition [. . .]. Editing is the art of expressing or signifying by the relation of two juxtaposed planes, so that this juxtaposition gives birth to the idea or expresses something that is not contained in either of the two planes taken separately. The whole is greater than the sum of the parts. (quoted in Betton 1983: 12)

As far as this work is concerned, the assembly is not directly analyzed. What is interesting to examine, within the framework of this research, is the way in which certain scenes are juxtaposed. What is being studied here is the transition and the sequence of scenes: understanding when the scene is cut, for what reason, and its relation to the subsequent scene, in order to bring out certain meaning effects.

Like the off-screen, the direct-transition technique also gives the director the opportunity to bring certain events to the viewer's mind, without showing them directly on screen. Direct transition is when the director cuts from one shot to another without any transition scene. For example, in one of the key scenes, when Nobar and Rasul are talking for the first time about their feelings, as Rasul, as previously discussed, places his hands on Nobar's shoes, music plays and we cut to the next shot: daytime, with cars moving across the road. The spectator is left to assume that they spent the night together. Alternatively, in the goodbye scene in the courtyard, they both put their hands on Rasul's coat, and the scene is cut. The next shot shows the factory, the day after. Finally, in the famous scene when they are crossing the water, the scene cuts to some house lights in the blackness of the night. In each of these scenes, locations are changed from one shot to the next.

SCENIC STRATUM: SPACE

Locations are a part of the scenic stratum which brings together elements participating in the staging of the "object." In other words, there are indices that create the context, the situation, and the atmosphere in which the message is produced. These indices can be the color, the light, the film set, or the location.

In cinema, the film set or the location presents an atmosphere, a place, an era, a social environment, and so on. It also situates the character in relation to his tastes, his social category, and other aspects. In Iranian cinema, with restrictions on the character's movement or clothes, the smallest detail in a setting, used intelligently, can express the inexpressible. Banietemad highlights the importance of the city of Tehran and the car as locations in her films by saying "the car is a space of intimacy for a certain social category and in particular for women. An interaction and a dialogue can have various influences in different spaces" (Banietemad 2010).

It must be mentioned here that the background location in distance shots and wide shots is significant, and moderates the sentimental, idealistic point of view of the film. The most important wide shot, in this regard, is the opening shot of *The Blue-veiled*. For approximately two minutes, whilst the credits appear, a real geographical location is filmed. This is the trace of Banietemad the documentarist that we can see and hear. Indeed, the spectator hears people shouting far away and babies crying. In the next eight minutes, location shots depict brickwork, farm, or factory, recalling the atmosphere of one of director's previous documentaries,

In Film-hā ro beh ki Neshun Midin? (*To Whom Do You Show These Films?*, 1993). Banietemad's social realist aesthetic is thus foregrounded in the film through the tension between exterior locations (conveying urban reality) and interior shots—the settings for artificial dramatic scenes.

Analyzing these oppositional interior and exterior spaces serves to highlight another spatial variable that we may call "intermediate" space. In *The Blue-veiled*, most of the male–female scenes are filmed neither inside nor outside the house. If interior represents the domestic realm and exterior the public domain, then the intermediate space is therefore neither outside nor inside, but situated between the two. Closed public spaces, such as an office or a personal car, as well as private open spaces like domestic courtyards or gardens, are part of the variable intermediate space. It should be noted that, in Iran, private spaces are private in so far as the neighborhood cannot observe them. From the moment a vis-à-vis exists, the laws imposed on public space must be respected there. Likewise, the personal car, being used in public space, is subject to the laws concerning it.

In *The Blue-veiled*, the two lovers are alone just twice in the interior space of the house. In the first instance, they are apart in the room; Nobar is cleaning and Rasul is awaiting guests to mark the anniversary of his wife's death. There is a glancing game between them in a shot/reverse-shot. Their love is not yet declared. The second instance takes place in a small room near the end of the film, as Nobar delivers a monologue directly to the camera. The same shot/reverse-shot is used here. Apart from these two instances, all other scenes featuring Nobar and Rasul are in intermediate places such as a field, his office, or his car, but mainly in the courtyard of the house.

The variable courtyard, as a private open-air space, highlights a capacity for intimacy on the one hand, but at the same time does not stress its likelihood, due to the non-enclosure of the space. As special rules of conduct are imposed by law for public spaces, the absence of contact does not upset the spectator, thanks to the outside effect of the court. On the other hand, when the courtyard space is combined with the transition or the off-screen, the interior effect allows for the suggestion of intimate relationships.

As already mentioned, the car space, though private, must still follow the rules imposed on public space. The fact that the couple is sitting side by side in a small and closed space gives an impression of proximity, even if characters are not permitted to kiss on screen. It is important to mention that, in Iran's urban areas, young people are challenging authority by creating spaces of semi-freedom in their cars, where romantic rendezvous are arranged and tactile exchanges are discreetly practiced.

In the goodbye scene in the car at night, Rasul drops Nobar and her sister off at their house. The child gets out and the conversation continues between the two adults. There is no light. They exchange affectionate words. The configuration of visual obscurity, a long moment of discussion, and the glancing game highlight the physical and emotional connection in this departure scene.

SOUND STRATUM

Linguistic

The affectionate words pronounced in the above scene hold their own importance and, as such, constitute a part of our formal grammar. Indeed, the sound stratum has two components: one linguistic—namely, everything that is said—and the other relating to music and sound effects.

Banietemad uses a key linguistic device in most of her films: the monologue. One of the main characters looks directly at the camera, talking to his or her counterpart via the spectator, due to the extreme close-up shot. This formula is a sentimental way to monopolize the spectator's attention and to highlight the fact that what is being said is incredibly important. In cinema, directors generally use the monologue to emphasize a message which is dear to them. However, the monologue format can be a double-edged sword. It can be very efficient and emotionally charged, because it dispenses with the conventional illusion of cinema by directly addressing the viewer as a confidant; but it can also be considered sentimental or superficial, in the same way that music can be.

Three essential monologues punctuate *The Blue-veiled*. The first one is Rasul's speech to Nobar during the famous suitcase scene in the courtyard. This monologue can be considered a love declaration, to which Nobar responds positively. It is accompanied by other cinematographic procedures—such as light, symbols, direct transition, music, and body language—which enhance the meaning and effect of the implicit love declaration. Through tears, disparate words, and sentences without verbs, he is painting the dark future of the couple if they decide to be together. Relying on John Langshaw Austin's theory of "speech acts" (1962), one can analyze the sentences pronounced by Rasul as follows: the "illocutionary act" (the speaker's intent) is a demand of Rasul to Nobar not to say yes to his love. The "perlocutionary act" (provoked reaction) is the fact that Nobar says yes to his love, as she understands the hidden love declaration between Rasul's implicit words:

> Say no. Say you don't want to. Say it and free me. My dignity! My reputation! I'll take care of you like my own daughter until I'm alive. Or maybe even more dear than them. That was my intention from the start anyway. I got caught off guard. Tell me: "You could be my father. It's frowned upon to say things like that. I don't want you to waste your youth for me. With a hidden life. Fear of getting caught. Visits without notice . . .

The last two monologues occur consecutively in the final ten minutes of the film. Firstly, there is Nobar's last speech in the film, addressed to her lover:

> I only stayed to see you and then leave. They're not wrong either. How dare a peasant fill the place of Talat, Rasul's wife, for him? But I was happy to just stay engaged [in temporary marriage] to you. They said: "you're like that at first, then you'll try and persuade him to marry you. Then you'll give birth and take all his money." They throw a bag of money in front of me, asking me to take it and to leave. I said: "I haven't come for anything to leave because of it. I've come for someone who has to tell me to leave himself." They hit me in the face for talking bigger than myself. That's when I realized, what difference does it make where they write your name [referring to permanent marriage, as opposed to a temporary one].

This second monologue is almost a response to the first one. We understand in the first monologue scene that Nobar has accepted the love declaration of Rasul and the conditions that he proposed. Thus, in between, they secretly perform a temporary marriage, in an attempt to legalize their love. But with this second monologue, we can understand that the couple cannot continue, as Rasul's family do not accept her. Here, the idealized love encounters a harsh reality. It is a discourse of disillusion and disappointment. One important element in this scene is the return of Nobar's blue scarf, the same one she wore in the first scenes of the film, whilst they were falling in love without declaring it to each other. The recurrence of this scarf can have the meaning effect of returning Nobar to her previous life situation. There is one important closing statement pronounced by Rasul, when he arrives at the firm. Romantic music plays and he shouts: "Hey! The blue-veiled!" (hence the title of the film). Nobar turns around, wearing a red scarf, whilst her little sister, Senobar, runs to join Rasul, wearing Nobar's blue scarf. As already noted, the evolution of their relationship was aided by the child. Confusion between Nobar and her sister bypasses the censorship regulations. With respect to the discourse analysis, as he calls her, he makes a step forward in the blossoming relationship. In the film's last monologue, Rasul addresses his family:

> Take everything I own. I raised you with all my heart. I took care of you like my own eyes. Even if I was your enemy instead of your father, we're even with what you've done. In order to save the family's reputation, and from the fear of bringing shame onto the family, you actually ruined my reputation. Now I leave the rest of my reputation here and go away. Rasul Rahmani dies today. The person standing here right now wishes to stay with Nobar Kordani, a peasant girl who's got no one, until he dies.

The fact that these are the last words pronounced in the film emphasizes the gravity of this monologue. Within this scene, we understand the significance of the character's name—Rasul Rahmani means "the clement prophet." Rasul (the prophet) is at the top of the stairs, looking down at his family who have betrayed him, just as Jesus was betrayed by his apostles, or as Muhammad mounted the camel to make an important declaration. Like a prophetic message, Rasul's discourse is gentle but firm, with his idealism and sentimentalism pitched in opposition to Nobar's previous monologue. It is also worth mentioning here that Nobar means "firstling fruit," alluding to both her youth and her position as "forbidden fruit."

The optimism and idealism of Rasul's last words dissipate with the harsh reality of the final scene. Indeed, the closing shot is less hopeful regarding a happy ending for this socially unequal relationship. Music plays and the film's closing credits begin to roll as the lovers try to join each other—Nobar on foot, as a sign of poverty, and Rasul in his car, signifying affluence—when a train separates them.

Music

In the early days of cinema, music—along with in-theatre narrators, live accompanying sound effects, and early experiments with sound (like operatic recitations)—played a key role in conveying a film's atmosphere and tone. With the advent of talking cinema, music had to negotiate its place alongside speech. According to Lo Duca, music has an aesthetic and psychological function, in creating a dream-like state, a climate, or an emotional shock (Duca 1948: 92). Music is by no means a furnishing element; it must denote something specific in the film. Banietemad considers music in her films as an element on its own, which must be mastered in harmony with the director's thought.

According to Gérard Betton, music in cinema fulfills a physiological function. Even during the era of silent film, it gave the spectator the feeling of a lived duration and of a "deliverance from the terrible weight of silence." It also has an aesthetic and psychological function, evidenced in fact that "by rhythm prevail eurythmic movements (dances, marches); through harmony, human expression, the harmonic and instrumental element suggested by moods." Elements such as pitch, duration, dynamics, melody, and intervention (or not) of a human voice are therefore decisive in the effect produced by a musical sequence (Betton 1983: 48).

In certain cases, the music can either co-structure the film, as in *Through a Glass Darkly* (Ingmar Bergman, 1961), where the musical interventions are there only to delineate the equivalent of theatrical acts in the film, or function in leitmotif to incarnate a movement of repetition, as in *Contempt* (Jean-Luc Godard, 1963), where the music of Georges Delerue brings drama to power.

Music in the cinema can then increase what Michel Chion calls the "empathic effect" of scenes (1995: 210), as in *La Dolce Vita* (Federico Fellini, 1960), where colorful music exacerbates the gaiety of the fountain scene. Conversely, an "empathic effect" might be achieved by music that is indifferent to the scene played, as in *Strangers on a Train* (Alfred Hitchcock, 1951), where scenes of crime and horror are juxtaposed with the sound of an organ.

Music has a preponderant and essential presence in *The Blue-veiled*. Here, music is like a trademark for each character, with Nobar and Rasul having their own music—sometimes slow and romantic, or, occasionally, more rhythmic, with music replacing language. Music in *The Blue-veiled* is a part of the film diegesis, accompanying the drama and the love story of the two protagonists. Banietemad confirms our hypothesis of meaning concerning music in her film:

> Yes, it's the same theme but with different variations that repeat themselves. [. . .] the musician, [Ahmad] Pejman, had composed it in a way to introduce and recall the relationship of each couple. It was a choice. [. . .] In any case, music has a particular definition in cinematographic culture and, then, there was a contract with the musician so that this melody comes back every time there is an ascent or a fall in the story around certain characters.

CINEMA AS CRITICAL PRAXIS

The force of Banietemad's career is based on her social realist yet romantic style, her pioneering role as one of the first female film directors after the Revolution, and the radical ways in which she chooses and depicts her stories. Through a focus on social problems, unconventional love, or women's issues in her films, she transcends a range of cultural, societal, and legal frameworks. Her work can be defined as what Roland Barthes (1985: 14) calls critical praxis, dealing with the "collective representations of sign systems" in order to understand "the mystification which transforms petty-bourgeois culture into universal nature." *The Blue-veiled* is the consecration of this idea, as is encapsulated at the end with Rasul leaving his family, petty-bourgeois culture, name, and fortune behind, in order to gain dignity and happiness by uniting with a poor girl. Like Barthes—who uses semiology as a tool to reveal underlying meanings by "targeting the symbolic and semantic system of our entire civilization"—one can see Banietemad's work in film as a responsible instrument for analyzing social objects. It therefore becomes a "fundamental method of ideological criticism." Banietemad herself does not miss an opportunity to declare that cinema is nothing more than a tool for her to help her society, her people, and her ideals.

CHAPTER 8

Masculinities in Banietemad's *Tales*: Reshuffling Gender Dynamics under Socio-economic Pressures

Nina Khamsy

Halfway through the film *Ghesseh-hā* (*Tales*, 2014), we embark with a documentary filmmaker in a minivan full of people conducting some industrial action. Their factory has closed down, but they have not been paid for months. The image switches to the documentary filmmaker's own camera; we witness a series of spontaneous testimonies from the workers. Their statements range from "I need my wage; I have a family to feed" to "I worked loyally all these years and now that's how they treat me?" Reza, one of the male leaders, expresses his despair: due to his lack of revenue, he has become dependent on the wage of his wife. Before the camera moves away, he rhetorically and repeatedly asks: "Is this acceptable?" Such testimonies of personal struggle echo larger social malaise. Eponymously, these stories form Banietemad's film, *Tales*, and highlight different aspects of gender subjectivities in Iranian society. The other stories showcase more situations of drug addiction, prostitution, abusive relationships, and financial desperation. In these intimate stories, Banietemad delineates the interplay of changing male and female subjectivities under socio-economic pressure. The film portrays how common people are squeezed in vicious circles of poverty and the battle to survive. "It's true that the questions we are dealing with are Iranian, but they are also global," said Banietemad in an interview in Venice (Roddy 2014). How does Banietemad portray gender reshuffling and representations of manliness in *Tales*? How does it echo her previous films? What does the actual production of this film tell us about today's politics of Iranian cinema?

These stories present how a lack of revenue brings Iranian ideals of manhood into sharper scrutiny. Thus, the film does not perpetuate the construction of a fixed gender, but, as noted by Pak-Shiraz (2017) regarding a series of post-2005 Iranian films, it instead challenges ideas of heroism, manliness, and patriarchy. It relates "tales of men's alienation and despair, presenting the diversity of performances of masculinity within Iran" (2017: 946). Thus, studies of masculinities in Iranian cinema have demonstrated the "diversity of the marginal experiences and the internal hierarchies of marginal masculinities" (ibid.) and have challenged stereotypes of Iranian or Middle Eastern masculinity more generally (Gow 2016: 175).

Importantly, *Tales* brings in another set of questions for the study of masculinities. Whilst Pak-Shiraz notes that in several recent films, including Saman Salur's *Chand Kilo Khormā Barāye Marāssem-e Tadfin* (*A Few Kilos of Dates for a Funeral*, 2006) and Majid Barzegar's *Parviz* (2012), "the dysfunctional relationship between the genders is evident in the absence of any form of conversation between them" (2017: 959), as many challenges come in the way of the men's repeated attempts to dialogue with women. Banietemad's film narrates long conversations or arguments between male and female protagonists. Her filmic language is famous for her capacity to successfully represent male/female intimacy in ways that circumvent the regulations of modesty. In *Tales*, she uses themes of private and public spaces, the negotiation of the male/female divide, and lyrical ambivalence to denaturalize the idea of masculinity as fixed by portraying it in dialogue with femininity. *Tales*' narrative resists simplification in readings of men's and women's roles. Instead, the film proposes a multi-faceted portrayal of men and women, and how they negotiate their position in their encounter.

In this chapter, I draw on masculinity studies as an object of knowledge that is always in relation to femininity, historically and contextually (Connell 2005). I will show how *Tales* problematizes the idea of a normative gender by "call[ing] to attention the construction of masculinity rather than concealing it" (Peberdy 2011: 29, cited in Pak-Shiraz 2017: 963). I argue that her films depict moments of crisis to better show the construction of masculinities and the possibility for alternatives, possibly based in openness and dialogue. Keeping this in mind, I draw on Pak-Shiraz (2017) to show that, in opposition to traditional depictions of male protagonists in pre-revolutionary Iranian cinema and to the hypermasculine hero of commercial cinema, there is no such hero in *Tales*. Following the same trend as other post-2005 Iranian films, it portrays the "conflicted man negotiating between the contradicting demands of tradition and modernity" (Pak-Shiraz 2017: 953). According to Pak-Shiraz, key binaries from the Iran–Iraq War, such as opposing enemy/friend, hero/traitor of the "sacred defense" cinema, have shifted (ibid.: 946). This change allows for more articulate elaborations of masculinity and alternative heroisms. Martyrdom is no longer conceived as an "ideal of masculinity and heroism from its male population" (ibid.). One can thus wonder what the performances of masculinity are for the young war generation that is now living in a swiftly changing Iranian society (ibid.). I respond to this call by showing the range of different masculinities represented in *Tales*. Thus, I contend that if Banietemad proposes a heroism in *Tales*, it comes from common people. With Khosrowjah (2011), I argue that these are post-modern urban heroes whose achievement is their capacity to survive amid difficulties and help each other in the urban jungle that is Tehran.

In *Tales*, the paths of the characters, including those from Banietemad's previous films, criss-cross. Those familiar with Banietemad's filmography know that she frequently features the same actors. This both broadens the horizon of *Tales* and provides her characters with increased breadth. In the scene described above, we meet Tooba (Golab Adineh), the respectable female laborer now in her sixties, who we previously saw in *Rusari Ābi* (*The Blue-veiled*, 1995) and *Zir-e Pust-e Shahr* (*Under the Skin of the City*, 2001). She is a hard-working and intelligent woman, even if she is illiterate.

Iranian films have portrayed how gender ideas have shifted with political changes throughout the last century. An assumption is that politics—stemming from power—infiltrates all aspects of life, and so does resistance (Laachir and Talajooy 2013). In this chapter, I will map masculinity theories in the context of Iranian cinema. The articulation of male characters is as important as that of female ones, yet it has received significantly less academic attention so far. This will provide me with the tools to examine gender dynamics linked to socio-economic processes in *Tales*. I will then move on to explore where this film stands in relation to Banietemad's earlier productions.

MASCULINITIES IN IRAN

Exploring masculinities requires some precautions since "masculinity as an object of knowledge is always masculinity-in-relation" (Connell 2005: 43). Thus, "masculinity and femininity are inherently relational concepts" (ibid.: 43). Butler's theory of gendered performativity (1988) suggests an emphasis on how everyday social practices reinforce or resist the wider cultural narratives of sexed and gendered subjects. In this view, masculinity is not a pre-existing or natural fact but an "effect" which is repeatedly achieved through discursive, embodied, and material performances (Butler 1988). Knowledge of masculinities arises within the larger project of knowing gender relations. Following Connell, "masculinities are configurations of practice structured by gender relations. They are inherently historical; and their making and remarking is a political process affecting the balance of interests in society and the direction of social change" (Connell 2005: 44). Thus, there are relations among masculinities: hegemony, subordination, complicity, marginalization (ibid.: 76). As we will turn towards later, socially dominant masculinities assert their position through the "marginalization or delegitimation of alternatives" (Connell and Messerschmidt 2005: 846).

In the context of modern Iran, *namus* (honor) is the concept that closely links maleness and femaleness. As shown by scholars (Najmabadi 1997; Tavakoli-Targhi 2001), it has shifted through history in tandem with Iranian nationhood. Iranian modernity, shaped discursively, went through a rearticulation of pivotal concepts crafted by gender, such as nation (*mellat*) and homeland (*vatan*; Najmabadi 1997: 444). *Namus*, primarily established in Islamic thought, shifted to a national concern. In parallel, so did *mellat* (understood as brotherhood). Thereafter, in a process of slippage, "*namus* constituted purity of woman and Iran as subjects of both male possession and protection" (ibid.). This is essential to understanding Iranian interpersonal expressions. As explained by Mir-Hosseini, *namus* "is a core value, so deeply ingrained in the dominant culture that it is rarely questioned . . . except when it is attacked or infringed" (Mir-Hosseini 2017: 211). The complex concept of *namus* is key to understanding gender dynamics in Iran. To insist on the way that both femininity and masculinity are dynamic and changing in Iran, one needs to look at gender changes throughout the nineteenth century and the role of the state as a pivotal cultural shift. As noted by Najmabadi (2005), masculine stereotypes are as dynamic as female ones. As we have witnessed, the state has an important role in shaping gender dynamics, but the rupture that the 1979 Islamic Revolution sometimes represents needs to be nuanced. The substitution of the figure of the Shah as head of state after the 1979 Islamic Revolution with that of Ayatollah Khomeini, as one that "rendered a different hierarchy of masculinities in Iranian society," was not completed to the point of replacing "the westernized with the religious as the new hegemonic order in post-Revolutionary Iran" (Pak-Shiraz 2017: 945). It was more complex; changes were already under way before the Revolution, and processes of rupture and continuity prevailed in the post-revolutionary period. This is also visible in cinema.

GENDER REPRESENTATION IN IRANIAN CINEMA

The representation of women in Iranian cinema has gone through a significant change since the early 1990s. From that time on, a number of rising female directors and actors began depicting their view of Iranian society, as well as the role of women within it (Ghorbankarimi 2015). The many studies of gender in Iranian cinema have focused on female representations, leaving men unconsidered (for example, Lahiji 2002). There is, however, a growing literature on masculinities in Iranian cinema. Scholars have recently aimed to address the gender imbalance in recent studies by incorporating studies of masculinities (Abedinifard 2019; Gerami 2003; Gow 2016; Pak-Shiraz 2017) because the representation of one gender tends to inform the other (Gow 2016: 166) and "non-female-centric films" can portray strong feminist perspectives (Abedinifard 2019). According to Pak-Shiraz, *film-farsi* (see below) created models of masculinity that reinterpreted the concept of *javanmardi* (chivalry) through its heroes and villains. It subverted the masculine hierarchies propagated by the state and "endowed marginalised men with the moral authority to take on the hypermasculine role without subverting the idea of hegemonic masculinity itself" (Pak-Shiraz 2018: 297). This sense, the "heroes of the 1950s and 1960s resembled a conventionally Iranian man" but "the hero of the 1970s *film-farsi* had the characteristics of the the western hero" (Pak-Shiraz 2018: 301).

The pre-revolutionary *film-farsi* genre is known for displaying song and dance, and female stars, at times semi-naked, appealing to a male gaze (Lahiji 2002). Male characters in *film-farsi* were as stereotyped as women. In the pre-revolutionary culture, the hierarchical order featured the merchants and professionals (engineers, doctors, professors) at the top, with the *jahel* (urban cowboys) and *lat-ha* (misfits) at the bottom (Gerami 2003). After the Islamic Revolution of 1979, the veiling and codes of modesty regulating society put an end to sexualized portrayals of women and also brought new models for male characters.

Scholars have drawn on theories of masculinity to analyze Iranian films. For Pak-Shiraz, the crisis of masculinity in pre-revolutionary Iranian cinema is not so much about

> masculinity's assertion of power and authority over female subjectivities but partly their struggle and ultimate failure to form a relationship with them. The gendered social and political discourse within Iran magnifies these obstacles ... and many recent art house films, including those discussed here, critically examine the challenges of establishing relationships and intimacy in a gendered society. (2017: 959)

For Pak-Shiraz, *film-farsi* subverted masculine hierarchies and presented the *luti*, or "tough guy," as the central heroic character and the rich Westernized man at the bottom of the hierarchy. Shahin Gerami explores post-revolutionary masculine models and argues that there is a new genre "devoted to the war efforts and the martyrs. The martyr is a young, unmarried (virgin, innocent) man, fearless and strong" (2003: 267) and she thus argues that the "glorified new masculinity types" include the clergy and martyrs. Drawing on this categorization, Gow (2016) examines different representations of masculinity in post-revolutionary Iranian films featuring male characters, following Gerami's conceptualization of masculinity in Iran. He highlights how Masud Kimiai's *Dash Akol* (1971) displays the *luti*, or "tough guy" genre, as a particular form of masculinity.

To contribute to this growing scholarship on masculinities in Iranian films, I will look specifically at instances of gender relationality in *Tales*. Previous works have mostly examined men and not their masculinity construction with regard to their women counterparts. Critiques of the concept of masculinity pointed to a "tendency, in research as well as in popular literature, to dichotomize the experiences of men and women" (Connell and Messerschmidt 2005: 838). Taking a consistently relational approach to gender is more favorable (ibid.), as

> women are central in many of the processes constructing masculinities—as mothers; as schoolmates; as girlfriends ... we consider that research on hegemonic masculinity now needs to give much closer attention to the practices of women and to the historical interplay of femininities and masculinities. (Connell and Messerschmidt 2005: 848)

Looking at instances of female–male dialogue might provide the most appropriate material to understand gender dynamics. Due to the scope and length of this chapter, I have applied a more limiting heteronormative framework to the research rather than a more fluid one.

TALES' SEVEN STORIES AS REALIST WINDOWS

Tales interconnects the stories of about fifteen characters in seven different shorts. Episodes take place chronologically, but no clear plot appears in their unfolding, reminiscent of French New Wave films. Characteristically, the figure of the upper-middle-class documentary filmmaker (Habib Rezaei) unites these chapters. He seems driven by an aim to portray society as it is in its most mundane expression. In the first scene of the film, seated in the back of a taxi, he films Tehran's nocturn urban landscape whilst listening to the cab driver's life story (which refers to *Under the Skin of the City*). The driver is intrigued and asks: "Have you been away for long?" "No, how come?," responds the filmmaker. "Well, you're filming the streets," the driver says, clearly finding this bizarre, as though only foreigners would find the landscape interesting. The filmmaker states: "This is how I look at the world." This sets the tone for the film. In *Tales*, we see portions of lives and hear stories without clear beginnings or ends, mere sneak peeks providing a taste of the broader social atmosphere. On this topic, Banietemad explains: "The documentary character is a representation of the position of the documentary that is constrained when making a film. It is, of course, a picture of a real filmmaker's situation" (Simorgh 2015). Further:

> the position of the documentary filmmaker in *Tales* represents the position of filmmaking in general, where his camera is not able to record the "real"—that is, in the sense that the perspective of the filmmaker and the way he views the world is through a camera lens only as a means to record and hold on to that moment. (Armatage and Khosroshahi 2017: 152–3)

In *Tales*, the documentary maker meets administrative restrictions on his work, but he persists.

The structure of *Tales* shows a cross-section of Iranian society. The characters circulate in a range of sites and socio-economic levels. We gradually learn how they skillfully navigate the social world. Moreover, the film's settings contribute to building the narrative. Half of the short stories take place in closed sites that are in motion: a cab, a minivan, or a subway. They also happen in private environments, such as a family household courtyard, or in semi-private ones, such as a non-governmental organization (NGO) sheltering female addicts or an administrator's office.

As films from the Iranian New Wave "tradition" tend to achieve in a similar manner to French New Wave films, *Tales* reaches a high degree of realism. The incorporation of the documentary style and the absence of non-diegetic sounds and music in the film (except at the very end) reinforce the sense of realism. To write, Banietemad takes inspiration from the conditions of real individuals, as she explains: "The different characters of *The Blue-veiled* were inspired by my research into the conditions of working women, and those who are marginalized" (Armatage and Khosroshahi 2017: 145). For the preparation of *Khun Bāzi* (*Mainline*, 2006), Banietemad explains that Baran Kosari, who plays Sara, the protagonist, spent considerable time in close contact with young people who were struggling with addiction in tension-filled rehabilitation centers and thus, "she gained knowledge of where drugs are sold and a deep understanding of addiction" (ibid.: 151). With regard to the construction of the film *Tales*, I now turn to the political context that influenced the filming style.

GUERRILLA-STYLE FILMING WITHOUT BREAKING ANY RULES

The final form the film took makes sense only when *Tales*' shooting conditions are considered. *Tales* was made in an uncommon way, and yet, according to Banietemad, no rules were broken in producing it. After *Mainline* in 2006, Banietemad made no feature films until *Tales* in 2014 because she boycotted filmmaking under the previous government (2005–13). As she explains:

> I didn't accept the new management of the Ministry of Arts and Culture, and I didn't want to make films under such conditions. Thus, *Tales* was made up of shorter films, which meant it didn't require a license, and as a result was made independently. (Armatage and Khosroshahi 2017: 152)

Tales was indeed created with a common short film license. Banietemad wrote these short stories in such a way as to produce a long film, which is not prohibited by law (Simorgh 2015). With this idea in mind, Banietemad structured the script so it could be filmed in a short amount of time, but it took her years to mature the script with her collaborator and co-author, Farid Mostafavi. To stay close to her values and ambitions, Banietemad did not refrain from casting two actresses who were banned from acting or appearing on screen at the time of filming (Fatemeh Motamed-Aria and Baran Kosari). It was possible for these actresses to feature in the film because it did not require a formal statement from the Ministry of Culture and Islamic Guidance (Simorgh 2015), which supervises all cultural activities.

The film met with challenges but was nevertheless a success that appealed to national and international audiences. As Banietemad explains:

> *Tales* wasn't screened until four years after completion. It didn't receive the right to be screened under the presidency of Ahmadinejad [2005–13]. Even with permission to be screened, which came under Hassan Rouhani's presidency [2013 to present], the immense pressure of opposing groups resulted in a two-year ban ... The main cinemas that belonged to government institutions in Tehran and other cities boycotted the film and prevented its screening. (Armatage and Khosroshahi 2017: 140)

In the end, with very few exhibiting slots, *Tales* was released and still "took in ten billion rials" (ibid.), or about 30,000 US dollars at the time. The film won three national awards at the 2014 Fajr International Film Festival, including one for Best Film and one for Best Actor in a Supporting Role for Farhad Aslani (acting as Reza), and six awards at other international festivals, including the prize for Best Screenplay in 2014 at Venice.

Whilst Banietemad strongly supports women's rights movements and organizations, and makes films challenging systems of patriarchy, she does not consider herself to be a feminist (Armatage and Khosroshahi 2017: 154–5). She explains that the

> term feminist in our society has been subject to confusing interpretations. Apart from progressive groups and intellectuals, it has created an inverted image that results in a feeling of disconnect between ordinary people and feminists. My job is to make social films, and what is most important for me is to have trust from the general public and to be able to communicate with them. (ibid.)

She reasons that her focus is more on women, "but that doesn't mean I just have to make films about women, as my look at male characters is no different to female characters. But it's natural that I know more about women than men" (Simorgh 2015).

MINGLING TALES OF TODAY AND YESTERDAY

In this section, I will focus on several scenes that meaningfully depict gender dynamics in resonance with Banietemad's previous films.

The shared burden of honor for men and woman: the episode where Abbas encounters his estranged neighbor, Massoumeh

Abbas (Mohammad Reza Forutan), the cab driver, picks up a young woman with a sick baby (Mehraveh Sharifinia). At first, he wants her to get out, thinking she is a prostitute, because she does not give him a destination. (Abbas asks: "Where do you want to go?" She replies, "Wherever you go." He yells, "Aren't you ashamed of yourself?" and "Don't you have a brother who's enough of a man to keep you from doing this?") But slowly he recognizes her as Massoumeh, his former neighbor when she was still a teenager. Whilst driving to a destination unknown to both the protagonist and the audience, Abbas recounts the story of *Under the Skin of the City*: after yet another fight between Massoumeh and her brother, in which he beats her and cuts her hair, Massoumeh runs away. The tension rises in the car as Abbas recalls the story whilst addressing Massoumeh in the front mirror, and she repeatedly asks him to stop the car because she wants to leave. It is implied that she took up what is considered a sinful life as a runaway girl, sleeping on the streets of Tehran. In his voice, Abbas displays a sense of resentment towards her "asshole junkie" brother and he shakes his head in disapproval. Although he chastises Massoumeh for the life she has led, he does not see her as the one to blame; he offers her a cigarette. At the end of his story, the two of them express their regret for the past. When he stops the car and gets out, one wonders whether Abbas will throw Massoumeh out of his car or hand her to the police. When he returns with a stuffed monkey for the baby and medications, he sees that she has gone. In Abbas's attempt to contribute to healing the baby, we can find a symbolic gesture of reconciliation and hope for what the future might hold. Perhaps the baby is the most palpable outcome of Massoumeh's tragedy but can still be healed and thus saved.

In this scene, it appears that Abbas harbors resentment towards Massoumeh's brother, but also towards himself for not preventing her tragedy from happening. A younger Abbas in *Under the Skin of the City* would fiercely react against men who beat their wives or sisters, including his own sister's husband. As he strove to lift his family out of poverty (his mother worked in a labor-intensive job in a factory), he took high risks that did not pay off in the end. His heroic intentions led to a tragic destiny that dragged himself and his family down. In failing to provide for his relatives, he failed to approximate to the ideal of the provider, the breadwinner. Abbas also offers an alternative masculinity with regard to the beatings. As shown by Pak-Shiraz (2018), *film-farsi* promoted a kind of eroticization of violence against women (as an erotic act of hegemonic masculinity), which boys were socialized to find erotic and entertaining. In this sense, boys understood that to display manhood involved committing acts of aggression. However, Abbas could not stand up to such hegemonic masculinity, as he now wished he had. In many ways, the *bi-namusi* (dishonor) of Massoumeh becoming a prostitute spills over to the men in her surroundings, who have proven unable to step in and protect her. As seen before, *namus* (honor) is closely linked to maleness. It conceives the purity of woman as subjects of male possession and protection (Mir-Hosseini 2017). Abbas, like other boys, was raised with the duty to protect the *namus* of his close female relatives. However, socio-economic inequality plays a major role in the multiple dynamics shaping gender relations, such as marital abuse. For example, poverty and lack of economic opportunity may lead to the reliance of common people on the black market.

Mocked hegemonic masculinities and institutional violence: the bittersweet encounter between Mr Halimi and a bureaucrat

A respectable retired civil servant in his sixties, Mr Halimi (Mehdi Hashemi) waits a whole day for his appointment with the administrative manager. Desperate to get his case fixed, he sneaks into the office of the busy bureaucrat (Hassan Mahjuni), who does not realize Mr Halimi has entered for several minutes. Mr Halimi hands the bureaucrat a dense folder and explains his Kafkaesque story. After working loyally for over thirty years as a civil servant, he requires financial support for some costly surgery and he has been asked to undress to prove the surgery has taken place in order for his claim to be accepted. As he speaks, the bureaucrat ignores him completely; his phone constantly rings, either to hold work-related discussions or to speak with his wife, who is organizing a dinner. When his mistress calls, the bureaucrat responds in a smarmy voice whilst Mr Halimi is still explaining his case. The bureaucrat turns back and says to Mr Halimi: "I'm drowning in work here!," preparing to leave the office. Mr Halimi becomes extremely frustrated and screams: "Now for a bill, I have to keep pulling my pants down in front of the likes of you?," thereby expressing his sense of "emasculation" and humiliation.

The contrast between the two men is blatant. Mr Halimi was the protagonist in Banietemad's first feature, *Khārej az Mahdudeh* (*Off Limits*, 1988). In that film, Mr Halimi, a modest employee, grappled with the municipal bureaucracy. Mr Halimi and his wife were robbed but could not seek support from the police because their neighborhood did not appear on the map due to a cartographic error. In *Tales*, Mr Halimi is still troubled with the cold and vicious bureaucracy of governmental officials. This tragi-comic scene shows two different masculinities. The bureaucrat is dressed smartly and is financially well off (he is hosting a party with lavish dishes), and in addition he can "afford" to have a mistress. Whilst he embodies the ideal of hegemonic masculinity, which is "related to particular ways of representing and using men's bodies" (Connell and Messerschmidt 2005: 581), the film mocks him. The intrusion of the popular song "Susan Khanoom" during the mistress's call is a tragi-comic instance. This song itself mocks men who compete to win a date with a classy woman. The situation echoes Connell and Messerschmidt's definition of masculinity as "essentially a collective process whereby men compete with other men for validation and confirmation. Masculinity is collectively enforced, protected, and threatened" (2005: 832). Hegemonic masculinity does not necessarily "mean violence" but can be supported by "ascendancy achieved through culture, institutions, and persuasion" (ibid.). In contrast with the previous scene's references to physical violence, here an *institutional* violence is experienced. According to Connell, "the top levels of business, the military and government provide a fairly convincing corporate display of masculinity . . . It is successful claim to authority, more than direct violence, that is the mark of hegemony" (2005: 77). Here, the bureaucrat embodies this hegemonic masculinity as he personifies power—even more so because it is a power that he seems to use arbitrarily.

Social class and love: the scene where Reza starts an argument with his wife, Nobar

Reza (Farhad Aslani) sits on the staircase in the courtyard of their home waiting for Nobar (Fatemeh Motamed Aria) to come home from work. She arrives, quite meaningfully, with a piece of bread. He is suspicious of her fidelity, as a letter has just arrived from her ex-husband. As the discussion becomes heated and filled with wrath, he grabs his wife's *chador* and pulls it down—displaying violence without physically touching her. He asks her to read the letter out loud, as he is illiterate. The letter at first is ambiguous and she stops halfway. Reza asks their son to continue reading. It is revealed that the letter expresses her ex-husband's last will. Realizing his unfounded mistake and faulty accusation, Reza holds his head under the running faucet at the sink whilst he cries. He may act in this way to cleanse himself from the offense he has done to Nobar (before prayer, a Muslim must perform ablutions and wash certain parts of the body as an act of purification). Reza then returns to the courtyard staircase, still crying. Nobar approaches him and gently leans her head on his shoulder. The scenes ends with this tender view.

Reza reveals his insecurity towards Nobar's ex-husband, the wealthy factory owner. In Reza, some will recognize the poor working-class laborer from *The Blue-veiled*. The film is about Rasul, a tomato sauce factory owner in his fifties and wealthy widower, whose love for Nobar, one of his farm workers who wears a blue veil, is taboo. Rasul's family rejects the union due to class and age differences and attempts to break off the relationship. As described at the beginning of this chapter, Reza has told the filmmaker in *Tales* that he depends on the wages of his wife. His jealousy is a reaction to his perceived "emasculation," as he has lost his status as *pater familias*. In the figure of the *pater familias*, manhood is strongly associated with the status of the breadwinner who provides for his family (Connell 1998), an ideal that defines patriarchal masculinity. This scene is highly allegorical, since Nobar literally bears a loaf of bread, portraying that she is the real breadwinner.

Matching male ideals is always challenging but is even more so at times of economic hardship, leading to perceived experiences of emasculation. As shown by Connell, we cannot talk about a "masculinity crisis" in this case (2005: 84). Masculinity is not a system but a configuration of practices within a system of gender relations; therefore, we may instead speak of the disruption or transformation of the system. There can be a "crisis of the gender order" (Connell 2005: 84), in which it is essential to look at the female roles in this reordering. Seen in this light, this transformation can be read as emancipatory.

Intimacy in dialogue: the final scene with Sara and Ahmad

Ahmad (Payman Maadi) is a driver waiting to pick up Sara (Baran Kosari), a volunteer at an NGO that shelters female addicts, from the hospital. We can sense a romantic charge in his behavior prior to her arrival: he examines himself in the mirror and fixes his hair. Nobar wheels Samira, a resident at the shelter who had attempted suicide, to Ahmad's minivan. What Nobar says to Samira in a motherly tone provides context: "Why would such a pretty girl slit her wrists? You have your whole life in front of you; you'll be a bride one day, then a mother." Then Sara arrives and the minivan departs; the conversation between her and Ahmad is riddled with tension. They accuse each other with provocative remarks. Sara hints at the fact that Ahmad studied Mechanical Engineering at university but was expelled due to his political inclinations, referring to Ahmad as *dāneshju-ye setāre dār* (star-holding student), a term that describes students who have been banned from university because of their political involvement or membership of particular groups. Ahmad expresses with disdain that, by helping addicts, Sara conducts herself like "Mother Theresa." They disagree about what "helping others" means. Ahmad says: "You should think of a situation where we can figure out how to keep 100 girls off the streets," to which Sara answers, "Okay, so since we can't save them all, I shouldn't help this one either?" Ahmad may be hinting that Sara should pursue politics instead of losing herself in petty charity work. They seem to disapprove of each other but show a high degree of attention all the same. Sara asks, "Why don't you do something in your field?" to which Ahmad answers sarcastically, "I hadn't thought of this at all!" Part of their conflict stems from their different class backgrounds, as Sara grew up in a middle-class family and Ahmad comes from a more disadvantaged background; he says, "you have always had things your way. Whilst everyone else, including me, have had no say in our lives."

As Sara justifies her choice to bring assistance to addicts, which she has experienced herself, Ahmad asserts she does not want to move on and says provocatively, "You've built a wall around yourself . . . and you won't even take a look beyond it." Sara wants to come to the core of the discussion and asks him if he likes her. He tries to dodge the real answer and asks her the same. Sara pauses and then says no. He looks hurt and asks her whether the problem lies with him. Sara, admitting it would not make a difference, confesses that the issue is herself.

Whilst Ahmad exposes his vulnerability in admitting his romantic emotions towards Sara, his persistence to reach her inner self comes to fruition. By the end of their confrontation, he manages to break down Sara's outer shell and renders her as exposed as he was, turning the intimate encounter into a shameful confession. With this move, he prevents his perceived "emasculation" and keeps a straight face. The dialogue ends as he asks the rhetorical question: "Do I need to know anything more than the fact that you can change the bandages on Samira's open sores despite her being HIV-positive—without wearing gloves?," disclosing that she is also HIV-positive.

Ahmad and Sara's confrontation displays the opposition of two stubborn people incapable of getting along and yet able to reach a mutual understanding. Intimacy is conveyed successfully in their provocations, jokes, and mockeries. Whilst Sara's assistance to drug addicts is deplored by Ahmad, it might be possible that, for Sara, her dedication to this work is her way of using her agency: that is, her capacity to act independently and to make her own decisions in an autonomous manner. She cares for the marginalized, and thus she positions herself against the dictated social structure mentioned by Nobar: "you need to get married and have children." This non-compliance with parental expectations echoes the theme of drugs that is central in *Mainline*, in which Sara conceals her drug addiction from the man she prepares to emigrate to Canada to marry. Filmed almost monochromatically to reflect the gray atmosphere, *Mainline* asks whether Sara's emigration would ever make her happy or would cause her problem to grow worse due to isolation. In *Tales*, Ahmad, in his well-intended attempt to "save" her, imposes his own vision of success upon her.

CONCLUSION: URBAN HEROES AND PRODUCTIVE ALTERNATIVE MASCULINITIES

Banietemad's depictions of masculinity in situations of drug addiction, prostitution, abusive relationships, and financial desperation offer a wide range of performances. There is something inherently subversive, even resistant (Laachir and Talajooy 2013), in showing spaces that deal with social issues such as drug addiction that the official state narrative tries to conceal. *Tales* offers slices of ordinary lives. Since masculinity is not a pre-existing or natural fact but an "effect" (Butler 1988), the film shows how it is achieved through different means. Due to poverty and lack of economic opportunities, "traditional" roles fragment and gender subjectivities as effects become ever more visible. If there is a hero in *Tales*, it is the one who survives the harsh life of Tehran. It may be Abbas and his behavior as a *javanmard*, who attempts to help Massoumeh's sick baby. It may also be Sara, who remains close to her ideals battling against "traditional" expectations. Tehran is the new battleground, no longer remote war fronts where soldiers fought and died for their ideals (Pak-Shiraz 2017: 954). In this vein, the anti-hero in *Tales* is the incompetent bureaucrat in the tragi-comic scene with Mr Halimi, where his hegemonic masculinity is mocked.

The camera often displays three protagonists: a man, a woman, and a vehicle. Khosrowjah describes the Kiarostamian male protagonist as

> increasingly alienated socially and culturally to the degree that the car is both a safe haven and a metaphor for uprootedness. This urban, middle-class, male protagonist has lost his home. His anchor, his car, is not a new dwelling, but a sign of his inability to stop, to rest. (Khosrowjah 2011: 57)

In several instances, such as in the last scene with Sara and Ahmad, a male and female character share the closed space of the minivan in ways that circumvent modesty regulations by opening up sealed thoughts. Banietemad uses the car, the subway, and the minivan as liminal spaces to navigate between the public and the private, the male and the female characters. These enclosed moving spaces are also spaces from which the characters cannot easily escape. The car and minivan in particular become spectacular capsules for building tension. The male character sitting in front of the female characters, usually driving, looks at her through the front mirror. They share a closed space and their own "battleground," renegotiating their positionalities in the tumultuous city of Tehran.

In *Tales*, as male/female characters argue, intimacy is conveyed successfully and produces mutual understanding. It is specifically in these encounters that this negotiation is made visible. Moments of crisis in gender systems are fecund moments of transformations and emancipation from assigned roles.

CHAPTER 9

Representing Sexuality on Screen in Walled Societies: A Comparative Analysis of Iranian Film (*The May Lady*) and Chinese Film (*Army Nurse*)

Yunzi Han

INTRODUCTION

"Am I a good mother?" "Am I a good comrade?" These are the questions that Forugh in *Bānu-ye Ordibehesht* (Banietemad, *The May Lady*, 1998) and Xiaoyu in *Nüer Lou* (Mei, *Army Nurse*, 1985) keep asking themselves. Both long for something that their roles—Iranian mother and Chinese comrade, respectively—do not support: personal desire and sexuality.

Forugh, a documentary filmmaker and also a single mother of a rebellious teenage son, is doing a project on "the exemplary mother." During her interviews with the candidates, she keeps comparing herself to them and struggling between her duty as a mother and her personal desire—she is in love with a man, Dr Rahbar. Caught between her son's rejection of her emotional life, her own desire to be with her lover, and the social norms and requirements for a mother, Forugh tries to negotiate a balance between them.

Xiaoyu, a young army nurse during the Cultural Revolution, falls in love with a soldier patient, Ding Zhu; however, the Party requires all comrades not to have personal desires and demands that they concentrate only on the construction of the nation. Therefore, Xiaoyu and Zhu cannot confess their love to each other. Whilst she tries to work hard to cover the pain of her loss, years later, still unable to move on, Xiaoyu gives up a suitable husband the Party has chosen for her and returns to the mountain hospital where she and Zhu had met to guard the memory of her futile love.

Both films are about the conflict between the social requirement—namely, to be a good mother and to be a good comrade—and individuality, and the attempts the female protagonists have made to seek a balance between them. Meanwhile, at first glance, one film represents and criticizes the contemporary situation at the time of filmmaking whilst the other takes a retrospective approach by looking back at the Cultural Revolution (1966–76) to reflect on the concerns of the present. Despite the different approaches, these reflections focus on the concerns over subjectivity and femininity of the present time. Moreover, both films are set in the context of a restricted environment, where the religious or the political takes precedence over individuality, sexuality, and more specifically, sexual desire. In addition, both reclaim subjectivity and femininity from the emphasized and prevailing notion of sacrifice prescribed to the roles of the protagonists: that is, a mother in post-revolutionary Iran and a Party member during China's Cultural Revolution.

In both films, patriarchal societies encourage the sacrifice of individual desire for greater values—the child and the nation—whilst the opposite—individual desire for love—is unacceptable and forbidden. In the two films, this repression is expressed by diverse and rich cinematic languages; however, two sartorial signs (Chen 2001) that the two female protagonists wear, the veil and the uniform, play very important roles in constructing and representing this restriction over individual (sexual) desire. These signs, which remind the protagonists of their roles and duties, and warn them to keep their emotions in check, are visually similar to the portable walls that have helped to construct "walled societies" (Milani 1992: 2) in an attempt to "wall in" sexual desire. However, the aim of this chapter is not to find an equivalent to the veil in the context of China or the uniform in the context of Iran, but rather, through a comparative reading of the two films, to seek the affinity of the notions that these sartorial signs carry in their own social backgrounds: namely, the idea of de-individualization. Moreover, the aim of this chapter is not to focus on restrained female desire and blame the man for causing it; undoubtedly, this de-individualization also applies to male desire. Instead, the aim is to unfold the discussion of de-individualization over sexuality from both sides in a heterosexual relationship; in this case, the cisgender man and woman. Through an analysis of the two films, *The May Lady* and *Army Nurse*, this chapter aims to answer the following questions. In the two films, how is the idea of sacrificing the personal and, furthermore, the notion of de-individualization of sexuality conveyed through the application of the two sartorial practices: namely, the veil and the uniform? How have the veil and the uniform constructed walled societies of individual sexual desire? How have the two female protagonists attempted to find positions for their desire in the two walled societies? Meanwhile, how does this de-individualization affect male sexuality? Finally, what is the attitude toward sexuality of the two societies, as reflected in their attempt at de-individualization in the two films?

CONSTRUCTING WALLED SOCIETIES FOR INDIVIDUAL DESIRE

"Maybe it (the exemplary mother) is yourself . . . You devoted your whole life to me, didn't you?" states Forugh's son. "You girls should especially note that you should be cautious about your personal life; you should focus on your studies and professional life. If you do not deal with this issue well, it will affect the future of your career," states the Party authorities. It seems that, in the contexts of the two films, sacrificing one's personal life is inherent to fulfilling the roles of a good mother and a good Party member; and this requirement of sacrifice, self-restriction, and the protagonists' resistance are subtly conveyed through the application of the veil and the uniform that Forugh and Xiaoyu wear in their daily lives.

It is known that, under Islamic doctrine, the function of the veil is to hide a woman from the forbidden gaze of men: that is, those men who could marry her and who are free of incest taboos (Milani 1992: 3). The veil is the most visible sign of restriction that the Iranian socio-cultural norm has applied to women to limit their bodily expression and, furthermore, their verbal self-expression (ibid.: 6). Therefore, this restriction also implies a power relation inherent to heterosexual relationships: issues of domination, exclusion, and unequal allocation of power (ibid.: 4). Through this deliberate attempt to keep the woman and anything related to her hidden, the topic of "women's issues" is categorized as belonging to the private realm and so should remain unseen (ibid.: 21). This idea is reflected and even strengthened by its representation in popular culture, especially the commercial film genre of *film-farsi*, which emerged in the late 1940s and enjoyed a boom in the 1950s. Most of the films in this genre engaged with the commercial elements of international popular cinemas at that time, such as Hollywood, European, Egyptian, and Indian films, in a haphazard and hotchpotch way. It is usually considered and criticized as "merely entertaining" and "debased" in the post-revolutionary scholarly literature. Admittedly, based on recent studies, this genre of films is not "merely entertaining," it also examined social problems such as unemployment, poverty, class division, and prostitution (Rekabtalaei 2019). However, one of the popular images of women in these films, as Shahla Lahiji asserts, is that of "chaste dolls," faceless and obedient women whose main duties are to keep the house for their father, husband, and son, to have babies and to take care of the children for their husband, and to be ready to sacrifice everything for their male superiors at any time without a complaint (Lahiji 2002: 216).

Corresponding to *The May Lady*, this is "the exemplary mother" that Forugh seeks in the film. But what about her own longing for love and happiness or her inner struggles underneath the veil? As Forugh says, "My own child thinks his mother was born one day and has lived long enough and everything has ended for her. That's it, you're alive, you breathe, then you're put in your grave." It assumes that motherhood, sexuality, and personal desire are incompatible under the social norms of Iran. A good mother should be de-individualized and sexually neutral inside, left only with her love for her children, her femininity only as a mother and not as a woman. In the film, out of the three times that Forugh visits the home of different candidates, she twice needs to walk down a narrow, high-walled pathway to reach the house, implying that these "exemplary mothers," whose husbands are dead or in prison, live in a hidden space isolated from the public, and more clearly, from other men and any possibility of being involved in emotional or sexual relationships. Also, most of them wear a *chador* to cover their whole body, which corresponds to the high-walled environment they live in, emphasizing their devotion to the Islamic religion and implying their enclosed emotional lives. Meanwhile, Forugh's own living environment also produces this enclosed feeling. Upon returning home, the film shows Forugh entering the front door, which is constructed with steel bars, and walking up the staircase, which is dark, narrow, and shadowed by the stair handrails on the wall. It creates an atmosphere of her entering a prison when she comes home, where she must face the conflict between her son Mani's aggressive attitude towards her love relationship and her own desire to be with her lover, that is, the struggle between fulfilling individual desire and the social standard of being a good mother in Iranian society. Therefore, the veil as a sartorial sign marks the boundary between a woman and others, covering her body as if she is enclosed by a wall, and preventing her from moving among and making contact with the opposite gender and expressing herself freely.

During China's Cultural Revolution (1966–76), the uniform, in addition to being an overt sartorial practice, was a visual marker of the socialist identity of the Chinese people. Robert Guillain described Chinese people as "blue ants" in this period because they all dressed the same, looked the same, and even walked the same (Guillain 1957: 3–8). This description implies the ideal image that a uniform aims to produce: specifically, a physically and ideologically controllable and disciplined society in which individuals voluntarily identify with Maoism and become a collective (Pang 2017: 242). After the establishment of the People's Republic of China (PRC) in 1949, as a nodal point in the interaction of citizenship, the politics of nation-building, and gender-formation, clothing and fashion played a significant role in the creation of socialist citizens to populate the new nation (Chen 2001: 144). Therefore, a new look was required to depart from the traditional colorful, hand-made, and embroidered blouses popular before the Chinese Communist Party's (CCP) liberation, which were associated with rural areas, the peasantry, and minority groups, and considered traditional and backward (ibid.: 149). As a result, the utilitarian work outfit of blouse and trousers or Mao jacket was the encouraged and dominant new look (ibid.: 153).

Until the mid-1960s, the military-styled Mao suit in blue, gray or army green, composed of long sleeves, long trousers, high necklines and buttons, made sure that little skin was exposed, and became the standard dress code of the masses, regardless of gender (ibid.: 161). Bright colors and prints were considered the reflection of individualistic and bourgeois interests, incompatible with the frugal, selfless commitment to the collective good required by the ideology of the Party (Evans 1997: 134; Chen 2001: 143). Interestingly, as Tina Mai Chen notes, during the 1950s, when the new nation was established, what contrasted sharply with the 1960s is the fact that wearing clothing made from factory-produced printed cloth during leisure time was encouraged and marked women as progressive and patriotic because these garments signified their participation both in the construction of socialist modernity and in support of the economy of the new regime (Chen 2001: 150–3). Fashion columns in the newspapers suggested new fashion styles for women and encouraged them to enrich their wardrobe (ibid.: 153). It is obvious that the desire for material goods, usually considered bourgeois and later criticized in the Cultural Revolution, was officially targeted at women in particular during this period, and women were encouraged to indulge this desire in order to support the new economy, which established an intimate gendered link between patriotic expression and consumption (ibid.: 147–8). More importantly, as Harriet Evans (1997) argues, the idea of encouraging women to complement the gendered components of their own wardrobe and lifestyle reasserted their role as belonging to the family sphere. Furthermore, it is important to note that the fashions encouraged in such columns usually appeared as alternatives to be enjoyed during leisure times and spaces, whereas at work, androgynous and utilitarian clothing still occupied a fundamental position (Chen 2001: 153). This emphasized how women and even their feminine image should remain in the private domain and were considered unserious and distracting in the public one, reinforcing the patriarchal notion of *nan zhu wai, nü zhu nei* ("men dominate the public, women stay in the domestic").

During the 1960s, although women were encouraged to come out of the domestic domain and join the frontline of industrial construction in building the new nation, they had to wear a uniform that concealed their feminine features. The dominant idea during this period was that a "communist should never care about the way she looked. The beauty of the soul was that which should be cared about" (Chen 2001: 148). As a true patriot, the socialist woman of the late 1960s should immerse herself in national construction projects without considering individual desires, which included her body, clothes, and sexuality (ibid.). However, the requirements for appearance ironically became one of the most important standards for measuring if an individual was a qualified socialist citizen (ibid.: 161), resulting in what would become one of the main impressions left by the Cultural Revolution, that is the uniformed "blue ants." Moreover, what should be noted here is that, whether wearing fashionable clothing or uniforms, it was not for women to highlight their individual beauty (ibid.: 154) but rather to contribute to the collective's benefit. The female body was similar to an object that could be used, endowed with different meanings, and even manipulated, due to different and changeable needs at any time.

In the film *Army Nurse*, similar to the living space of "the exemplary mothers," Xiaoyu and the other nurses are all living in a remote hospital in the mountains. There are frequent scenes depicting her walking or running up and down in this high-walled, isolated building. This is also the place where she encounters her love, though it is deemed futile in this isolated and enclosed space. During the two scenes of her walking down the corridor to turn off the light of each ward at night, she always stops at Zhu's ward to check his bed secretly, even after he has left. Both scenes start with a long shot of her wearing full military uniform underneath her medical one, with only her face showing (her hair is covered by a surgical hat), walking in the empty but enclosed space of the corridor with her steps heard clearly in the silence. She always slows down when reaching Zhu's ward, then the film cuts to a close-up of her face when she opens the door of his ward secretly and looks at his bed in the darkness. The deep and full close-up with her head cutting the frame of the image conveys a sense of nervousness and breathlessness. Moreover, in both scenes she is watched or warned; in the first, a girl approaches Xiaoyu to check on her mother, and in the second, Xiaoyu turns to exit the corridor and sees the two big red characters, *sujing* ("solemn and silent"), written on the gate in the background, which overwhelm the whole image and warn her to control her emotions. Her duty as a nurse and the requirement of self-restraint as a Party member enclose her individual desire for love in the double layers of uniform, and at the same time, the high walls trap her mobility and constrain her in this mountain hospital. Meanwhile, the warning words are constant reminders that she must practice self-control. Even the Chinese title of the film, *Nüer Lou*, in which "Nüer" means girls and "Lou" means high-walled building, implies that women's bodies, dreams, hopes, and desires are all walled in and confined in this isolated place.

Am I a good mother? Am I a good comrade? In the two films, the veil and the uniform represent the duties and the social requirements of the two roles of mother and Party member. By putting them on, the two individuals are obliged to take up the duties and requirements of the roles that society has prescribed for them, forcing them to repress and even sacrifice their individual desires (in this case, sexual) for the child and the nation through constructing conceptual and physical portable walls to enclose their personal emotions from growing and expressing. In the context of Iran, being a good mother means Forugh needs to devote herself completely to her child and give up her identity as a sexually desirable and desired woman. In the context of China, being a good comrade means she should not think about her personal desire, especially sexual desire, as the Party authorities have warned, and instead must devote herself to building her career, which will make her serve the construction of the nation better. As a result, desires and struggles over sexuality are repressed in hearts, judgmental and surveillant eyes are at every corner, conceptually walled societies are constructed, visually represented by the veil and the uniform.

THE VEIL AND THE UNIFORM: DE-INDIVIDUALIZATION OVER SEXUALITY

As stated above, the function of the veil is to hide women from the view of men. Therefore, "seeing" has become the obvious but subtle bridge connecting the desire of men and women. Milani further observes that "in a veiled society, seeing, far from being considered a mere physiological process, takes on a socially determined, potentially dangerous, and highly charged meaning" (Milani 1992: 24). As a result, eyes have become subject to the strictest regulations for both men and women, and men's eyes are considered to attain phallic power; thus, men's forbidden act of seeing becomes a sin, a violation, a visual rape that women must protect themselves against by donning veils (ibid.: 22–5). However, this raises a fundamental question: why is the male gaze unequivocally considered sexual and evil? Who can make the judgment that all male gaze is sexual and detrimental? Following this arbitrary decision, all women in society must veil themselves to prevent the "sexual and evil gaze" of men. For a mother, even though her husband is absent, irrespective of whether that is due to death or divorce, she should consider herself only as a mother to her child and forget that she is also a woman with a desire to love and be loved. In this logic, the gaze of forbidden men may distract her from her duty and pure love towards her child and drag her into a trap of individual and sexual desire. This is one of the reasons why most of "the exemplary mothers" in Forugh's project live in high-walled spaces, isolated from the public, and wear *chadors*. A strong sense of de-individualization over sexuality has been ascribed to the role of mother. But what needs to be noted here is that the notion of "de-individualization over sexuality" should not be confused with "desexualization." Even though the veil functions to hide a woman's sexual features from the gaze of men and sexual conduct is highly monitored by the authorities, such as the morality police and clerics, and gossiping neighbors, it is perhaps through these devices that society becomes sexualized rather than desexualized. For example, secret codes of courtship have developed among young people, wherein cars become a semi-private space of sexual conduct in an intensively monitored public space (Mahdavi 2009).

To return to de-individualization in *The May Lady*, Forough's son refuses to accept that she has another man in her life, as shown in this exchange between Mani and Forough's friend:

Mani: For as long as I remember, it's been only me and Forugh. We shared everything, joy, sickness, travels. Now the idea that someone else would stand by her drives me mad.
Friend: Are you always going to remain single? You think that when you get married, you will forget your mother?
Mani: Obviously, I can't always be with her as I am now.
Friend: Naturally. Then should she expect you to always remain by her side?
Mani: What you say is true, but I can't come to terms with it.

Mani has become used to the idea that Forugh is just his mother, which is her one and only role, and he considers it unnatural for her to live another role as a woman who desires love and an intimate relationship with another man in her life. However, as shown by his quick reaction when asked if he would remain single, it is natural for him to desire to be not just a son but also a man who desires an intimate relationship with someone else. This contrast clearly shows that even he admits that his mother is also a woman who has desires; however, growing up with the socio-cultural norms that maintain that a mother should not have individuality but only devotion to her child, Mani cannot emotionally accept her "affair." Moreover, he reminds Forugh that she herself is probably "the exemplary mother" because she has devoted her whole life to him, applying the degree to which she sacrificed her individual desire as a woman to the standard by which to measure "exemplary mothers." Furthermore, when Forugh is conducting the interviews with the candidate mothers, she constantly struggles to place herself among them. Compared to them, has she sacrificed enough for motherhood? How much is enough?

Forugh's way of approaching a solution is to negotiate a balance, as she tells Dr Rahbar: "The dilemma I face is because I don't want one of them at the expense of the other." In the space of Forugh's living room, where most of the conflicts take place, there is a set of three paintings of *yinyang*, a Chinese sign of balance, hanging on the wall. The first (from right to left) is one full white circle against a black background, the second is one small white circle on a big black circle against a white background, and the third shows equal amounts of black and white intertwining to form a perfect circle. The three paintings show the progression to perfect balance, implying Forugh's wish of achieving a balance that will not harm either side. However, will she ever succeed? Can her motherhood and her desire to pursue an intimate relationship co-exist?

Her relationship with Dr Rahbar is a secret, and they speak only in private spaces where no one overhears or sees her. Dr Rahbar never appears in the film;

we only ever hear his voice. Forugh does not even dare show her emotion to him in public. For example, when she receives his letter via a colleague, her face shows no change in emotion; only when she moves closer to the camera do we notice a slight smile. After reading the letter, she returns home, enters the prison-like staircase, and closes the open window, which implies that she worries in her subconsciousness about this relationship being found out by the outside world. The next scene cuts to Forugh expressing her love to Dr Rahbar in her diary, with her voice-over changing from the normal volume to a repressed whisper. This editing clearly shows the boundary between private and public spaces and her cautiousness in preventing her love relationship from becoming public. It seems that her motherhood and her personal desire as a woman can co-exist, but one has to remain underground.

Moreover, veiling also affects and regulates daily interactions among people. These regulated interactions indicate modes of being and behavior that are shaped or misshaped by different degrees and kinds of protection, or as Milani states, it can be called censorship, both external and internal (1992: 22–3). Veiling is one of the most significant symbols in Iranian society that expresses the nation's prevailing attitude toward the self and the other (ibid.: 23). Similar to the walls that enclose houses and separate inner and outer spaces, the veil makes a clear statement of the disjunction between the private and the public, and has profoundly influenced the way people interact with each other, and ultimately, with themselves (ibid.). The practice of *ta'arof* (ritualistic mode of discourse) perfectly explains this duality, as it involves thinking one thing but appearing to say another, which shows the disjunction between people's inner and outer worlds (ibid.: 5; Honarbin-Holliday 2008: 66–7). Similar to this regulated and coded way of communicating, which leads to a ritualistic and supposedly civilized mode of discourse in daily life, veiling, also a quotidian practice, is a ritualistic expression of culturally defined boundaries that physically sanctify a system of censorship and self-censorship (Milani 1992: 23).

This censorship of individuality over self and other is emphasized during the last scene of *The May Lady*. A still long shot shows Mani and Forugh sitting under the *yinyang* paintings. The phone between them rings; it is Dr Rahbar. Forugh cautiously looks at Mani; however, he remains indifferent and does not answer the phone. Forugh returns the call in the next shot when she is alone. It seems that a balance between her motherhood and her individuality has been reached on the surface; at least Mani no longer displays any strong objection to the phone call. However, what is implied in this seeming balance is that Forugh's contribution to the greater value—that is, her child and her family—stays in the public domain whilst her sexual individuality remains veiled and hidden in a secret corner of her life. To maintain this superficial balance, she continues living in this duality—or dilemma, as she depicts it—of her inner and outer worlds. Therefore, when concealing thoughts, hiding the personal, and covering the body, veiling is a strong indication of de-individualization (ibid.).

A similar logic can be found in the sartorial practice of uniform wearing during China's Cultural Revolution. As previously stated, during the mid-1960s, a wave of militarism took over the civilian life of Chinese people (Chen 2001: 161), with the military uniform becoming the standard dress code for men and women, visibly marking the socialist identity of Chinese people. However, although women were encouraged to leave the domestic domain to work in the frontline of construction of the socialist nation, this involved concealing their femininity. Admittedly, the emancipation of women has constituted one of the central legitimating discourses of the CCP since its very beginning (Zheng 1999: 359). For example, women were acknowledged as full citizens (Chen 2001: 163) and were emancipated from the feudal patriarchal system by a new Marriage Law in 1950, supporting free-choice monogamous marriage (Evans 1997: 4–5). As a result, uniformed women signified the success of this emancipation (Chen 2001: 162). Mao's famous dicta, "The times are different; men and women are now all the same" and "anything a male comrade can do, a female comrade can do as well" (Mao 1969: 243), strengthened the masculinized image of socialist Chinese women. Moreover, in photographs and pictorial depictions of this period, the clothing of female role models, "advanced" women chosen from different professional areas for the masses to admire and learn from, replicated the appearance of the male industrial workers pictured next to them (Chen 2001: 151). Therefore, to be qualified to work on the frontline and earn respect in the professional arena, women needed to mask their feminine features, concealing that the person underneath the uniform was a woman. During this period, cultivated beauty signified weakness of character, and femininity was undesired; as a result, this hyper-masculinity even conflated undesirable features, such as bright colors and bourgeois classes, into feminized bodies (ibid.: 161). This has conveyed a strong sense of de-individualization and disrespect over sexuality, and especially femininity. Here also, the notion of "de-individualization over sexuality" should not be confused with "desexualization." Similar to the veil in Iran, although the uniform attempts to cultivate desexualized subjects, in reality, women styled the uniform to highlight the shape of their bodies, and the sexual difference evidenced through clothing was greater than intended (Berry and Shujuan 2019).

Furthermore, the period of the Cultural Revolution was a time when new fashion was both suppressed and encouraged (Pang 2017: 43): that is, the new standard dress code of the masses was encouraged whilst new fashions created by individuals were prohibited. Also, as argued above, this uniformity extended from the look to the mind, and people thought and acted in ways that connected them with Mao and the unified collective (ibid.: 1). In this highly monitored society, people who moved out of line with the mainstream would pay an exceptionally high price for flaunting their difference (ibid.). Therefore, this demand for a strictly regulated and well-disciplined society sanctioned a system of censorship and self-censorship over individual desire, and especially sexual desire. The film

Army Nurse shows a subtle play of the use of uniform to convey this sense of censorship.

The arrival of Ding Zhu had stirred gossip because the nurses had noticed the handsome young soldier. Whilst they had internalized the socialist moral code of giving up sexual desire, their self-censored expression tells a different, opposing story, which implies the duality of their inner and outer worlds. A scene in which the nurses discuss Zhu whilst hanging sheets on washing lines begins with a long shot, which shows each nurse stands at one washing line, alluring to the activity as a relaxing occasion of exchanging gossip, but barriers between them are slowly exposed:

"He is a platoon leader, from Beijing, has one brother."
"Another guy told me his father is a plane design expert."
"He does not talk much, but there is something different in his eyes: Aloof! Proud!"
"Conceited! Looking down on people! But, Xiaoyu, have you noticed his teeth are very nice. Oh my! Why do I talk about him like this?! So shameless!"
"It does not matter if his teeth are nice, what is more important is his character."
"Why do you pay attention to his character? It is not about matchmaking for you!"

The camera then focuses on Xiaoyu's face, happy but embarrassed and cautious, worrying that other girls will notice her interest in him. The hanging sheets hide her face from the other girls, symbolizing the boundaries between each of them. It is obvious that every girl is interested in Ding Zhu; however, the hanging sheets are like the uniforms they wear, veiling their personal feelings, setting walls between them, attempting to make them only have comrade love and look plain, simple, and even the same. From the conversation they have, as one may notice, when one girl speaks of Zhu's character, another girl quickly criticizes her and becomes suspicious of her thinking about matchmaking. This conversation conveys a strong sensitivity and an attempt at censorship and self-censorhip specifically targets on personal desire and sexuality.

Meanwhile, the constraints over personal desire and sexuality that the two sartorial practices imply apply not only to the female protagonists Xiaoyu and Forugh, but also to the male characters in the films. Despite the efforts of de-individualization in their respective contexts to secure the social hierarchy of "male domination and female subordination," they emasculate men in both cases. Being in a so-called dominant position is not always an advantage because it is the patriarchal gender system itself that is in the genuinely dominant position, not the people living under it. Men's inability in a hyper-masculinized society is expressed in both *The May Lady* and *Army Nurse*.

Dr Rahbar is an example of this; as the most emasculated man in the film, he is deprived of the right to appear. Seemingly, he has achieved a closeness to the hegemonic pattern of masculinity: that is, an ascendancy over social class (Connell 1987: 184). In his professional arena, he has obtained the highest academic degree, which is respected in society, and has the power to decide the result of "the exemplary mother" project, judging which mother has sacrificed most. Ironically, despite this high position in his professional life, he can express his affection and desire for his lover only through reading letters together over the phone and is otherwise powerless to change the situation. In one scene, after Forugh has brought Mani home from the police, Dr Rahbar calls her to ask why she did not ask him for help. She says, "nothing important; I solved it." He says, "as usual, right?" Her independence makes him unneeded; also, he is unable to make any effective changes regarding Mani's attitude towards him; he even leaves for a while because of the lack of agency that he feels in this relationship. Ultimately, to achieve a reasonable balance according to social norms, this relationship must be kept private. Even a man with a prestigious position in this hyper-masculinized society must veil his desires which fall outside the mainstream marriage in order to avoid "polluting" the normative sexual pattern and maintain the seeming "balance" of society.

In *Army Nurse*, Zhu also holds a prestigious position in the army and has a reputable family name, which poses a sharp contrast to his emasculated attitude towards personal desire. It is interesting to note that when he is in patient clothes, he is more expressive, especially with his eyes. For example, in the scene in which Xiaoyu and Zhu first meet, Xiaoyu delivers medicine but twice calls him by the wrong name before Zhu, who has an arm injury, corrects her. When Xiaoyu approaches his bed to give him the medicine, a close-up of his face reveals that his eyes are gazing at her boldly and have changed to interested and curious. The next shot is a close-up of Xiaoyu's face, who looks back cautiously and tries to conceal her nervousness. Even though he is physically emasculated, Zhu actively pursues love. Later in the film, there are several instances in which the pair bump into each other, as if expressing their unwillingly walled desire for each other. Days later, their emotion grows, but Zhu leaves without notice. Xiaoyu runs down the mountain to chase him but sees a different version of Zhu wearing an army uniform and escaping her eyes. Ironically, he looks spiritually weakened in this masculine uniform and refuses to express himself—he is physically recovered but emotionally tied. Yet this is Xiaoyu's first time not wearing her uniform in front of him, and he has no answer to her questions and looks embarrassed. His uniform distances them, symbolizing the requirement to be a good comrade, that is, to emasculate oneself from sexual desire and de-individualize the personal.

CONCLUSION

Hiding the personal, sacrificing desire, contributing to the greater value—in both films, the roles of good mother and good comrade have been ascribed to these requirements, which seem to have become a social convention in their respective contexts. The veil from post-revolutionary Iran and the uniform from China's Cultural Revolution become the most visible symbols of self-restriction. The two sartorial signs, visually similar to portable walls, are a reminder, not only to women but also to men, of their roles and duties, warning them to restrict their emotions as the walled societies attempt to "wall in" individual desires. Moreover, the two sartorial practices convey a strong affinity of de-individualization, especially over sexuality, which has sanctified a system of censorship and self-censorship of sexual desire among people.

Interestingly, it can be demonstrated in the two films that not all kinds of individuality are unwanted. Apart from being a mother, Forugh is also a successful documentary filmmaker, whilst Xiaoyu is encouraged to pursue her career. These are also individual desires, but since they are not for sexuality but for success in professional life, they are supported. This special de-individualization over sexuality implies a strong anxiety about sexuality in the two societies, and the reasons for this may be worth exploring in further studies. At the end of the two films, Forugh decides to keep her love relationship hidden in order to achieve peace to the conflict between her duty and her individuality; Xiaoyu chooses to serve in the mountain hospital for the rest of her life to keep the memory of her futile love alive. However, what should be noted here is that neither Forugh nor Xiaoyu give up on their love and (sexual) desire in the end but instead show a nuanced resistance to de-individualization by hiding, but not discarding, their inner desires to keep them safe.

PART IV

Fact, Fiction, and Society

CHAPTER 10

Rakhshan Banietemad's Art of Social Realism: Bridging Realism and Fiction

Maryam Ghorbankarimi

Throughout the history of Iranian cinema, successful films have tended to be based on a realist approach to contemporary life. The "New Wave" of Iranian cinema witnessed in the 1960s with films such as Forugh Farrokhzad's poetic documentary *Khāneh Siyāh Ast* (*The House is Black*, 1962) or Dariush Mehrjui's symbolic drama *Gāv* (*The Cow*, 1969), among others, was directly paralleled by the "committed literature" movement that began in early 1950s. Writing about this period, Kamran Talattof asserts that "Marxist ideology shaped the works of the majority of writers, whose themes revolved around issues of equality, justice, and freedom, colored by Iran's own cultural particularities" (Talattof 2000: 5). This sense of commitment was not confined to the literary realm, but also affected the independent cinema of the 1960s and the Iranian intelligentsia in general. The focus on social injustices and inequalities gave birth to Iranian social realist films. Since then, social realism has flourished and become a prominent style in Iranian cinema.

The works of Rakhshan Banietemad—both her documentaries and her fiction dramas—are considered as social realist. Through undertaking a close reading and analysis of a number of Banietemad's documentaries, illustrating her mastery of social realism, this chapter offers an auteurist reading of her work. This is not to turn a blind eye to the problematic nature of auteur theory in film, in that it is a collaborative artistic endeavor. However, I still believe that it is an effective way to classify and identify a certain recurring trait in a filmmaker's work, especially when studying the filmmaker's entire œuvre. I would also agree with Andrew Sarris's observations concerning British cinema, when he argues that auteurism "has less to do with the way movies are made than with the way they are elucidated and evaluated" (Sarris 2011: 360).

For a variety of reasons which are beyond the scope of this chapter, film criticism and scholarship over the years has tended to favor certain films and directors over others. These evaluations have formed the canon in film studies, which has historically left out women, and Iranian cinema is no exception in this regard.

In positioning the study of auteurs within an academic field, it is crucial to distinguish between the various author functions (Foucault 1997: 205–22), including the agency of the director in constructing an image of the auteur; the academic and popular discourses that promote an auteurist approach to film studies; and the types of spectatorship and viewing positions interpellated in the circuit of auteur theory. This chapter will distinguish Banietemad's position as an auteur and will discuss the ways in which she, as a filmmaker, consciously or unconsciously adopts practices which confirm her status as an auteur. It will then ultimately address how we, as both audiences and researchers, construct discourses which frame her as an auteur.

Rakhshan Banietemad has developed a hybrid style of social realism in her films. Whilst dealing with the harsh social realities of her subjects in present-day Iran, her films also offer a level of entertainment. In their book *Realism and Popular Cinema*, reviewing the social realism genre, Julia Hallam and Margaret Marshment identify a set of films that respond to the economic restructuring of the global economy during the 1980s and 1990s. They assert that "[t]hese films are characterised by a stylistic hybridity that engages a spectrum of realist strategies . . . formerly associated with European art cinema to an embracing of popular generic forms" (Hallam and Marshment 2000: 185). I believe this stylistic hybridity is also evident in Banietemad's filmmaking.

Her fictional films incorporate melodramatic narrative devices and employ well-known actors, whilst they represent true-to-life characters in believable settings and locations. Although they depict heartfelt social issues and perhaps some harsh facts and figures, they still enjoy a level of popularity. One could argue that this is the result of casting well-known actors and portraying tangible social themes in a form that speaks to the average viewer. Hallam and Marshment note that Italian neorealism, although championed by Bazin at the time for its ability to reveal reality, was often a blend of realism and generic elements (Hallam and Marshment 2000: 40). Banietemad's films, too, "using the socio-economic matric of . . . localised situations as background . . . play out dramas of 'universal' human significance: coming-of-age stories, oedipal scenarios of growth, development and conflict between the generations, domestic relationships and the trauma of everyday family life" (Hallam and Marshment 2000: 185). Similar to John Hill's assertion of British social realism, Banietemad's films also remain "attached to the basic conventions of 'realism', the 'habitual' versions of 'dramatic reality', made familiar by the mainstream fiction film" (Hill 1986: 60), whilst also incorporating more subtle avant-garde traits, such as an open-ended narrative structure.

Throughout her career, Banietemad has applied herself to working on a variety of documentary projects. The access and knowledge which she obtains through her research and documentary films are also employed to create a believable "realistic" setting for her fictional features. If one surveys her documentary body of work, Banietemad has been an artist in constant search of her next topic, and has patiently developed her subsequent feature films through inspiration from her documentaries. There is a thematic and stylistic unity between her documentaries and her fictional work. Although her auteurship is evident in her films through recurring links and themes, it is through her documentaries that we really observe her critical approach and the fundamental issues she tends to focus her lens on. The next section will look at three of her early documentary works: *Tamarkoz* (*Centralization*, 1986), *In Film-hā ro beh ki Neshun Midin?* (*To Whom Do You Show These Films?*, 1993), and *Zir-e Pust-e Shahr* (*Under the Skin of the City*, 1996), which I believe exemplify the source and drive of her unique style of filmmaking.

This chapter first examines *Centralization*, one of her earliest documentaries available in digitized format. This short documentary both establishes her filmmaking approach and style, and demonstrates her ideological and political view of Iranian society. The documentary is not a straightforward report on the social conditions of urbanization and centralization of wealth and amenities that attract migrants to the mega-cities; rather, it is a complex film with some poetic qualities. Whilst employing several key aspects of an expository documentary—namely, voice-of-God narration and interviews—it is actually a subjective work. Alisa Lebow defines subjective documentary as being poetic, political, prophetic, or absurd. She asserts that it does not always require to be about a person, but could depict a neighborhood or a community—in this case, a metropolis, Tehran. Subjective documentary is about the "mode of address" and "films 'speak' from the articulated point of view of the filmmaker who readily acknowledges her subjective position" (Lebow 2012: 1). The narration in this film is largely subjective and delivers a specific political perspective, though it is impersonal and, because it is a male voice, cannot directly be associated with Banietemad.

With a running time of just over half an hour, *Centralization* has a post-apocalyptic feel to it in both sound and image. The music is a melancholic, digital futuristic soundtrack accompanying the slightly washed-out 16mm footage of the polluted Tehran of the 1980s. It is almost unbelievable how polluted Tehran already looks in this decade, when the population was considerably lower than it is today. The film begins with two-minute aerial traveling shots of Tehran, where, on the horizon, the clusters of concrete buildings merge into the sky. Whilst the images depict a chaotic cityscape, gray skies, dusty trees, and junctions with cars haphazardly crossing, the narration begins with a quotation from Mahatma Gandhi: "Indian cities were exploited by Britons and villages by the city. Big cities were built at the cost of villager's misery and blood." The narrator pronounces this the best and most valid description of mega-cities in developing countries. It then continues: "Huge cities cancerously expand inharmoniously against the social patterns of these countries, growing even bigger by using up all economical resources. And devour the villagers who abandon the ruined countryside." The filmmaker, through her subjective narration, condemns the modern economic and political situation that makes developing countries dependent on a single production economy, exporting their remaining national wealth. Designating cities as the "means of domination," it lists "skyscrapers, highways, clinics, and universities" alongside "slums, poverty, illiteracy, hunger, disease, and unemployment." At the end of this introduction, the narration introduces the main subject of the film: "Tehran in the autumn of 1986," and the title and main credits appear. After the titles, the view changes to eye-level shots of the city. It starts with the shot of the iconic Azadi tower in the largest square in Tehran, standing tall and almost disappearing into the smoke and smog in the background, with cars and trucks crossing in the foreground (Figure 10.1).

Figure 10.1 The Azadi Tower in *Centralization* (1986)

The narration, whilst pointing out some issues which are relevant to the images depicted, does not offer a factual voice-of-God type of narration. The images do not act as illustrations of the information that the narration delivers. The narration offers a subjective and a rather pessimistic interpretation of the issue of urbanization. One could venture that the film does not attempt to see any good in this expansion, focusing solely on its negative impact. This type of narration resonates with what Bill Nichols terms the poetic (Nichols 2017). At times, the narration does venture into poetic territory and creates a rhymed prose. For instance, in an early montage sequence of close-up shots of heavy traffic, slow-moving vehicles, and people commuting, the narration introduces the city state:

> A city filled with dust and pollution. Pollution and smoke. Smoke . . . smoke.
> A city poisoned, overcrowded and immethodical [sic].
> A city of iron, steel, and concrete.
> A city of suffering, struggles, and competitions.
> A city of marathons for little gain.
> A city jammed, a city of centralization.
> A city of endurance, inflation.
> A city so busy and so noisy. Noise and noise and noise.
> A city of melancholy in search of bread, seeking shelter and remedies.
> Looking for culture, a city for hunting jobs.
> A city of contrasts, modernity versus traditions, poverty and credibility side by side.
> Imitation and imitations.
> A city in chaos. Disordered, out of shape, and cruel.
> The devouring city. So much for nothing.
> A city of interactions and business.
> A place ideal for trade, for brokers and dealers.
> A city for smugglers, for black markets.
> A city of hopes and illusions.
> A city of great expectations and sad endings.

This type of narration could almost be a love letter, mourning a city that has lost its way, similar to how the narration functions in Chris Marker's seminal work *Sans Soleil* (1983).

After this introduction to the city, the film shifts its focus to the migrant inhabitants who are devoured by the gloomy metropolis, living with hardship and homesickness, far away from their roots and cultures and loved ones. The transition to the individual, brief, on-camera interviews is a shot of a few men alighting from a bus. This, in conjunction with the narration addressing temporary workers coming into town on a daily basis, makes the viewer see those men as representations of the influx of temporary workers to Tehran. This shot is framed in such close proximity that the workers cannot ignore the camera; many look directly at the lens whilst leaving the bus. The shot then freezes on one man as the narrator poses the question of what they are after, coming to the big city. The incorporation of these two reflexive elements—the freeze-frame and the subjects acknowledging the camera—is the first instance of Banietemad using this device; indeed, it is the first of many more instances throughout her work, both fictional and documentary. This direct questioning or contemplation on behalf of the narrator, in juxtaposition with these reflexive devices, concretely demonstrates this film subjectivity of style. The male narrator is a surrogate for the filmmaker in her absence.

The scene continues with a number of men stating their reasons for being in Tehran, whether for work or for medical reasons. Each speaks in his regional accent or language. What is interesting is that no Persian subtitle is provided for instances when a social actor speaks in other languages, such as Azeri, further distancing and isolating the migrant's position in the unknown mega-city. Recognizing the diversity of cultures and languages in films is a much more contemporary addition to Iranian cinema. Historically, Iranian cinema has been quite Tehran-centric, with an incredibly sparse representation of regional languages and accents. Even in the war films of 1980s, which sought to adopt an inclusive approach to support their mission to mobilize troops from all around Iran, the characters from different provinces were acknowledged in the plot, yet the spoken language, aside from a couple of words, would always remain standard Persian.

The film continues by exploring the impact of the oil industry on the agricultural industry, which resulted in many farmers going out of business and therefore moving to the big cities in search of alternative work. The next section is introduced through aerial shots of the industrial developments on the city outskirts, showing snapshots of some of the most important factories and companies that are located in and around Tehran. It focuses on Melli Shoe Factory as a case study, only 18km outside Tehran: a factory which, as is stated by the narrator, imports all its raw material from abroad, with the majority of its 13,000-strong workforce not being from Tehran. This example illustrates the main reason that workers are drawn to the big cities: there are more opportunities. One of the factory employees expresses his difficulties with making ends meet on his low income, sharing that he has spoken to his manager and is contemplating moving back home to his farm. Whilst he is still speaking, his words are overlaid by the narrator, imposing his skeptical point of view by calling his wish to go back to farming a delusion.

The next section of the film focuses on the living conditions of the migrant workers who, as the narrator observes, are "trapped in the outskirts" of Tehran because they cannot afford to live in the city. In Persian, the narrator literally states that they are "thrown out to the off-limits of the city." This is not only reminiscent of the title of Banietemad's very first feature film *Khārej az Mahdudeh* (*Off Limits*, 1988); it also demonstrates that this is a persistent issue in Iranian society, and one that Banietemad is particularly concerned about, for she selected this script only a couple of years after making her *Centralization* documentary. Whilst *Off-limits* is a comedic film, it strikes the same notes and is critical of the unruly expansion of the city without proper planning. The people living in slums and on the outskirts of the city are a recurring leitmotif in Banietemad's later films, such as *Narges* (*Nargess*, 1992) and *Rusari Ābi* (*The Blue-Veiled*, 1995), and in her documentaries *To Whom Do You Show These Films?* and *Ruzegār-e Ma* (*Our Times, 2002*).

Moving to the Ghale Hassan Khan area, which lies 20km outside Tehran, the film for the first time turns its attention to women and children. Their harsh living conditions and the daily challenges they face, such as lack of water and electricity supply and access to medical care, amongst other things, are exposed. In this section, a well-spoken man in a crowd of people talks about the issue of education and lack of sufficient schools in the area. He addresses the Ministry of Education and says, "if they hear our voice then they can come, and I will show them the conditions." Of course, to address the camera in this way, the man must have believed the film crew was making a report on their conditions for broadcasting on television. But again, choosing to include this reflexive element in the final cut of the film adds to its political message, calling for an infrastructural change in society which will provide for all in an equal manner. This also confirms Banietemad's personal belief that cinema is simply a device to help disseminate information that is lost or otherwise overlooked. She comes from the same background that was shaped by the committed literary movement of the 1960s, and believes that films are a means of communication and that filmmakers have a social responsibility towards their fellow citizens.

The well-spoken man also complains about the fact that the city council demolishes houses that people have built with their own money without prior notice. Following this statement, the film depicts many shots of half-demolished, one-room brick houses which people still reside in. This particular topic is one which Banietemad would return to a few years after, in her documentary *To Whom Do You Show These Films?*, which will be examined in more detail later in this chapter.

The concluding section of the film focuses on Tehran's Grand Bazaar, calling it "the heart of the country's economy." The documentary claims that investments from the provinces are drawn to Tehran and, due to the city's dominance over the country's trade, it swallows the funds of everywhere else. This part concludes with images of the main bureaucratic, governmental, and financial buildings. At the end of the section, the image and sound are speeded up and the focus moves to the hustle and bustle and transactions taking place in the open entrance of a bureaucratic building—the busy hallways filled with people waiting, the archive rooms, and so on—and the narrator says:

> Thousands of people are confused in the labyrinth of bureaucracy in offices, searching for a key to their problems among the files.
> A waste of time, a waste of workforce, a waste of money, a waste of lifetime, a waste of energy . . .

The narration concludes with a strong statement that none of the issues addressed in the film can be resolved in the short term, for that would require fundamental and infrastructural change. As long as the villagers and provinces depend on the big cities for jobs, supplies, healthcare, and education, the issue of centralization cannot be resolved. Centralization established the thematic preoccupation of Rakhshan Banietemad as a social filmmaker and also some of her stylistic traits, such as subjectivity and reflexivity, which we see recurring in her subsequent films. The next documentary we will consider, *To Whom Do You Show These Films?*, confirms her fully as an essayist filmmaker, evident through her self-reflexive play with film form and her subjective authorial use of voice-over (Kuhn and Westwell 2012).

To Whom Do You Show These Films? is a feature-length documentary following the lives and living conditions of the residents in Shahrak-e Fatemiyeh, a temporary camp that was built twelve years prior to when Banietemad and her crew went there. This engaging documentary combines a number of documentary modes at once. The nature of filming is observational and, as is stated in the script, the filmmakers actually stumbled upon the story whilst working on another project, subsequently making a decision to follow this new thread, which would take them over two years to complete. The documentary revisits a number of the residents we first meet at the camp several times across a period of two years; some lives are changed for the better, whilst others have not taken the best turn. Yet this is not purely observational, because the film was itself used as a catalyst of change. It was by sharing the footage they had initially filmed with the mayor that the municipality became involved in finding a solution to the problem. Banietemad's commitment to the people and the social actors she met is evident in her participatory involvement with their cause and her continuous pursuit of their wellbeing, on and off camera.

The documentary is, at the same time, an essay film, with Banietemad's voice-over weaving the narrative together and filling in the blanks. Her own voice narrates, and she constantly refers to herself as the filmmaker and to her crew, whom we see on the screen. It is her subjectivity that we follow throughout. She facilitates a space for all those affected people to have a chance to tell their stories. She offers an unbiased narrative throughout and holds the municipality responsible, yet she does not end the film once they respond positively to people's needs, continuing filming to see the end result. The story is brought to a close, but she does not, in any shape or form, suggest that the issue is fully resolved. Banietemad does not believe in black and white storytelling; what she cares about is creating a ripple of change where possible, no matter how big or small. She holds herself responsible as the filmmaker in the same way that she holds those in charge responsible.

The title, *To Whom Do You Show These Films?*, the same words with which the film begins, is her demonstration of self-reflexivity, whilst ensuring that, from the onset, the spectator is also playing an active role. She believes in cinema that can make a difference, and this film portrays the achievement of a tiny fraction of this hope. This is evident in her future documentaries too, for, in one way or another, they are also self-reflexive and participatory. For instance, in her forty-six-minute documentary *Mā Nimi az Jame'yat-e Irānim* (*We Are Half of Iran's Population*, 2009) she creates a forum where requests from different female representatives, syndicates, groups, and non-governmental organizations that she had filmed in advance could be heard by the presidential candidates, giving them a chance to respond. This was meant to help women, who constitute half of the population, to make choices based on what would benefit them. Of course, the film did not end in the way she intended. All the candidates but Ahmadinejad, who would become the disputed elected president in 2009, turned up to listen and respond to the women's wishes and demands. This self-reflexivity is a trait that is also evident, to varying degrees, in many of her fictional films.

The question of ethics is also an important aspect of this documentary. Banietemad teases the spectator at a few points in the film, particularly in the opening and final sequences. In the opening scene, the camera crew, seemingly descending upon the people in the camp, create an uncomfortable viewing experience. The camera appears to be intruding on their privacy, even capturing them off guard: one elderly lady sharing intimate issues, for example, whilst Banietemad on camera directs her and asks her several times to walk the crew to her house and show the house to the camera. This is before the spectators even know where they are and how the film crew is going to treat the subjects. Of course, soon after, we observe how welcoming they are, and how willingly everyone admits them into their privacy. In the closing scene, which will be treated in more detail later, Banietemad admits in the voice-over that the social actor is not aware of being filmed, again creating a sense of discomfort to convey the message she wants to deliver. It is only a minute later that the social actor looks at the camera, laughs after recognizing that it is on, and repeats that segment.

The film begins with only the audio of the memorable words: "Who do you show these films to anyway? Help us!" on black. These piercing words, questioning the role of film as a whole, are reused in the feature film *Under the Skin of the City* (2001), when the female protagonist Tooba is being interviewed about working conditions at the factory. The same words are also uttered by Mehri, one of the female social actors we get to meet later in the film. The opening scene depicts a crew using a 16mm camera and a boom operator, plus Banietemad herself talking to an elderly woman, Leila, on the streets of Shahrak-e Fatemiyeh. A crowd of people, adults and children, watch them from the back of the alleyway, following them wherever the camera goes. This chaotic opening, full of movement and with Banietemad's physical appearance on the screen directing Leila, asking her to take them to her house and show it to them, creates a sense of intimacy and immediacy rarely witnessed in any other Iranian documentary. Shot by a behind-the-scene videographer, this opening drops the spectator right into the middle of story. Banietemad's own voice is then overlaid on the diegetic on-location sound, explaining how they came about making this film. They had been shooting the project *Healthy City* in the area when they arrived at the camp. The poor conditions and the standard of living, which seemed to be at odds with the rest of the area, motivated them to shoot a few rolls of film there. She further explains that some of these people had come from the slums that were destroyed in 1979–80, whilst others were those affected by flooding at Barut Kuhi Channel a few years before. Apparently, they were relocated there for temporary shelter, but up until 1992, when the film crew turned up, they were still living in this temporary housing. Over those twelve years, the population had increased but the capacity of the camp had not. The voice-over was accompanied by shots of different people eagerly guiding the crew into their little shacks, showing them their impoverished conditions. We are then taken to the house of Mehri, whose voice opened the film, and a woman who people claimed spoke well. She talks of their poverty and unemployment, and the fact that the government's financial support was not sufficient to live off. Her summary of their living conditions, Banietemad claims, was what made them more curious to spend more time there.

After showing the clips to Tehran's mayor, Banietemad explains, he promised to look into their situation. As for herself, seeing as they were already involved with the lives of the people in the camp, she decided to continue filming, but using a cheaper digital camera and only a skeleton crew. What they had already shot on 16mm forms the exposition to the camp after the first scene, taken in the early morning when the alleyways were still quite empty. Most of the individuals in the film are women and children, because it was mostly shot during the day when the men were at work. On average, four to eight people were living in each room; many did not even have private toilet facilities and had to use the communal bathrooms on the block. The sewage was shallow, exposed, and located very close to their drinking-water pipes.

The film continues by getting closer to a few families and individuals, offering a more detailed exposure of their daily challenges. Slightly later, the voice-over explains that, after an initial survey, the mayor announced that there was nothing that could be done to improve living standards, and so the residents had to be evacuated. The film crew were also advised not go there for a while, as residents might be angry with the decision and hold them responsible. Banietemad explains that, once she was able to go back, the demolition had already started. There are many scenes depicting people packing and children playing in the rubble.

Since the municipality was well aware of the bad effects of previous relocation projects, which had resulted in the creation of such camps, Banietemad further explains that they had decided in this instance to take a new route. They formed a committee out of the people and asked those living there to fill out a questionnaire. They based their action on mutual respect and people were given money to buy another place in accordance with their needs. Of course, the money would not be enough to buy property in Tehran; most of them had to relocate to villages outside the city. Residents were going to demolish their homes to help the city, and would also be permitted to take away the building material if they wanted. For some of the elderly single women, like Leila, the municipality rented rooms elsewhere.

The film continues by following the people in their new residences. They each live in varying levels of comfort and satisfaction. The film, although evincing some improvement from where they had started, shows that their conditions are still far from ideal. It also focuses on the uncertain future of individuals and families who were resisting leaving the camp because relocation for them meant moving far away from Tehran.

Later, the film revisits the cleared site of the camp and shows a single man, Seyyed, and his mute wife and six children still remaining. He has refused to move until he could buy a house for his family. In the voice-over, Banietemad confirms that he stayed there for an extra ten months. The film flashes back to the first time the crew had met Seyyed at his work and then walked to their house. Switching back to the present day, the crew travel to visit him at his new place. They find Seyyed working as a cobbler in a small shop; he smiles and is excited to see the crew, asking why they had been away for so long. Later, they go to his house, where we see there is a new addition to the family. This time, we see them as a happy and smiling family—quite the opposite of their first encounter. They speak with Banietemad; she asks about the house and they show their satisfaction. She and the crew are welcomed into their house like family members or old friends (Figure 10.2). Off camera, Banietemad's voice is heard as she greets them all individually, remembering each person's name.

Figure 10.2 Banietemad in Seyyed's house, behind the scenes of *To Whom Do You Show These Films?* (1993)

At first, they sit and look at printed photographs of the camp, which Banietemad's crew have brought with them, identifying people they know. Banietemad asks them to sit and watch the edit of the first half of the film and their first visit to the family. This brings excitement to the family at first, having never before seen footage of themselves. Soon, this visible excitement is replaced by a sense of melancholy and nostalgia. Whilst the family are watching the film on their small TV, the camera observes their reactions and the sounds of the film are heard off screen. The act of watching their own film within a film brings their relationship with the crew to a satisfying close, and also helps them reflect on how far they have come since leaving the camp. At the same time, it highlights how the filmmakers were not simply exploiting the people in the camp for the sake of making a socially critical film; rather, the care and respect they feel for every single individual they have filmed are what stands out.

Banietemad repeats the action of showing footage with Mehri as well. This brings tears to Mehri's eyes, and she confirms her prior statements, saying she really was right about it all. The film crew subsequently go to visit her in her new home to check on her conditions. She admits that it is much better, but she complains of her loneliness under the new living arrangements. This scene becomes quite playful, for in the beginning Banietmad says Mehri was not aware of being filmed and spoke freely; then she laughs, upon realizing that they are filming. There is a cut, and she is next depicted after adjusting her headscarf to look more modest and repeating her issues but in far more conservative fashion. Banietemad has left both versions in the film, commenting on how the camera causes the social actors to self-censor. Including this right at the close of the film is highly effective, inviting spectators to contemplate all that they have heard from the beginning of the film and to wonder if they heard the "real" or the self-censored versions of each narrative. Mehri, immediately after asserting that she is much more comfortable in her new surroundings, turns towards Banietemad with a huge grin and says, "I'm kidding," then laughs. The shot goes to black, then comes back to her as she pours her heart out, looking directly at the camera and repeating the true sentiments she feels. She regrets not having her own place at this age, what with all the work she has done since she was seven years old. She finishes by saying, "And you're here filming and taking pictures. I don't even know what's in that camera! Who do you show these films to anyway? Help us!" The same lines that began the film are now ending it, bringing it full circle. Both this direct address and these words are testament to the film's reflexive and subjective style.

The final narration of the film, on black, reports on the state of the remaining people from the camp. Declaring that the hour-and-a-half film was the edited version of the thirty hours of footage that they had shot over two years, Banietemad ends by saying that the story of the camp is over; but, she goes on, what about the story of its people? She then begins naming all of the individuals that they have met over the period of making the film, and the credits roll.

The short documentary *Under the Skin of the City* (1996), with a running time of just over half an hour and dealing with the issue of addiction, also combines several documentary modes. Above all, Banietemad structures her film through her subjective lens. Reflexivity and self-awareness are key elements employed, with lots of camera angles pointed elsewhere or playing with exposure to avoid depicting people who do not wish to be recognized. The film also incorporates the camera crew's presence. For instance, an early scene shot from a distance shows Banietemad talking to a group of young men in what appears to be a park. The cameraman and the sound person's voices off camera speculate as to whether or not she will be successful in convincing any of them to be filmed. The camera follows Banietemad and one of the young men approaching a car and getting in. From that shot, zoomed in from a distance, it cuts to another of a moving car out of the front window whilst we hear Banietemad having a conversation about smoking with the young man. He admits he smokes up to a pack a day, but claims his family do not know that he smokes. He adds that he has never tried any other drugs. She asks him if he knows what addiction is and he offers his understanding of it. He talks about how addicts look and how their faces change and become ugly. She asks him if he could think of those addicts being people like his friends, to which he responds immediately: "Oh no, God forbid!"

In the narration, Banietemad explains that that day she also spoke to the boy's mother, who was aware of him smoking and did not approve. This short narration confirms the filmmaker's ethical consciousness. She must have driven the boy home and asked to speak with his parents, as it is unclear whether or not he is a minor; had this been the case, she would have needed to obtain his parents' approval to use the material, even anonymously. Banietemad adds that, after speaking further with his mother, she became worried about her son, whilst other mothers she spoke with were not taking this issue as seriously—as if addiction were something that could only happen to others and not themselves. In the next scene, she talks to a young mother who is confident that, through family awareness and support, children are not in any danger of becoming addicts. Banietemad voices her fear of this mother's overconfidence, for in the rehabilitation centers she has met many boys who came from financially secure and supportive families and had still been exposed to addiction. At this moment, we can see the roots of the script forming for her film *Khun Bāzi* (*Mainline*, 2006), which tells the story of an addicted girl from a middle-class family whose mother is struggling to help her quit.

The film opens with a narration read by Banietemad, defining addiction as not just an illness, but a social illness, and claiming that it is the outcome of a sick society. She ends by asserting that addiction has many aspects to it, but this film is going to function only as a warning for families. This opening sequence is very reminiscent of the opening narration of Farrokhzad's *The House is Black*, where a male voice, that of Ebrahim Golestan, explains the purpose, hopes, and motivations of the filmmakers who made this piece about leprosy. In this essay film, two voice-overs are employed: a male one representing the factual information, as in an expository documentary, and a female-voice one, by Farrokhzad herself, representing a more subjective and poetic reflection of the people living in the leper colony. *Under the Skin of the City* also incorporates a second narrator—the male voice of Jahangir Kosari. But this other voice does not exactly create the same effect as in *The House is Black*; instead, it mirrors Banietemad's voice, and could be read as an attempt to create a balance and shared experience for all the family members, with the male voice-over representing the fathers' perspective.

The film intercuts scenes from the rehabilitation center, the visiting halls, and interviews with young boys at the center and some mothers (Figure 10.3). At a pivotal moment, we hear a mother's story as she sits with her back to the camera. She had divorced her husband because he was an addict, and now she is struggling with her son's addiction, saying that she could divorce her husband but what could she possibly do with her son? She could not give him

Figure 10.3 Banietemad at the rehabilitation center, behind the scenes of *Under the Skin of the City* (1996)

up. A little later, she says they should get rid of them all. She then becomes embarrassed and stands up and leaves. Banietemad's voice-over adds, "How desperate must a mother be to wish for her own son's death?"

In the next section, a female rehabilitation practitioner talks about the issue of families underestimating the chances of their children becoming involved with drugs, which she asserts is due to a lack of knowledge and education. Banietemad adds that many families she spoke with believed that it is best not to speak of these topics too openly, as though knowing about it would entice children to try them. However, disagreeing with this view, she continues by posing the question: if there is no education about something that is readily available in society, where will the children be able to satisfy their curiosity, if not at home or school? The film then introduces the helpline by showing the counsellors responding to a few calls. The latter half of the film tries to demystify conceptions about who can become an addict, and encourages families to play a more active role in understanding their children and the different reasons why they may turn to drugs. This section also encourages families to employ different methods to prevent their teenagers from using drugs.

The film ends with the departure of one of the young men from the rehabilitation center, whose journey we had come to know. But Banietemad's voice shares the unfortunate information that she had gleaned a few weeks after he left the center that he began misusing again. She ends the film with the comment that it is only now that she realizes how easy it is for one to become addicted, but how difficult it is to overcome addiction for good. In this documentary, Banietemad offers personal reflection and perspective, backed up by individual experiences of dealing with addiction, whether in the form of a user, a relative of a user, or a doctor helping a patient to stop using.

Banietemad's essayist style of documentaries translates into her social realist fictional narratives, which rely on real and tangible social issues. The care and respect she demonstrates towards the social actors in her documentaries are carried across to her feature films. No one individual is ever assigned the blame; it is society as a whole that is to be held responsible for the ailments of the people. In *Centralization*, as discussed earlier, she concludes that until the infrastructure is changed or fixed, the issue of migration to the big cities will not be resolved. In the documentary *Under the Skin of the City*, addiction is presented as the consequence of a sick society.

Having closely considered some of Banietemad's early documentaries, it is my hope that this chapter has managed to highlight some of the main stylistic strategies that she has incorporated in her films and which allow us to see her auteurial signature. This is also evident in the subjects she has focused her lens on, which are ignited in her documentaries and realized in her fiction films. It is small wonder that, when one is talking to her, she always says her heart is with the documentary project she is working on. Her creativity lies in reflections on real issues in society. In this regard, my other hope is that the present study will help extend knowledge of and access to films that have rarely been viewed outside Iran.

Through offering detailed textual analysis, this chapter has sought to further scholarship on Banietemad's documentaries, which have been largely neglected in scholarship. It is only through examining the whole spectrum of her work that one can construct a discourse to help frame her as an auteur.

The combination of reflexivity, intertextuality, and playing with the film form has become an iconic trait throughout the entirety of her work. This may be a lot more evident in her documentaries, as the style of narration, or the presence of herself and the film crew on camera, are features which, by their own merit, draw attention to the fact that we are watching a film. In her feature films, especially her later ones, this reflexivity takes the form of self-referential intertextuality. This intertextuality can be witnessed crossing over from her documentaries into her fiction, as, for example, when the mother with her paralyzed war veteran son in *Bānu-ye Ordibehesht* (*The May Lady*, 1998) becomes the main protagonist of *Gilāneh* (*Gilane*, 2005), or the living conditions and similar people to those we met in *To Whom Do You Show These Film?* form the setting of *The Blue-veiled and Under the Skin of the City*. And, of course, in her latest feature, *Ghesseh-hā (Tales,* 2014), where many of the characters from her very first feature film appear over twenty years after their respective stories have ended, and still encounter the same social issues as a couple of decades before. The most striking example concerns *The May Lady*, in which sections of Banietemad's earlier documentaries are used as documentaries that the protagonist has supposedly produced. Yet Banietemad does not stop there: she goes and films fictional documentary-style footage of the protagonists of her films *Nargess* and *The Blue-veiled*, depicting them in the post-plot reality of their stories and blending this with her actual documentaries.

This, in itself, is a commentary on the constructed nature of film, inviting a reflection on what is real and what is made up. The juxtaposition of actual documentary footage with what the documentary is meant to look like reminds us of the final scene with Mehri in *To Whom Do You Show These Films?*, posing the question as to which of her speeches represents her "real" self. Perhaps Banietemad is trying to show that films, documentaries or otherwise, may not only be realist in approach, but also reflect reality itself. Perhaps this further explains why she has developed such a unique hybrid style of social realism: because the classical narrative conventions she employs help make the harsh realism of her stories more palatable.

CHAPTER II

Embracing *All My Trees*: An Ecocritical Reading

Fatemeh-Mehr Khansalar

> "I suffer too much . . . perhaps this old woman is being a fool . . ."
> Mahlagha mumbles and looks at the filmmaker behind the camera and
> continues: "I believe I must raise my voice [on behalf of nature].
> No matter what."
> Mahlagha Mallah in *Hame-ye Derakhtān-e Man*
> (*All My Trees*, 2015; Figure 11.1)

In recent years, the development of a cinema that provides "cinematic experiences of being immersed within the natural world" (Rust 2012: 19) has started to come to light. Scott Macdonald, in *Ecocinema Theory and Practice*, explains that, although this trend has not attracted large audiences, the works of filmmakers and visual artists in this field can provide visual training in "appreciating the experience of an immersion within natural process" (ibid.). In the field of ecological documentary, all filmmakers, regardless of their place and time, have to find a cinematic language to express their environmental concerns and, in turn, invite their spectators to reflect on the matter. Macdonald believes that the job of ecocinema is to create "a new kind of film experience that demonstrates an alternative to conventional media-spectatorship and helps to nurture a more environmentally progressive mindset" (ibid.: 20). This new ecocentric mindset is the main goal of ecological filmmakers and ecocritics, because raising awareness about the environment, no matter how small this action might be, will ultimately lead to a healthier planet.

The films construct the sense of the city and environment yet can never fully represent what is real. "Cinematic texts, with their audio-visual presentations of individuals and their habitats, affect our imaginations of the world around us, and thus, potentially, our actions towards this world" (ibid.: 2). Therefore,

Figure 11.1 Mahlagha Mallah among her friends and colleagues in *All My Trees* (2015)

the cinematic city—in Rakhshan Banietemad's case, Tehran—is never the real Tehran, and the real Tehran is never simply its architecture. The cityscape and urbanization are at the heart of most of Banietemad's fictional films, if not serving as the foreground of the plot. In *Khārej az Mahdudeh* (*Off Limits*, 1988), the protagonists cannot file the burglary of their house with the police because their property is not registered and therefore does not exist on the map. Further examples include the main character in *Nargess* (*Nargess*, 1992), who lives in an unlicensed abandoned house on the peripheries of the city; the protagonist in *Rusari Ābi* (*The Blue-veiled*, 1995), who lives in the slums next to a brick factory; and the protagonist in *Zir-e Pust-e Shahr* (*Under the Skin of the City*, 2001), who sells his small two-room house on the outskirts of the city, the family's only possession, to a developer without his mother's consent. This sense of awareness of individuals and their habitat is not confined to Banietemad's feature films, but is, in fact, even more evident in her documentaries, which I will discuss later in the chapter. A Tehran ecocinema not only approximates the real Tehran more closely by debunking its misrepresentations; it also appropriates cinema as a tool to hold us accountable for our society and environment. I argue that Banietemad's socially conscious films move the Tehran urban cinema towards a Tehran ecocinema. Ecocinema studies both focus on films that have an environmental message, and "[investigate] the breadth of cinema . . . in which producers, consumers, and texts interact" (ibid.).

Whilst it is possible to look at Banietemad's œuvre from an ecocritical lens, this chapter, as briefly illustrated above, will focus on the more conventional ecocinematic examples which directly address environmental issues. Although making documentaries about ecology and nature has a short history in Iran, the body of ecodocumentary production has accelerated in the last few decades. This is reflected in Iranian filmmakers' decision to investigate ecological topics such as underground water, forests, waste, pollution, and agriculture. Among these filmmakers, Rakhshan Banietemad constitutes one of the pioneers. As part of my research in the field of ecological criticism, my intention in this chapter is to investigate Banietemad's documentaries, following her journey towards environmental concerns and the Karestan project. In the first part of this chapter, I will analyze her ecodocumentaries from a "green" point of view and investigate how her works concerning iconic ecological activists have engaged audiences' attention. In the second part, I will focus on her ecodocumentary *All My Trees*, to observe how it communicates with audiences and examine the way in which she attempts to raise awareness about issues in Iran relating to nature and the environment.

BANIETEMAD'S ECODOCUMENTARIES

Examination of Banietemad's works indicates that the environment has been one of her key areas of interest since the 1980s. Banietemad's journey towards harnessing environmental matters has, I believe, followed the same path as her concern for women and other oppressed groups, marginalized because of their health, poverty, gender, and struggles with addiction. Nature, and also non-humans, are marginalized and silenced entities in our current world, yet Banietemad endeavors to give them a voice and bring their issues to light. In *Mohājerin-e Roustāi dar Shahr* (*Occupation of Migrant Peasants in the City*, 1980), and especially in *Tamarkoz* (*Centralization*, 1986), Banietemad depicts displaced villagers who, working in Tehran and other big cities in the hope of finding a better life, encounter only the harshness and poor quality of urban living conditions. Far from their farms, these miserable villagers are framed by the surroundings of the polluted city. Although in *Centralization* the main purpose of the documentary is to analyze the exploitative role of big cities (especially Tehran), the first fifteen minutes of the documentary instead depict the environmental issues caused by this centralization in Iran since the Land Reform in 1960s. In Centralization, the towering buildings and Tehran's smoky atmosphere are highlighted by the camera, contextualizing the narrator's explanation of how the city's excessive growth generates chaos, disaster, and noise. In addition, by framing and interviewing the tired peasants at Tehran's main bus station, awaiting a new life in the city, Banietemad portrays how the giant metropolis is swallowing these hopeful people who "have already been expelled from their ruined villages," as the narrator of the film asserts. In *Centralization*, no beautiful scenes of rural areas have been framed, and it is left to the audience's imagination to create those landscapes and nature. However, as the migrant peasant labor is shown tanning leather in Kafsh-e Melli (Melli Shoe Company), the audience can see directly how these farmers and their descendants are destined to clean the filth of this industrial city. The camera, placed on the ground, captures the two workers washing away all the greasy refuse from the shoe factory. The juxtaposition of the images of natural scenery (which is now out of reach) and this dirty, industrial center (which is currently at hand) forces the viewer to reconsider the environment of big cities and villages.

After *Centralization*, the only documentary by Banietemad fully dedicated to environmental concerns was produced in 2015. Nevertheless, in most of Banietemad's documentaries, city issues, nature, plants, and birds are always included as a part of her narrative. Whilst not significant enough to characterize the film as an ecodocumentary, scenes which feature nature (such as watering indoor plants, singing birds, and the appreciation of gardens) appear regularly in her work, as seen in *Fardā Mibinamet Elinā* (*See You Tomorrow Elina*, 2010), *Touran Khanom* (2018), and *Āy, Ādamhā (Hey, Humans, 2016)*.

In 2007, Banietemad initiated a project in collaboration with a number of other prominent Iranian documentary filmmakers, called Kārestān (Karestan), which has produced ecodocumentaries featuring four iconic environmental activists. The Karestan Project, working under the Kārgāh-e Film Kārā (Kara Film Studio), was founded by Rakhshan Banietemad and Mojtaba Mirtahmasb, a prominent Iranian documentary filmmaker. Karestan intended to bring stories about, and introduce successful Iranian entrepreneurs to, audiences. Kara Film Studio is an independent, non-commercial collaborative institute that invites both small and large groups of filmmakers to come together to pitch ideas and see them produced professionally (Kara Film Studio 2013). These like-minded filmmakers have, to date, produced nineteen documentaries, according to the Kara Film website. Six of these can be categorized as environmental or green documentaries because their main theme is the environment: *Roodkhāneh Hanooz Māhi Darad* (*The River Still Has Fish*, 2002) and *Bānooye Gole Sorkh* (*Lady of the Roses*, 2009) by Mojtaba Mirtahmasb; *Shāerane Zendegi* (*Poets of Life*, 2017) by Shirin Barghnavard; *Mādare Zamin* (*Mother of the Earth*, 2017) by Mahnaz Afzali; *Yek Sāat az Yek Omr* (*A Lifetime in an Hour*, 2015); and *Hamehye Derakhtāne Man* (*All My Trees*, 2015) by Rakhshan Banietemad.

In a visual interview made by Artebox and directed by Hassan Salamat (Banietemad 2017), Banietemad states that, although she could not make the ecological documentary based on her idea and her vast consultations with scholars and activists (due to budget restrictions), she decided to document a few individuals who had dedicated their lives to speaking on behalf of nature in Iran. Whilst she acknowledged that "one may say that these are interviews, rather than films," she goes on: "I believe that these activists are such influential individuals that I prefer to add these films to my body of work" (ibid.). *A Lifetime in an Hour* is a fifty-minute interview with Eskandar Firouz, the founder of Sāzmān-e Hefāzat-e Mohit-e Zist (Department of Environment) in Iran, who is known as Iran's "father of the environment." Banietemad explains that, due to financial and other restrictions, an interview during a short visit was all she could gather for documenting Mr Firouz's achievements. Banietemad and her crew could obtain only one appointment with him, and she failed to find any usable archival footage of him. As a consequence, she decided to adopt a straightforward approach, editing the interview along with some family archival photos and images from his books (Banietemad 2017). Although it was simple, Banietemad succeeded in creating a reflective piece of work through one mere encounter. She has incorporated the crew members walking into Mr Firouz's house and setting up and interacting with him. These shots not only function as a good technique to bookend the film and award it structure; they also add a certain feeling of intimacy and immediacy. The film is not just a standard interview: it is a visit to the house of an icon. As a viewer, you are welcomed into his house and given the opportunity to spend just over an hour with him, listening to him sharing some personal memories about his work and as the director of the Department of Environment.

Likewise, *All My Trees is a documentary about Mahlagha Mallah*, Iran's longest-campaigning environmental activist and founder of the first environmental non-governmental organization (NGO) in Iran. However, in this case, the director has had some time to follow Mahlagha in her day-to-day activities. In this film as well, the crew are participating and interacting with the social actor. *All My Trees* manages to communicate with its audience directly and draw their attention toward the main concerns of the film: demonstrating how Mahlagha enacts change in her society in an attempt to save the environment. Banietemad acknowledges in her notes on the web page for this film that "though these two films may not stand out in my body of work, they are among the films whose completion and screening has made me very proud and happy" (Kara Film Studio 2013). She also states that these two documentaries have attracted the biggest audiences of all her documentaries. This is in spite of the fact that, in Iran, environmental concerns can still be regarded as a "luxury" (Banietemad 2017).

Along with the two aforementioned documentaries, Banietemad has also participated as an artistic consultant in the two other ecodocumentaries produced by Kara Film Studio: *Poets of Life and Mother of the Earth*. These are also centered on two female environmental activists and entrepreneurs. The first documentary is about Shirin Parsi, the founder of organic agriculture in the north of Iran. The second presents Hayedeh Shirzadi, the founder of a recycling center for domestic waste in the province of Kermanshah, Iran. Similarly, in these two films the filmmaker (in addition to conducting interviews with the main character) follows the social actors to capture their lives, concerns, ideas, and the struggles which they have faced.

The Karestan project has been one of the leading initiatives to help celebrate and preserve the legacy of notable individuals, most of whom, as indicated above, are key figures in environmental projects. Banietemad's role in this initiative as both a consultant and a participant is unparalleled. The next section will focus on Banietemad's film *All My Trees*.

All My Trees is a fifty-one-minute documentary, written and directed by Rakhshan Banietemad, edited by Shirin Barghnavard, and produced by Mojtaba Mirtahmasb. Banietemad utilizes an observational mode of documentary filmmaking, following Mahlagha Mallah (b. 1917), a female environmental activist, for a few days during her still professionally active life at the age of ninety-seven. The documentary presents a short introduction to Mahlagha's works and achievements during the title sequence of the film. She is known as the "mother of Iran's environment" and has devoted her life to raising awareness about environmental issues. Mahlagha received a PhD from the Sorbonne after completing her MA in Sociology at Tehran University. She became interested in environmental issues whilst in her role as head librarian of the Psychology Research Institute Library at Tehran University, where she worked upon her return from studying in Paris. From 1973, she began collaborating with the newly established Department of Environment. In 1993 she founded Jamiat-e Zanān-e Mobāreze bā mohit-e zist (Women's Society Against Environmental Pollution), hereafter referred to as the Women's Society. Mahlagha's approach in addressing environmental issues cuts across public and private sectors. She promotes comprehensive education about the environment for families, local communities, and schools, believing that, with sufficient knowledge, people are capable of helping with environmental issues.

Banietemad's camera captures the activities, members, and achievements of the Women's Society as the first environmental protection association in Iran. The documentary begins by illustrating Tehran's polluted air and continues by entering Mahlagha's house, where she has been living for sixty years. Her living room is bright, cozy, and full of plants, with a window overlooking her garden, in which she has diligently composted her domestic waste over the years. With this opening, the audience has already engaged with Mahlagha's mission of raising awareness of environmental issues.

In *All My Trees*, instead of explaining the environmental issues via a narrator, similar to Centralization, Banietemad becomes a social actor like her subject and participates in her own work. For a few days, she actively engages in Mahlagha's private and social life. She participates in Mahlagha's daily activities and follows her from home to the different conferences and meetings she attends. As Bill Nichols states, the participatory documentary helps filmmakers who seek to represent broad social issues "through interviews and compilation footage" (Nichols 2010: 123). The director's sole aim in documenting Mahlagha's life and activities is to show how this woman has effected change in her community through finding her own voice and speaking out on behalf of the environment.

This approach, again, reveals that Banietemad accesses environmental issues through her concerns about empowering women and about the way that this empowerment can influence society. In her works, she has always identified marginalized figures and gives voice to women and other individuals who are silenced or ignored. In *All My Trees*, Banietemad provides a platform for Mahlagha to communicate her message to a larger audience and depict how devoted she still is to the Women's Society, despite the limitations imposed by her age and health. Banietemad demonstrates how Mahlagha and other members of the Women's Society are making inroads into changing power relations within wider society in relation to the environment and women. In line with other feminist documentaries, in this ecodocumentary Banietemad identifies herself with Mahlagha and documents her activities in order to establish a close relationship with her and, ultimately, the audience. In feminist documentaries, the filmmaker has a "close identification with their subjects, participation in the women's movement, and sense of the films' intended effect" (Kahana 2016: 678).

Employing an observational approach, Banietemad, for the most part, regards Mahlagha without interruption, letting her talk and live as she wishes. Her camera follows Mahlagha from one room to another; from home to conferences and to various events which celebrate nature, clean air, and forestation. Consequently, whilst Mahlagha is the intended focal point of the film, the environmental concerns which unfold before the audience as we follow her are given center-stage. Everything that she speaks about is somehow connected to the environment. Even when speaking about her husband's death, she acknowledges how he was her friend and supporter, admitting that she preferred to plant trees for his funeral ceremony. She enthusiastically suggests that, as with her husband's death, we must use all major life events to extend nature's domain within the environment. As with this example, we see clearly how Mahlagha's private life is interconnected with both the environment and her public life; making a prewritten biographical documentary about Mahlagha's private life would thus seem redundant.

As Mahlagha's own life is so intertwined with the life of Iran's environment, Banietemad invites her protagonist to steer the plot of the film, allowing it to be adapted to her own subject of choice: the environment. It is this shift, from a biography of Mahlagha to an investigation of Tehran's pollution and forestation, which leads me to consider this film an ecodocumentary. Banietemad's decision to open her film by introducing Mahlagha and then permitting her to make environmental issues the core theme of the narrative demonstrates Banietemad's equal concern with these issues. In order to see an ecodocumentary from the "green film criticism" or "ecocriticism" perspective, one must concentrate on how visual elements allow nature and natural elements to be framed and positioned in front of the camera (Willoquet-Maricondi 2010: 8). Banietemad's ecodocumentary highlights environmental issues by exploring Mahlagha's lived experience as an environmental activist.

To depict Mahlagha's lived experience, Banietemad uses a linear narrative structure and thus illustrates how the character has enabled herself and others to engage with the environment. A linear narrative, as Julia Lesage states, attracts feminist and *cinéma verité* filmmakers because "filming often is collaborative, with both subject and filmmaker sharing the political goals of the project" (Lesage 2016: 674). The filmmakers use the medium of cinema to defamiliarize what is familiarized within society. As we will see here with *All My Trees*, Banietemad portrays Mahlagha's identity and engagement with environmental issues in a manner which encourages audiences to watch from an alternative point of view. Through the narrative of the film, the audience are exposed to news items which they would otherwise be unaware of, such as the construction of roads in preserved forests, instances of pollution, dams, and the like. A visual report of companies and NGOs featuring in the Thirteenth International Environmental Exhibition of Tehran is also included in the film. This side information is inserted into Mahlagha's interview in order to attract the audience's attention towards issues such as the use of pollutant materials and polluting companies, forest fires, and so on. The clarity of this linear narrative structure, therefore, is beneficial in conveying Mahlagha's concerns about education and environmental awareness, as well as her personal character, to the audience. Mahlagha is depicted as a kind, educated, and energetic woman who has dedicated her life to her passion. The audience can see how, over the course of the last fifty years, Mahlagha's private and public life have become strikingly intertwined: her dining room has been turned into a classroom for children and young people with ecological interests, and her house is brimming with paperwork for the Women's Society.

To emphasize the delicate border between the private and public life of Mahlagha, Banietemad incorporates the film crew into the documentary. The presence of a film crew in front of the camera first and foremost reminds audiences that they are watching a film; although the footage conveys the reality of Mahlagha's life, the presence of the cameras for the purpose of the documentary means that it cannot replicate her life exactly. However, this aspect in itself serves to mirror her intertwined public and private life: just as she has always shared her living room with students and activists, and the compost heap in her garden with friends and family, she now opens her home to all audiences. In one scene, whilst the camera is positioned outside her house and shoots over the shoulder of a guest ringing her doorbell, Mahlagha opens her door to the friend. When her friend enters, Mahlagha pauses for a few seconds to look at the camera, and then asks: "Aren't you coming in?" It is almost as if she is inviting us, as the viewers, into her home. In a couple of other scenes, too, she acknowledges the cameraman and sound recordist who are following her from the dining room to her bedroom. She offers tea to the crew and builds a cheerful and light-hearted relationship with them. This cherished relationship sets an intimate tone for the documentary, allowing it to flow more naturally. The close and very personal depiction of Mahlagha's day-to-day activities presents not only the joyful side of her life, but also the setbacks she has faced in her career and all the disappointments that she has had to endure. In a very touching scene, a young female activist, one of her protégées, points out one of Mahlagha's achievements for the environment when she saved a forest and natural habitat. This, however, only makes Mahlagha emotional, reminding her instead about the campaigns she has lost.

Banietemad's success in *All My Trees* is her illustration of the unseen elements of Mahlagha's multi-faceted character: an environmental activist who is both a joyfully hard-working woman and someone who must fight back tears in order to continue her battle to protect the environment.

In addition to the emotional communication between the character and her audiences (which I will reflect upon later), one can observe that, for Mahlagha and the Women's Society, education and engagement with the environment are indispensable, for each individual has the capacity to prevent damage to the nature around them. This is a "specific thematic manifestation of environmental–ethical concern," as Pat Brereton asserts (Brereton 2016: 37). The focus of this film—like that of other ecodocumentaries—involves a proactive engagement with the environment. In order to be proactive in relation to Iranian environmental issues, the role of education cannot be ignored, and Mahlagha is a forerunner in this area. As the film develops, the audience witnesses how Mahlagha is actively engaging in education, both with teachers and students, and with local communities and households. The audience learns that Mahlagha and her society have been responsible for spreading knowledge not only in Tehran, but in the city of Urmia and a number of other provinces. She states that, in a district in Tehran with 26,000 households, for example, "we knocked on each door and talked to women to explain what 'trash' is, what 'the environment' is . . . over the course of three months." Mahlagha engages with her audiences, from children to educated activists, explaining problems and offering solutions through her interviews and her use of photo archives.

The main element of Mahlagha's education plan is the management of waste and the raising of awareness of deforestation and air pollutants. In addition to raising awareness through education, an ecological plan must also build an emotional relationship with audiences if it is to mobilize individuals to act. For an ecocritic, the effects of nostalgia are influential; as Murray and Heumann assert, it helps to create a "tipping point" in audience engagement and the legitimization of environmentalism as a primary ethical imperative (cited in Brereton 2016: 35). Similarly, invoking empathy in *All My Trees* helps the audience to pause for a moment and consider reality from a different perspective. In this documentary, Banietemad invokes the audience's emotions by conveying the extent to which air pollution in Tehran causes citizens to suffer and how it has developed into an invisible killer. The statistics presented by Mahlagha support her concerns about the irrigation of farms and the deforestation of a northern forest in Iran and communicate these to the audience. All of these subjects have been ignored and it is highly unlikely that any villager or urban citizen considers such matters in their day-to-day life. As I will demonstrate, in addition to statistics, Banietemad successfully shares emotional, nostalgic ecocentric moments and scenes to trigger the audience's emotions. In this ecodocumentary, Banietemad utilizes not only content, but also structural means to arouse emotive responses at audience level. In the remainder of this chapter, I will initially present elements of the content which the filmmaker uses, including both subtle emotional moments and bigger events. I will then explain how she makes use of structural tools, such as slow narrative and personal language, to attract the audience's attention.

The moment that the audience identifies themselves with the main character is the point of connection between them. As such, in every moment which demonstrates a shift in Mahlagha's emotions, whether she is disappointed, joyful, or hopeful, the filmmaker creates that connection. Banietemad focuses on and highlights these moments through highly effective editing and, at times, her own participation in the scene. For instance, when the camera captures a medium shot of Mahlagha's face holding back tears, Banietemad reads a sentence from Mahlagha's book, saying: "it's not about a leaf dying. Look! They're turning forests into deserts!" Or, in another close-up shot, Mahlagha's hands are framed pressing a handkerchief between her fingers in order to express her disappointment and anger as she explains how, with the appointment of a new Minister of Education, permission to provide environmental training for schoolteachers was revoked.

In addition to these subtly emotional instances, Banietemad also creates publicly emotional moments in *All My Trees*. For instance, in a project on top of Milad Tower, Mount Damavand, the highest peak in Iran, is reconstructed out of plastic cars painted by students from six different cities in Iran. At the end of the showcasing ceremony, Mahlagha, who is in a wheelchair, is wheeled closer to the installation, her fragile body wrapped up warmly in her shawl and blankets. She struggles to get out of her wheelchair. We see Banietemad next to her asking her: "What do you want to do?" Mahlagha says nothing. She asks again: "Do you want to get up?" Again, Mahlagha does not reply but, almost falling out of her wheelchair, she goes to the groups and, kneeling close to the reconstructed Damavand, prostrates herself and kisses the ground. After a moment of silence, the crowd applauds, and we hear Mahlagha crying. This scene cuts to an aerial shot filmed by a drone. The blue and white plastic cars have perfectly recreated the beautiful Damavand. For each individual Iranian, Damavand is a symbol of Iran's integration and strength, as it shines through in Persian literature and mythology. This sequence of people surrounding the blue Damavand installation, with its white summit at the top of the tallest man-made tower in Iran, combined with Mahlagha's gesture, has the potential to bring tears to the spectator's eyes. Mahlagha's voice is heard in this frame as she exclaims: "Oh God, save this homeland! Save this homeland!" Although Mahlagha's action was clearly not an anticipated part of the filmmaker's schedule, the film cleverly captures this moment, making it the most powerful part of the documentary—one which arouses strong emotion in its audience.

By the same token, the filmmaker also uses intimate language and a slow narrative to sustain an emotional and affective bond with her audience. As mentioned before, the language of *All My Trees* is natural and intimate. It seems that there is no prewritten transcript for the film, other than a loose outline of the subject. Therefore, Mahlagha becomes the one who steers the conversation and Banietemad gives her space to speak and behave as she wishes. This natural communication creates a direct relationship with her audience, and draws their attention to environmental matters. In addition to the language, the slow pace of the film promotes contemplation about ecological aspects (Brereton 2016: 30). In *All My Trees*, Banietemad's aim is to enable her audiences to consider the world from an ecological point of view. Banietemad has slowed down the pace of the narrative to offer the audience space to contemplate certain issues and to engage with the environment and ethical sensibilities, albeit just for a moment. This slower style of ecodocumentary can in turn "encourage the retraining of perception as a necessary condition for greater ecological awareness" (Brereton 2016: 31). This more gradual pace of narrative is a result not only of the combination of interviews, indoor scenes, and lectures, but also of Mahlagha's own physical limitations. For instance, in the sequence in which Mahlagha displays the archive album of the Women's Society, she sits in a two shot beside Banietemad on a couch. When no one can find Mahlagha's magnifier, she decides to find it herself. In an action shot, the camera leaves the filmmaker behind and focuses on Mahlagha, who gets up slowly and says: "wait a moment." Then she teasingly adds: "wait two hours." The camera follows Mahlagha as she slowly walks to her bedroom. When she is looking for her magnifier behind the drawer, the audience can see her photo table, full of pictures of her husband. Then Mahlagha, with one magnifier in hand, slowly turns and looks around. Ignoring the cameraman, she takes another magnifier and comes back to the living room. Now, in a medium shot, Mahlagha is alone on the couch, burying her face and magnifier in her archive album and trying to read the captions to the photographs. During these stretched-out moments, the audience silently follows Mahlagha, whose slow movements contrast sharply with her mental agility. After observing Mahlagha as she contemplates the album, carefully turning its pages and explaining about school protests for clean air, forestation in the semi-arid areas, and so on, the audience has had enough time to understand Mahlagha's concerns and is now emotionally attached to her.

Banietemad similarly plays upon viewers' emotions when presenting statistics in this documentary. Visualizing numbers and talking about ecological impacts require special attention because data visualization aims to translate the empirical data of experts into symbols to make them legible for the mass population, in order to mobilize them at an effective level (Rust 2012: 282). In *All My Trees*, there are no graphs or maps to explain the statistics provided by Mahlagha and other experts about Tehran's pollution or the deforestation of northern Iran's woodlands. The filmmaker does not attempt to make this visualization because, in her film, delivering any maps, graphs, or tables implies a hidden narrator and distances the narrative from the audience. Instead of data visualization, Banietemad incorporates these statistics into Mahlagha's daily routine, thereby linking them with the emotional moments. For instance, the audience is able to comprehend the scale of carbon emission in Tehran when family and friends are eating at Mahlagha's dinner table, or when one of the activists celebrates her birthday in Mahlagha's living room. Even the annual report of the Women's Society is delivered when members are gathering at Mahlagha's home to celebrate *Norouz*, the Iranian new year. Through such examples, Banietemad links the pure, scientific statistics with occasions in Mahlagha's ordinary life to trigger the audience's emotion. At the end of the film, audiences may forget the numbers, but they will remember the impact of these numbers on their everyday lives.

Indeed, Banietemad's ecodocumentary has been watched by a significant audience in Iran. Banietemad has been able to turn her restrictions, such as a low budget and limited time for shooting in Mahlagha's house, into advantages, resulting in the production of an influential ecodocumentary. She accomplishes this not only by listing the protagonist's achievements, but by capturing the vitality that Mahlagha spreads through her diligence, engagement, and humor. The filmmaker focuses on the educational side of Mahlagha's life and depicts how she has passionately imparted her experience and knowledge to a new generation of environmental activists. To illustrate this aspect, Banietemad reveals how the private and public lives of this pioneering environmental activist have so often intertwined, as she offers her home to the Women's Society to find solutions for environmental issues and runs classes about the simple ways that citizens can save the planet. As with all other ecodocumentaries, the filmmaker uses various means (conceptual and structural) to arouse her audiences' emotions and to raise their awareness of nature and non-humans (such as animals, air, and soil). Therefore, by virtue of the documentary's slow narrative and the exposure of the previously unobserved features of pollution and deforestation, the audience has time to reflect on the matter and to connect emotionally with Mahlagha's life and character. After experiencing the close relationship developed by *All My Trees*, no one could conceive that discussing environmental issues is a luxury.

Furthermore, as previously mentioned, there are two other documentaries within the Karestan project which share common ground with *All My Trees*. Although beyond the scope of this chapter, writing about these three ecodocumentaries—as an expanded project—in a comparative manner not only would help to bridge the gap between Iranian ecofilms, but would also be beneficial in creating a textual-based corpus of Iranian ecocritical writing. I believe that writing about ecocinema in Iran should be prioritized because, unlike in developed countries, there are only limited textual bodies on this subject. The lack of scholarly work on ecocinema, however, does not mean that there are no noteworthy examples of ecocinema in Iran. Looking closely at Banietemad's work, one can observe her engagement with environmental issues not only in *All My Trees*, the case study in this chapter, but indeed in many of her films. I am certain that many more examples could be brought to light, if a comprehensive study of Iranian cinema from an ecocritical perspective were to be undertaken. On the other hand, in *Iranian Studies Journal*, for instance, within the special issue on "Environment in Iran" (2016, issue 49:6), not one single article (out of a total of ten) addressed ecological representation within Iranian cinema, literature, or any other art form. As far as I have found, only a small number of ecocriticial studies on contemporary Persian literature have been published in Iran. This limited body of textual analysis will compound the lack of communication artists, scholars, and critics, and, consequently, will affect the creation of ecological cultural products such as cinema and literature. In other words, the smaller the textual corpus we have at hand, the less we stimulate communication in the domain of the cinema, literature, and other arts on issues relating to the environment. A text about an ecological film can reveal voices echoed through the narrative and visual elements of the film, thereby creating a space for contemplation about silenced nature and ignored environmental issues. From this perspective, scholars, critics, and writers have to compensate for the lack of a corpus of environmental products, such as ecocinema. They must not only investigate how Iranian ecological representations depict the exploitation of nature, but also consider their vital role in spreading environmental consciousness among audiences by constructing an active, multi-layered consideration of the relationship between humans and their environment.

CHAPTER 12

Hidden Transcripts of Subordinates and the Art of Resistance in *Our Times*

Bahar Abdi

Rakhshan Banietemad always speaks of the filmmaker's responsibility, claiming that, for her,

> cinema is not the aim but the tool . . . in countries such as Iran, where the podiums are not loud enough, and democracy is not yet fully institutionalised, artists—and not just filmmakers—are put in a responsible situation when taking the podium. (Ghorbankarimi 2015: 20)

This assertion demonstrates Banietemad's position concerning the production of films, but it is also part of her wider philosophy. Not only does she claim the podium herself in her films, through addressing persisting social issues in Iran, but she also provides a platform for others to voice their concerns. As such, Banietemad is one of the leading female writer–directors in Iran, renowned for her focus on female characters and social issues in both fiction and documentary genres. In this chapter, looking at the documentary *Ruzegār-e Ma* (*Our Times*, 2002), I would like to focus on how Banietemad overcomes the obstacles to addressing significant issues by constructing a direct criticism of the dominant power.

James C. Scott, in *Domination and the Arts of Resistance*, whilst discussing the power relations between the dominant and the subordinate, introduces two theoretical concepts" "public transcript" and "hidden transcript." He argues that the subordinate's public performance tends to fit the expectations of the powerful, and he uses "the term public transcript as a shorthand way of describing the open interaction between subordinates and those who dominate" (Scott 1990: 2). According to Scott, every subordinate creates a hidden transcript which comes to represent a critique of those in power. The hidden transcript, as he suggests, is what the subordinate uses out of sight of the dominant force and is different from their public transcript (ibid.).

At the outset of his book, Scott asks: how does one examine power relations "when the powerless are often obliged to adopt a strategic pose in the presence of the powerful and when the powerful may have an interest in overdramatizing their reputation and mastery?" (ibid.: xii). Scott's main thesis is that resistance is created somewhere in between the strategic pose of the subordinate and the overdramatization of the dominant power. The opposing messages, the means of resistance, are developed and disguised as hidden transcript until they can make their way into public transcript. I would argue that film as a medium, due to its wide reach, is a public transcript: hence the authoritative powers' need for tight control and censorship in order to dictate what it delivers to the masses. The filmmakers can insinuate their resistance through their films by making use of the hidden transcript within this public transcript. The hidden transcript is not a secret, but it is disguised. Scott argues that the political life of the subordinate is "neither in overt collective defiance of power holders nor in complete hegemonic compliance" (ibid.: 136) but somewhere in between. He argues that there are many "strategies by which subordinate groups manage to insinuate their resistance, in disguised forms, into the public transcript" (ibid.).

There are multiple layers of the hidden transcript at play in Banietemad's *Our Times*, especially when it comes to the matter of voice and agency. In fact, one could argue that Banietemad's films constitute her direct negotiation with the ruling power, the government. Moreover, what we can read between the lines and her indirect address of various issues is the hidden transcript in her work, which, if cultivated fully, can become public transcript. Employing James Scott's theory of hidden transcript as a mode of resistance, I will demonstrate how, in her polemic documentary *Our Times*, Banietemad has subtly managed to give voice and agency to young people, and particularly to female presidential candidates. I will also examine how, through various coping strategies, the social actors carve out a space to create an equal society, one which allows women also to be acknowledged and seen. Finally, I will demonstrate how Banietemad, through capturing these struggles and releasing them in the form of a film, makes these experiences accessible to a larger audience. Consequently, through her film she pushes boundaries and enters the public transcript, which directly criticizes the dominant power.

To convey her message to a broader audience and to bring the hidden transcript of marginalized groups into the public transcript, Banietemad must deal with some logistical obstacles which could affect the scope of her work's reach. The most significant of these obstacles is the limited number of theaters which are willing to show non-commercial and non-fictional films. As a result, most documentaries may not reach large audiences and consequently may not have the intended impact on the process of social, cultural, and political change in society. However, as Naficy observes, *Our Times* was one of the few documentaries to have a commercial distribution, with screenings at fourteen different theaters throughout the country (Naficy 2012b: 46). This makes the film one of the most successful and well-received documentaries produced in recent years.

The documentary depicts a few weeks leading up to the eighth presidential elections in Tehran, when society was characterized by mingled senses of fear, hope, doubt, and trust. It adopts a hybrid documentary mode; using Bill Nichols's (2017) classifications, it switches between observational and participatory, and, at times, between poetic and reflexive, modes of documentary production. The first section of the film follows the young, newly eligible teens campaigning for the re-election of the current president, Mohammad Khatami, through an observational mode, with the camera functioning as a fly on the wall. The second section, following the female presidential candidate, is more participatory, and we sense Banietemad's presence with her probing and questioning. There are reflective elements throughout the film, be it through the narration or through the actual presence of the filmmaker. This is achieved subtly, through her use of an omniscient narrative voice that vocalizes inner contemplation, thus creating a narrative which is informative but also personal.

In the opening narration of *Our Times*, Banietemad informs the viewer about the atmosphere in Tehran before the presidential election whilst expressing her concerns as a mother for the future of young people in the society. In the voice-over at the very beginning of the documentary, Banietemad says that, at the time of candidacy registration, society was experiencing natural anxieties around the election. Some people were ready to boycott the election, and others supported the existing candidates, particularly the re-election of President Khatami. She goes on to mention some surprising phenomena about the presidential election of 2001, which made it an even more significant event. The number of registered candidates exceeded 700, and there were 48 women among them. Additionally, she witnessed the excitement of her own teenage daughter, who could vote for the first time and who wanted to organize a campaign of support for President Khatami. Therefore, Banietemad decided to make a film to capture the spirit of that particular election by focusing on the presence of young people and women.

The voice-over narration in this documentary doubles as both poetic and reflexive. Throughout the film, the narrations at each interval inform the audience that they are following the filmmaker in her attempt to gain access to her next social actor, reminding the audience of the fact that they are watching a film. The first section of the documentary begins by celebrating young people's enthusiasm to vote in the eighth presidential election in Iran. They had been given the chance to vote at the age of sixteen only four years previously, during the seventh presidential election in 1997. Capturing a group of sixteen-year-olds who were excited to be able to vote for the first time, including her own daughter, Banietemad highlights the youthful and optimistic nature of Iranian society. The film follows this group of teenagers as they organize a campaign of support for President Khatami's re-election. In this section, Banietemad's camera observes the young campaigners from a comfortable distance over a period of eight weeks, without much interaction and interference, which follows Nichols's definition of observational documentary, or observing the subjects with an unobtrusive camera (Nichols 2017: 22).

The documentary smoothly shifts its focus and moves on from the hopeful young people to the voiceless women fighting to be heard. Banietemad begins this section by interviewing some of the women who had put themselves forward as candidates. The film then gradually narrows its focus to a unique candidate, Arezoo Bayat, whose eligibility was rejected by the Guardian Council (Figure 12.1). We will look at this in more detail later in the chapter, as it is well known that all women (to this day) have been denied presidential candidacy by the Guardian Council. This second section of the film, which focuses on Arezoo, is done very differently from the first. Not only does the subject matter change, but the style shifts to focus much more on the interaction between Banietemad and Arezoo. The film turns from a broad focus to a much more personal and specific subject. The filmmaker is physically present in this section and spends time with Arezoo for an extended period, focusing on the latter's experiences and her everyday life challenges.

Figure 12.1 *Our Times*, Arezoo explaining why she decided to become a candidate

Arezoo is a twenty-five-year-old single mother from a working-class background. She is divorced and now takes care of her daughter and her blind mother. Banietemad finds Arezoo at a crossroads; she has to move houses in the few days leading up to the election and is searching for a new home on a limited budget when she should have been preparing for the election (should she have qualified). Banietemad's camera follows Arezoo intently wherever she goes, on her quest to find a home.

Banietemad in *Our Times* gives Arezoo the podium and space to express her views. Whilst facing her personal and immediate struggles, Arezoo expresses and hypothesizes her wishes and views on how to resolve the country's problems if she were to be the next president. In this section, the filmmaker takes a more participatory role and collaborates with the social actor. The filmmaker addresses the interviewee through on-screen conversations (even though Banietmad might not be in the shot), rather than narrating a voice-over commentary.

The film conveys the power relations between different groups of subordinates and the dominant power. It shows the different perspectives of various women and young people through the presidential election and the surrounding atmosphere in the city of Tehran. Despite capturing events that occurred in the same place and time, the film offers an insightful portrayal of the life of different people and how they engaged with this event. One can argue that, in part one, the film portrays the relationships between the young campaigners and the state, in addition to the relationship between them and the skeptical older generations who have already had the experience of voting in the Islamic Republic. Through this seemingly generational commentary, the filmmaker refers to the general public's perception of the election, highlighting the relationship between them and the state. The second half of the documentary offers a more head-on dialogue with the state. It focuses on Arezoo, her unique position as presidential candidate, and her constant negotiation with figures of power: the state, her boss, and potential landlords.

According to Rini Cobbey, "Banietemad highlights how individual people and families are embedded in the social and political system . . . [She] is drawn to stories of individuals and families, not to slogans or overly simplified, direct critique" (Cobbey 2011: 92). That is to say, instead of merely showing the events happening on the surface, Banietemad takes her inquisitive camera to different layers of society and observes them from within. Scott distinguished between two levels of resistance among the subordinate groups: the "open, declared forms of resistance which attract most attention, and the disguised, low-profile, undeclared resistance" (Scott 1990: 198). Banietemad portrays what is happening off stage beyond the direct surveillance of the powerholders in order to reveal the undeclared forms of resistance of the subordinates. Arezoo's position as the most unlikely candidate for presidency best portrays the general public's desire to defy the state and its oppressive rule against women.

Amongst these undeclared resistances, we witness the echoes of the sense of doubt relayed from the general public in the first half of the film. The narration at the start declares that there are groups of people who are willing to boycott the election, and many who said that they would cast blank votes. Furthermore, when the young campaigners confront people on streets and ask them who they would vote for in the election, there are many who directly criticize Khatami's first term of presidency and the policies of the regime in general, whilst some admit their refusal to participate at all in the upcoming election.

By capturing the excitement of the young campaigners as well as the opposing views, Banietemad creates a space for dialogue between different perspectives, which is what political debates in Iran lack. In one scene, after showing the excitement of the young campaigners about organizing the election campaign office for Khatami, Banietemad speaks with a young man standing in front of Khatami's office. He says that "Khatami is the last person to vote for. I won't vote this year . . . I won't cast my vote for any candidate." This is an abridged interview with an opponent, captured after a scene showing enthusiastic campaigners furnishing the campaign office. It is succeeded by another scene of the young campaigners in the office, accompanied by the energetic music usually used in propaganda videos for the elections on Iranian national TV. Through capturing the young opponent looking at the group of campaigners from the margins, the film reveals another existing perspective from the same generation. Therefore, his presence can be seen as a form of disguised—but symbolic—resistance to the dominant power. Although the young man does not declare his opposition by disturbing the campaigners, he resists them by not participating in their activities.

In another scene, when the young campaigners distribute flyers on the streets of Tehran and negotiate for more participation in the election, some people avoid accepting their views and say they would not vote in the election. In response to a passer-by saying that she would cast a blank vote, Baran (one of the campaigners and Banietemad's daughter) implies that the authorities might fill in the blank voting papers with the name of their desired candidate. Both the opponents and the campaigners are speaking of their concerns off stage. Although they have opposite perspectives about voting, they both speak as subordinates who criticize the powerholders. Those against participating in the election think that all candidates are similar, and it does not matter which one is elected because nothing would change for the better in the country anyway. Contrastingly, the campaigners believe that, by voting, they can defend their right to be involved in the politics of the state and to voice their ideas about their own future. In doing so, they attempt to change their status from marginalized subjects to active citizens who are able to interrupt the distribution of power, as dictated by the hierarchical regime of the Islamic Republic.

Others in this scene suggest that the young campaigners should not support the election, having already personally witnessed the negative consequences of their earlier support for the Islamic Republic. A woman says, "Four years ago I told my son everything would be all right. He is now a university graduate selling napkins on street corners." A young man asks the campaigners if they can justify the crimes he believes the regime has committed. Another person says that he will not vote, as he already knows that nothing good can come from the statesmen. When the campaigners respond that nothing would change if people did not vote, he replies, "At least they cannot boast about winning the election by 20 million votes," a reference to the 1997 election. Because the government considers the number of people turning up to vote as a sign of support for, and validation of, the state by the people, abstaining from participating in the election can thus be interpreted as utilizing a disguised form of resistance to challenge the legitimacy of the state. Additionally, although the film is supposedly focusing on the young campaigner's point of view, it also gives a voice to those who oppose the election entirely. As street demonstrations and other kinds of direct protest are usually prohibited in Iran, this film shows the other means that people turn to in order to let their dissatisfaction be known. By boycotting the election, not only do they avoid the troubles that direct protest may bring them, but they also undermine the legitimacy of the election and the political regime that holds it.

The film creates an intimate space in which the social actors and the filmmaker can find a common language for criticism. In *Our Times*, all those featured, particularly those who have issues with the current government and intend not to vote, find the chance to manifest their ideas transparently before the camera. The streets in the film become the social site for the hidden transcript of the subordinates, where they represent a critique of the dominant powers beyond their direct observation. Declaring the hidden transcript in social spaces such as streets, as Scott writes, is an achievement of resistance. Indeed, people who criticize the state in the scenes captured on the streets have conquered the public space for a few minutes and manage to defend it, despite the will of the dominant power (Scott 1990: 15).

One of the most significant segments in the first part of the documentary is that in which young campaigners attend a large convention in support of President Khatami. In this scene, a young antagonist who sits among the crowd listening to Khatami's speech starts shouting: "Yes to reform but no more empty talks! Liars, get out of here!" On the one hand, one may simply assume that the young man is a supporter of other competitors or is connected with anti-reform fundamentalists. On the other hand, one may see him as a subordinate who cannot control his anger anymore and shouts out his objections directly before the eyes of the powerholder. This is the moment in which the subordinates find the chance to unveil their hidden transcript before the eyes of the dominant force.

According to Scott, "A shouted insult seems hardly a hidden transcript. What is crucial here is the 'safe distance' that makes the insulter anonymous: the message is public, but the messenger is hidden" (ibid.). Although the criticism does not take place off stage and the powerholder is present, it is made by an anonymous person with a safe distance between him and the dominant power. Whilst this antagonist is located near the front of the crowd and thus is not far removed from the view of the oppressor, the crowd enables him to maintain a safe distance and therefore avoid identification. Consequently, the disobedience becomes public whilst refraining from becoming a visible, hazardous form of resistance due to the anonymity of the actor.

If one looks from another perspective, despite dissatisfaction with the current government and whispers about a potential boycott of the election, a great number of people voted in the 2001 presidential election. According to Ervand Abrahamian, "Khatemi won a second term as president increasing his vote by two million and receiving 80 percent of all votes cast. More than 67 percent of the electorate participated" (Abrahamian 2008: 188).

In the voice-over at the end of the first part of the film, Banietemad states that people considered the election an opportunity to articulate their demands and desires. Indeed, one can argue that the general public's dissatisfaction is not a secret but rather concealed from those who are in power. They avoid showing their defiance before the eyes of powerholders for two reasons. First of all, the powerholders have the authority to give and retract privileges. For example, after the Iranian Revolution in 1979, it became a common belief amongst Iranians that they would face difficulties in receiving governmental services or finding jobs if they did not participate in elections and did not provide evidence of having done so via their birth certificates. Secondly, by participating in the election and supporting the elected candidate, people use peaceful means of achieving a better future. Candidates' promises prior to the election articulate their priorities, should they come into power, and electorates vote for the candidate whose interests align most closely with their demands. In other words, even people who live under totalitarian regimes may prefer to vote for a candidate who can facilitate their connection to power, even when they do not believe he will fulfill his promises entirely.

As mentioned earlier, the second half of the documentary involves interviews with some of the women who had put themselves forward for candidacy but had been denied eligibility by the Guardian Council. According to Minoo Moallem, in an article entitled "The Unintended Consequences of Equality within Difference," although the constitution of the Islamic Republic has not forbidden women to take up high-profile political positions, severe obstacles are created by the Guardian Council to prevent women's participation as political leaders (Moallem 2015: 342). According to Articles 107 and 108 of the Iranian Constitution, anyone who is known to have a sound moral and ethical reputation, who believes in the fundamentals of the Islamic Republic, and has good knowledge of Islamic jurisprudence, as well as current political issues and the system of governance, is eligible to be nominated for the presidential election (Guardian Council 2013). Another criterion mentioned in the Iranian Constitution is that the president should be a *rajol-e siāsi* ("a learned politician"). The borrowed Arabic word *rajol* is used ambiguously in Persian, and although there is no direct reference to the gender of the candidates in the article, the word *rajol* is interpreted by many to mean "man." According to Bahramitash and Esfahani, this interpretation of the term used in the Constitution and the consequent assumption that the president must be a man has caused much debate and raised many objections. They write about the terms and conditions for women serving as high-profile officials in the Islamic Republic:

> Women have quietly been resisting by nominating themselves and running for president, despite the fact that it was common knowledge that the Guardian Council would automatically strike down their candidacy. To have been arguing that rajol-e siasi means any person, either male or female, with sufficient knowledge of public affairs and refined political skills. The issue unified women of different backgrounds, Islamist and secular women alike. (Bahramitash and Esfahani 2011: 88–9)

Also, in reaction to the imposition of Islamic veiling in the aftermath of the Revolution, as Moallem writes, women endeavored to resist their marginalization. The slogan "with my veil but everywhere" was frequently used by female Islamist activists to establish their dynamic presence in society. According to Moallem, the mass participation and involvement of women in the 1979 Revolution "changed their position as objects of modernization and Westernization into subjects of citizenship" (Moallem 2015: 342). Therefore, despite facing severe and relentless restrictions on their engagement in social, political, and even cultural realms, "Iranian women have taken and used power allocated through both the normative framework and the constitution of the Islamic Republic to negotiate their own situations" (ibid.). One may argue that the disqualification of women in the presidential election and the misinterpretation of the Constitution by the legislative authorities are both due to the patriarchal ideology that forms the basis of most social structures in Iran, which maintains that women should be kept busy with their domestic roles and should be excluded from state affairs. Nonetheless, Moallem claims that "while the patriarchal male elite has consistently disqualified women from running in presidential elections, this has not intimidated them from nominating themselves for political offices, even that of president" (ibid.).

Therefore, one can argue that, by registering for presidential candidacy, these women engage in a form of undeclared disguised resistance. Registering for candidacy is a relatively safe way for women to express their opposition to the restrictive laws for women in the patriarchal society of Iran. However, some may interpret this action as a sign of subordination and compliance with the powerholders. Women's participation (even if unsuccessful) can be used as evidence of the "epic presence" of a diverse range of people engaging with the presidential election. Indeed, the state frequently uses the statistics relating to people's participation in political events to prove that they have a decent democracy. These statistics are material for a kind of public transcript which, as Scott defines, is "the open interaction between subordinates and those who dominate" (Scott 1990: 2). According to Scott, it is "the self-portrait of dominant elites as they would have themselves seen," and "it is designed to be impressive, to affirm and naturalise the power of dominant elites" (ibid.: 18). Taking advantage of these statistics in order to make themselves look good can also be interpreted as "overdramatizing their reputation," as previously noted (ibid.: xii).

Arezoo is one of the female candidates who is resisting the unfair constitutional law by nominating herself for the presidency. The film positions her as one who has been deprived of her rights in society by introducing her as one of the disqualified candidates. Later in the second half of the documentary, when Banietemad follows Arezoo as the main subject, the spectator witnesses other aspects of her life wherein she is marginalized and disadvantaged in society, as seen in the two weeks that Banietemad spends with Arezoo as she looks for housing. The documentary shows the difficulties she faces in renting a proper house, mostly stemming from the fact that she is a single mother with a low income. The spectator sees Arezoo struggling with landlords, who prefer to let their houses to families rather than single mothers as they would prefer to deal with a male figure within the family. Amidst all this, Arezoo shares with the documentary her experience of two unsuccessful marriages, which have resulted in poverty and hardship. She is also fired from work because of her absence over several days when she is looking for a house. Each of these facets of her life demonstrates her position as a subordinate who suffers both from her financial status and from the patriarchal structure of her society.

However, progressing through the second half of the documentary, one can see that Arezoo's strategies for survival become her means of resisting the unequal distribution of power in society. She negotiates ways to survive collectively and individually whilst preserving her right to communicate her condition of marginalization, and deals with her problems by finding ways to adapt and surpass them, such as working extra shifts to manage her living expenses and aiming to return to university to complete her studies, in order to make the future better for her family and herself.

Arezoo's other survival strategy is to discuss her difficulties with other people, particularly women in a similar situation to her. In one scene, Arezoo speaks with the current tenant of a house she is willing to rent, saying that, as women, they should be unified and support each other in negotiating their rights with those in power. In this scene, just before they start speaking, we hear the voice of a radio presenter discussing the start of the campaigns for presidential candidates. The tenant first responds to Arezoo by saying that it is the responsibility of the government to facilitate comfort for its citizens, which indicates her awareness of the right of citizens in society. Then she subtly faces the camera, confronting Banietemad and asking if she would help Arezoo or if she is just the subject of the filmmaker's project. The female tenant recognizes a kind of superiority in Banietemad and assumes that she can help. However, Arezoo has a different perspective. Whilst the tenant believes that those from the upper social class should mediate working-class obtainment of their rights, Arezoo believes that their rights could be achievable if working-class people found a way to express their demands and negotiate for them. This is also shown in her relationship with her colleague when she asks for help in reversing her dismissal from work.

Our Times concludes with Arezoo reading aloud her letter to Rakhshan Banietemad, layered over a fixed frame of Arezoo's despairing face, having just lost her job and, thus, her only means of livelihood. The letter is written when the presidential election is over and the results have been determined. Arezoo has also moved to her new house. In the letter, Arezoo expresses her gratitude toward Banietemad for providing her with this opportunity to convey the words and experiences that she wished to share with everyone in the first place when she had registered for presidential candidacy. She states her wish to speak about her other life experiences, asserting:

> When I went to register, I thought that people should hear what I had to say. Because my thoughts were similar to theirs. And that of my life experience was similar to theirs. On the day of elections in my midst of moving house, I lost my birth certificate, I couldn't vote and the president was elected anyway. And you made a film and said some things but there is still a great deal more I want to say. Maybe one day I will write it all . . . or maybe . . .

Leaving the last sentence open, Arezoo indicates her wish to publicize her personal life experiences in some way, perhaps by writing a memoir or even participating in the documentary. Banietemad, as the filmmaker, gives Arezoo, the lead of the film, the power to close it. She concludes with Arezoo's voice instead of her own, which is the only time in the documentary that somebody else's voice-over is heard. Indeed, by giving her the authority to end the film, Banietemad allows Arezoo to appropriate the public space, the podium, in order to resist her subordination further.

In this scene, the filmmaker and subject become one. That is to say, Arezoo and the director are integrated as if they are one person. This integration is rooted in both Banietemad and Arezoo's tendency to raise the common concerns of women: gaining their voice and being acknowledged by society. This recurring factor can be distinguished in all works which adopt a feminist approach. According to Chandra Talpade Mohanty:

> In any piece of feminist analysis, women are characterised as a singular group on the basis of a shared oppression. What binds women together is a sociological notion of the "sameness" of their oppression. It is at this point that an illusion takes place between "women" as a discursively constructed group and "women" as material subject of their own history. (Mohanty 2006: 244)

Together, Banietemad and Arezoo create a piece in which they demonstrate their shared oppression and attempt to declare their disobedience against the status quo openly. *Our Times* becomes a site of empowerment for them by which they acknowledge the patriarchal domination pervading society.

This documentary is made by a woman, and in most parts, it highlights the status of women as second-class citizens. In general, many documentaries by women are inclined to uncover social problems and heighten awareness of the marginalization of women, as well as acknowledging the need for women's rights. According to Lisa French, "Female documentarians have used their practice to lobby for women's access to social, political, cultural, creative and economic spheres whilst advocating for positive change in women's social and economic conditions" (French 2019: 16). Arezoo's narrative, as well as the silenced voices of the young people captured in the documentary, occupies the public space in order to question their social and legal status within society. Moreover, these social actors pave the way for further negotiations that will enable all members of society to enjoy the privileges of citizenship.

By capturing the collective activities of different people around one of the most momentous political events in the country and shedding light on the forgotten aspects of their lives, Banietemad unfolds their hidden transcript of resistance. Moreover, by presenting them in the form of a documentary, she allows different narratives of the subordinates in the form of individual and collective resistance to openly question the distribution of power in society. According to Scott, "The most explosive realm of politics is the rupture of the political cordon sanitaire between the hidden and the public transcript" (Scott 1990: 19). Banietemad, in *Our Times*, publicizes multiple hidden transcripts of resistance. Thus, the documentary can be considered a creative, rebellious act which openly resists the power relations of society and draws public attention to the hierarchies operating within it.

More importantly, this documentary records and reveals the neglected narratives surrounding a very notable political event. Therefore, it constructs a public archive out of various aspects of this stage in socio-political history that would have otherwise been forgotten. Through this documentary, Banietemad and her subjects question the performance of the state and provoke a debate about the ways that the state should handle political dissidence. The documentary, as an archive, continues the resistance in the public sphere, which requires the state to implement an appropriate reaction: that is, the state's narrative, which contrasts with the reality presented in the documentary, should be somehow amended. Thus, the state needs either to discredit the pieces of evidence through its propaganda agents or to correct the faults being exposed by this archive.

To conclude, in *Our Times*, Banietemad questions the distribution of power in Iranian society by highlighting the hidden transcript of marginalized groups in the final weeks leading up to the 2001 presidential election. On the surface, the public transcript of the film reveals Khatami's popularity with young people, despite the general public's dissatisfaction at the conclusion of the first term of his presidency. After portraying the general atmosphere of the city before such a significant event and showing the enthusiasm of the younger generation for electing a reformist president, the documentary concentrates on the lives of marginalized groups, revealing the reality of society. The film includes the hidden transcripts of people who are, by various means, denied and disadvantaged in society. Moreover, it shows how these different groups of people perform resistance against the state in their hidden transcript. There are many opposing opinions shown in the general public, through those who expressed their decision to boycott the election due to their mistrust of the state or disapproval of the power relations within society. These oppositional views take place mostly off stage because of the potentially dramatic and detrimental effects they may have on people's lives if expressed openly.

The second part of the documentary begins with a few interviews with some of the female candidates who were all disqualified by the Guardian Council. These women had already known that their eligibility would be rejected, yet they nominated themselves for the presidential candidacy anyway. The political engagement attempted by female candidates can be interpreted as part of their covert strategy in challenging the institutionalized inequality of Iran's patriarchal society. Arezoo's attempts to survive can also be demarcated as her strategy of resistance. She tries to actively play a role and overcome her individual and social problems using appropriate solutions. She also engages with others in order to achieve her rights and overcome her difficulties.

These are samples of resistance which are applied by people off stage. All these people are, by some means, marginalized by societal power relations, and their insights are overlooked in the existing narrative of that particular era in history. This is a collection of hidden transcripts of subordinates, presenting their protestations against those in power which cannot be readily disclosed. By creating an archive out of these hidden transcripts, the documentary makes them an accessible public resource, as well as continuing to challenge the state on a more visible level through the film itself. These hidden transcripts are recorded as realities happening under the skin of society and serve to contradict the harmony of the narrative offered by the powerholders.

Filmography

FICTION FILMS/DIRECTOR

Ghesseh-hā (*Tales*, 2014)
Khun Bāzi (*Mainline*, 2006)
Gilāneh (*Gilane*, 2005)
Zir-e Pust-e Shahr (*Under the Skin of the City*, 2001)
Bārān va Bumi (*Baran and the Native, Kish Tales*, 1999)
Bānu-ye Ordibehesht (*The May Lady*, 1998)
Rusari Ābi (*The Blue-veiled*, 1995)
Nargess (*Nargess*, 1992)
Pul-e Khāreji (*Foreign Currency*, 1989)
Zard-e Ghanāri (*Canary Yellow*, 1989)
Khārej az Mahdudeh (*Off Limits*, 1988)

DOCUMENTARIES/DIRECTOR

Touran Khanom (Co-director Mojtaba Mirtahmasb, 2018)
Āy, Ādam-hā (*Hey, Humans*, 2016)
Yek Sāat az Yek Omr (*One Hour in a Lifetime*, 2015)
Hame-ye Derakhtān-e Man (*All My Trees*, 2015)
Ān Suy-e Ayeneh-ha (*The Other Side of Mirrors*, 2014)
Concert-e Ayeneh-ha (*The Mirrors Recital*, 2014)
Concert-e khodāvandān-e Asrār (*The Concert of the Lords of Secrets*, 2014)
Otāgh-e 202 (*The Room No. 202*, Part of *Kahrizak 4 Views*, 2012)
Fardā Mibinamet Elinā (See You Tomorrow Elina, 2010)

Mā Nimi az Jame'yat-e Irānim (*We Are Half of Iran's Population*, 2009)
Hayāt Khalvate Khāneh-ye Khorshid (*Angels of the House of Sun*, 2009)
Farsh-e 3 Bodi (*3D Carpet*, Part of *Iranian Carpet*, 2007)
Ruzegār-e Ma (*Our Times*, 2002)
Zir-e Pust-e Shahr (*Under the Skin of the City*, 1996)
Ākharin Didār bā Irān Daftari (*The Last Visit with Iran Daftari*, 1995)
In Film-hā ro beh ki Neshun Midin? (*To Whom Do You Show These Films?*, 1993)
Bahār tā bahār (*Spring to Spring*, 1993)
Gozāresh-e 71 (*The 1992 Report*, 1993)
Tamarkoz (*Centralization*, 1986)
Tadbirhā-ye Eqtesādi-e Jang (*The War Economic Planning*, 1981)
Mohājerin-e Rustāi dar Shahr (*Occupation of Migrant Peasants in the City*, 1980)

PRODUCER/ARTISTIC CONSULTANT/COLLABORATIONS

Khāneh-ye Man Mahak (*Mahak My Home*, a collaboration, 2014)
Karestan Documentary films as follows (Artistic consultant, 2013):

- *Poets of Life*
- *Puzzles*
- *Mother of the Earth*
- *MAHAK: A World She*
- *Friends at Work*
- *Flax to Fire*

Bacheh-hā rā dar Madreseh Negahdārim (*Keep Children in School*, a collaboration, 2012)
Heiran (Producer) (Director: Shalizeh Arefpour, 2009)
Second Home (Producer) (Director: Mahvash Sheikholeslami, 2008)

Bibliography

Abedinifard, Mostafa (2019) "Asghar Farhadi's nuanced feminism: Gender and marriage in Farhadi's films from *Dancing in the Dust* to *A Separation*," *Asian Cinema*, 30: 1, pp. 109–27.
Abrahamian, Ervand (2008) *A History of Modern Iran*. Cambridge: Cambridge University Press.
Aghighi, Saeed (2016) *Zir-e Pust-e Ghesse-ha: Cinema-ye Rakhshan Banietemad*. Tehran: Rozahen.
"Annual figures for the sale of Iranian films and cinemas in the year 1988," Ministry of Culture and Islamic Guidance, September 2017, <https://apf.farhang.gov.ir/ershad_content/media/image/2017/09/531237_orig.pdf> (last accessed 22 January 2020).
"Annual figures for the sale of Iranian films and cinemas in the year 1989," Ministry of Culture and Islamic Guidance, September 2017, <https://apf.farhang.gov.ir/ershad_content/media/image/2017/09/531238_orig.pdf> (last accessed 22 January 2020).
Anvar, Fakhreddin (2014) *The New Iranian Cinema* [Sinema-ye novin-e Iran], Interview by Amir Farzollahi. Tehran: Afraz.
Armatage, Kay, and Zahra Khosroshahi (2017) "An interview with Rakhshan Banietemad," *Feminist Media Histories*, 3: 1, pp. 140–55.
Atwood, Blake (2016) *Reform Cinema in Iran: Film and Political Change in the Islamic Republic*. New York: Columbia University Press.
Austin, John Langshaw (1962) *How to Do Things with Words*. Cambridge and London: Harvard University Press.
Bagheri, Asal (2012) "Les Relations homme/femme dans le cinéma iranien postrévolutionnaire: Stratégies des réalisateurs, analyse sémiologique, vol. 1, 2," PhD dissertation, Université René Descartes, Paris.

Bagheri, Asal (2017) "The image of women," in Parviz Jahed (ed.), *Directory of World Cinema: Iran 2*. Bristol and Chicago: Intellect, pp. 384–91.

Bahramitash, Roksana, and Hadi Salehi Esfahani (2011) *Veiled Employment: Islamism and the Political Economy of Women's Employment in Iran*. Syracuse, NY: Syracuse University Press.

Banietemad, Rakhshan (2010) Personal interview by Asal Bagheri, Persian, Tehran.

Banietemad, Rakhshan (2016a) *The 1980s Filmmaker's Views* [Az negah-e sinemagaran-e daheh-ye 1360], Interview by Mohammad Ali Heidari. Tehran: Rozaneh.

Banietemad, Rakhshan (2016b) "Cinema as a Mirror of the Urban Image," in Shiva Rahbaran (ed.), *Iranian Cinema Uncensored: Contemporary Film-Makers since the Islamic Revolution*. London and New York: Tauris, pp. 127–46.

Banietemad, Rakhshan (2017) "Rakhshan Banietemad," Arte: The Contemporary Art and Culture Oral History [Arteh: Tarikh-e Shafahi-ye honar va farhang], on-line video, <http://artebox.ir/vi/> (last accessed 1 January 2020).

Barthes, Roland (1977) "The grain of the voice," in *Image–Music–Text*. Essays selected and translated from the French by Stephen Heath. London: Fontana, pp. 179–89.

Barthes, Roland (1985) *L'Aventure sémiologique*, Paris: Seuil.

Bayat, Asef (1997) *Street Politics: Poor People's Movements in Iran*. New York: Columbia University Press.

Bayat, Asef (2017) *Revolution without Revolutionaries: Making Sense of the Arab Spring*. Stanford: Stanford University Press.

Bazin, André (2005 [1961]) *What is Cinema?* Essays selected and translated by Hugh Grant, vol. 2. Berkeley, Los Angeles, and London: University of California Press.

Berry, Chris, and Zhang Shujuan (2019) "Film and fashion in Shanghai: What (not) to wear during the Cultural Revolution," *Journal of Chinese Cinemas*, 13: 1 (March), 1–25.

Betton, Gérard (1983) *Esthétique du cinema*. Paris: PUF, "Que sais-je?"

Birdwhistell, Ray L. (1968) "Kinesics: Inter- and intra-channel communication research," *Information (International Social Science Council)*, 7: 6 (December), 9–26.

Booth, Wayne (2002) "Is There an 'Implied' Author in Every Film?", *College Literature*, 29: 2, 124–31.

Bordwell, David (2008) *Poetics of Cinema*. New York and London: Routledge.

Bourdieu, Pierre (1992) *The Rules of Art: Genesis and Structure of the Literary Field*. Stanford: Stanford University Press.

Bourdieu, Pierre (1997) Outline of a Theory of Practice. Cambridge: Cambridge University Press.

Brecht, Bertolt (1990 [1940]) "Notizen über realistische Schreibweise," in *Gesammelte Werke 19*. Frankfurt am Main: Suhrkamp, pp. 349–73.
Brereton, Pat (2016) *Environmental Ethics and Film*. London and New York: Routledge.
Butler, J. (1988), "Performative acts and gender constitution: An essay in phenomenology and feminist theory," *Theatre Journal*, 40: 4, 519–31.
Chaudhuri, Shohini (2006) *Feminist Film Theorists*. London: Routledge.
Chaudhuri, Shohini, and Howard Finn (2003), "The open image: Poetic realism and the New Iranian cinema," in Catherine Grant and Annette Kuhn (eds), *Screening World Cinema*. London: Routledge, pp. 163–82.
Chen, Tina Mai (2001) "Dressing for the Party: Clothing, citizenship, and gender-formation in Mao's China," *Fashion Theory*, 5: 2 (June), 143–171.
Chion, Michel (1994) *Audio-Vision: Sound on Screen*. New York: Columbia University Press.
Chion, Michel (1995), *La Musique au cinéma*. Paris: Fayard.
Chion, Michel (1999), *The Voice in Cinema*, edited and translated by Claudia Gorbman. New York: Columbia University Press.
Cobbey, Rini (2011) "*Under the Skin of the City* (Rakhshan Bani-Etemad): Under the surface contrasts," in Josef Gugler (ed.), *Film in the Middle East and North Africa: Creative Dissidence*. Austin: University of Texas Press.
Connell, Raewyn W. (1987) *Gender and Power: Society, the Person, and Sexual Politics*. Stanford: Stanford University Press.
Connell, Raewyn W. (1998) "Masculinities and globalization," *Men and Masculinities*, 1: 1, 3–23.
Connell, Raewyn W. (2005), *Masculinities*, 2nd edn. Cambridge: Polity Press.
Connell, Raewyn W., and James Messerschmidt (2005) "Hegemonic masculinity: Rethinking the concept," *Gender & Society*, 19, 829–59.
Corbin, Henri (1971) *The Man of Light in Iranian Sufism*. New York: Omega.
Crow, Barbara A. (2000) *Radical Feminism: A Documentary Reader*. New York: New York University Press.
Dabashi, Hamid (2001) *Close up: Iranian Cinema, Past, Present and Future*. London: Verso.
Dabashi, Hamid (2018) "Why Iran creates some of the world's best films," 16 November, <http://www.bbc.com/culture/story/20181115-the-great-films-that-define-iran> (last accessed 1 March 2020).
Davari, Arash (2014) "A return to which self?: Ali Shari'ati and Frantz Fanon on the political ethics of insurrectionary violence," *Comparative Studies of South Asia, Africa and the Middle East*, 34: 1, 86–105.
de Bruijn, J. T. P. (2012) "Fiction, i," *Encyclopedia Iranica*, <http://www.iranicaonline.org/articles/fiction-i-traditional> (last accessed 1 August 2019).

Decherney, P., and Blake Atwood (2014) *Iranian Cinema in a Global Context: Policy, Politics, and Form* (Routledge Advances in Film Studies). London: Routledge.
Deleuze, Gilles (1986) *Cinema 1: The Movement-image*. Minneapolis: University of Minnesota Press.
Deleuze, Gilles (1989) *Cinema 2: The Time-image*. London: Athlone Press.
Doane, Mary Ann (1980) "The voice in cinema: The articulation of body and space," *Yale French Studies*, 60: 33–50, 35.
Doane, Mary Ann (1987), "The 'woman's film': Possession and address," in Christine Gledhill (ed.), *Home is Where the Heart Is: Studies in Melodrama and the Woman's Film*, London: British Film Institue, pp. 283–98.
Dönmez-Colin, Gönül (2019) *Women in the Cinemas of Iran and Turkey: As Images and Image-makers*. London: Routledge.
Duca, Lo (1948) *Technique du cinéma*. Paris: PUF, "Que sais-je?," no. 118.
Elphick, Jeremy (2015) "Tales—An Interview with Director Rakhshan Bani-Etemad," 16 June <https://fourthreefilm.com/2015/06/tales-an-interview-with-director-rakhshan-bani-etemad/> (last accessed 1 July 2019).
Entezari, Mahyar (2011) "'Azādārān-e Bayal," *Encyclopedia Iranica*, <http://www.iranicaonline.org/articles/azadaran-e-bayal> (last accessed 1 August 2019).
Eslami, Mazyar (2017) "Iranian Realist Cinema: Formal Style or a Social Subject?," unpublished paper given at *Where the Truth Lies* workshop, Basel, December, in the framework of the Swiss National Science Foundation-funded research project *Afterimages of Revolution and War: Trauma- and Memoryscapes in Iranian Cinema*.
Evans, Harriet (1997) *Women and Sexuality in China: Female Sexuality and Gender Since 1949*. Cambridge: Cambridge University Press.
Ferro, Marc (1988) *Cinema and History*. Detroit: Wayne State University Press.
Foucault, Michel (1977) "Nietzsche, Genealogy, History," in Donald F. Bouchard (ed.), *Language, Counter-Memory, Practice: Selected Essays and Interviews*. Ithaca, NY: Cornell University Press, pp. 139–64.
Foucault, Michel (1984) "What is Enlightenment?", in Paul Rabinow (ed.), *The Foucault Reader*. New York: Pantheon, pp. 32–50.
French, Lisa (2019) "Women documentary filmmakers as transnational 'advocate change agents,'" *Interdisciplina*, 7: 17, 15–29.
Gaudreault, André, and François Jost (1990) *Cinéma et récit: Le récit cinématographique*, vol. II. Paris: Nathan.
Gerami, Shahin (2003) "Mullahs, martyrs, and men: Conceptualizing masculinity in the Islamic Republic of Iran," *Men and Masculinities*, 5: 3, pp. 257–74.

Ghorbankarimi, Maryam (2012) *Colourful Presence: An Analysis of the Evolution in the Representation of Women in Iranian Cinema Since the 1990s*. PhD, University of Edinburgh.
Ghorbankarimi, Maryam (2015) *A Colourful Presence: The Evolution of Women's Representation in Iranian Cinema*. Newcastle upon Tyne: Cambridge Scholars.
Gow, C. (2016) "Real men—Representations of masculinity in Iranian cinema," *Asian Cinema*, 27: 2, pp. 165–76.
Guardian Council (2013), "Article 107 and 108 The Islamic Republic of Iran Constitution," Guardian Council, <https://www.shora-gc.ir/fa/news/2952> (last accessed 20 December 2019).
Guillain, Robert (1957) *The Blue Ants: 600 Million Chinese under the Red Flag*. London: Secker & Warburg.
Hallam, Julia, and Margaret Marshment (2000) *Realism and Popular Film*. Manchester: Manchester University Press.
Hill, John (1986) *Sex, Class and Realism*. London: BFI.
Holman, Rosa (2016) "Leprosy and the Dialectical Body in Forugh Farrokhzad's *The House is Black*," in B. Fraser (ed.), *Cultures of Representation*. New York: Wall Flower, pp. 247–63.
Honarbin-Holliday, Mehri (2008) *Becoming Visible in Iran: Women in Contemporary Iranian Society*. London: Tauris Academic Studies.
Houdebine, Anne-Marie (2009) "Sémiologie des indices," in Driss Ablali and Dominique Ducard (eds), *Vocabulaire des études sémiotiques et sémiologiques*. Paris: Honoré Champion; Besançon: Presses Universitaires de Franche-Comté, pp. 121–6.
Hutcheon, Linda (2013) *Narcissistic Narrative: The Metafictional Paradox*. Waterloo: Wilfrid Laurier Press.
Issa, Rose, and Sheila Whitaker (1999) *Life and Art: The New Iranian Cinema*. London: National Film Theatre.
Jahid, Parvaz (2012) *Directory of World Cinema: Iran*. Bristol and Chicago: Intellect.
Juhasz, Alexandra (2003) "No Women is an Object: Realizing the Feminist Collaborative Video," *Camera Obscura*, 54: 18.3, 70–9.
Kahana, Jonathan (ed.) (2016) *The Documentary Film Reader: History, Theory, Criticism*. New York: Oxford University Press.
Kaplan, E. Ann (1988 [1983]) *Women and Film: Both Sides of the Camera*. New York: Routledge.
Kara Film Studio (2013) "All my Trees," <https://karafilm.ir/en/films/released/24-all-my-trees> (last accessed 1 January 2020).
Karami, Sepideh (2018) *Interruption: Writing a Dissident Architecture*, Stockholm: KTH Royal Institute of Technology.

Kassabian, Anahid (2013) *Ubiquitous Listening: Affect, Attention, and Distributed Subjectivity*. Berkeley: University of California Press.

Khosrowjah, Hossein (2011) "Neither a victim nor a crusading heroine: Kiarostami's feminist turn in 10," *Situations: Project of the Radical Imagination*, 4: 1, pp. 53–65.

Kiarostami, Abbas (2016) "Where is the Revolution?," in Shiva Rahbaran (ed.), *Iranian Cinema Uncensored: Contemporary Film-Makers since the Islamic Revolution*. London and New York: Tauris.

Kracauer, Siegfried (1960) *Theory of Film. The Redemption of Physical Reality*. Princeton: Princeton University Press.

Kuhn, Annette, and Guy Westwell (2012), "Essay film," in *A Dictionary of Film Studies*. Oxford: Oxford University Press.

Laachir, Karima, and Saeed Talajooy (eds) (2013) *Resistance in Contemporary Middle Eastern Cultures*. New York: Routledge.

Lahiji, Shahla (2002) "Chaste dolls and unchaste dolls: Women in Iranian cinema since 1979," in Richard Tapper (ed.), *The New Iranian Cinema: Politics, Representation and Identity*, London and New York: I. B. Tauris, pp. 215–26.

Langford Michelle (2012) "Tending the wounds of the nation: Gender in contemporary Iranian war cinema," *Screening the Past*, <http://www.screeningthepast.com/2012/12/tending-the-wounds-of-the-nation-gender-in-contemporary-iranian-war-cinema/> (last accessed 1 January 2020).

Langford, Michelle (2019) *Allegory in Iranian Cinema: The Aesthetics of Poetry and Resistance*. London: Bloomsbury.

Langford, Michelle (forthcoming) "Seeking love in the interstices: Acousmatic listening as counter-memory in Abbas Kiarostami's *Shirin* (2008)," in Matthias Wittmann and Ute Holl (eds), *Countermemories in Iranian Cinema*. Edinburgh: Edinburgh University Press.

Lebow, Alisa (2012) *The Cinema of Me: The Self and Subjectivity in First Person Documentary*. London: Wallflower Press.

Lesage, Julia (1978) "The political aesthetics of the feminist documentary film," in Jonathan Kahana (ed.) (2016), *The Documentary Film Reader: History, Theory, Criticism*. New York: Oxford University Press.

Lesage, Julia (1984) "Feminist documentary: Aesthetics and politics," in Thomas Warne (ed.), *Show Us Life: Towards a History and Aesthetics of the Committed Documentary*. New York: Scarecrow Press, pp. 224–40.

McLuhan, Marshall (2013) *Understanding Media: The Extensions of Man*. New York: Gingko Press.

Mahdavi, Pardis (2009), *Passionate Uprisings: Iran's Sexual Revolution*. Stanford: Stanford University Press.

Mao, Zedong (1969) *Mao Zedong sixiang shengli wansui* [Long Live Mao Zedong Thought], Beijing: Renmin chubanshe.

Martinet, Jeanne (1974) "La Sémiologie du geste," *La Linguistique*, 10: 2, 137–9.
Milani, Farzaneh (1992) *Veils and Words: The Emerging Voices of Iranian Women Writers*. Syracuse, NY: Syracuse University Press.
Mir-Hosseini, Ziba (2004) "Sexuality, rights and Islam: Competing gender discourse in post-revolutionary Iran," in Lois Beck and Guity Neshat (eds), *Women in Iran from 1800 to the Islamic Republic*. Champaign: University of Illinois, pp. 204–40.
Mir-Hosseini, Ziba (2017) "Islam, gender and democracy in Iran," in Jocelyn Cesari and Jose Casanova (eds), *Islam, Gender and Democracy*. Oxford: Oxford University Press, pp. 211–36.
Mirmohammadi, Seyedkeyvan (2017) "Realism without a Ceiling: The Hidden Idleness and the Violence of the Street," unpublished paper given at *Where the Truth Lies* workshop, Basel, December, in the framework of the Swiss National Science Foundation-funded research project *Afterimages of Revolution and War: Trauma- and Memoryscapes in Iranian Cinema*.
Mirsepassi, Ali (2003) *Intellectual Discourse and the Politics of Modernization: Negotiating Modernity in Iran*. New York: Cambridge University Press.
Moallem, Minoo (2015) "The unintended consequences of equality within difference," *Brown Journal of World Affairs*, 22: 1, 335–50.
Mohanty, Chandra Talpade (2006) "Under Western eyes: Feminist scholarship and colonial discourses," in B. Ashcroft, G. Griffiths and H. Tiffin (eds), *The Post-colonial Studies Reader*. London: Routledge.
Mohseni, Hamid (2018) "'I do not fear them. I have nothing to lose'—Iran's current 'No Future'-movement challenges the Islamic Republic," *Beyond Europe*, 4 January, <https://beyondeurope.net/707/irans-current-movement/> (last accessed 24 September 2020).
Moradiyan Rizi, Najmeh (2016) "The acoustic screen: The dynamics of the female look and voice in Abbas Kiarostami's *Shirin*," *Synoptique*, 5: 6, 44–56.
Mottahedah, Negar (2008) *Displaced Allegories: Post-Revolutionary Iranian Cinema*. Durham, NC: Duke University Press.
Mottadeheh, Negar (2017) "Crude Extractions: The Voice in Iranian Cinema; Introduction," in Tom Whittaker and Sarah Wright (eds), *Locating the Voice in Film: Critical Approaches and Global Practices*. Oxford: Oxford University Press.
Mulvey, Laura (1986) "Visual Pleasure and Narrative Cinema," in Philip Rosen (ed.), *Narrative, Apparatus, Ideology: A Film Theory Reader*. New York: Columbia University Press, pp. 198–209.
Mulvey, Laura (2001) "Between Melodrama and Realism: *Under the Skin of the City*," <http://www.thecine-files.com/current-issue-2/guest-scholars/laura-mulvey/> (last accessed 1 January 2020).

Mulvey, Laura (2002) "Afterword," in Richard Tapper (ed.), *The New Iranian Cinema: Politics, Representation and Identity*. London: I. B. Tauris, pp. 254–61.

Mulvey, Laura (2019), *Afterimages: On Cinema, Women and Changing Times*. London: Reaktion.

Naficy, Hamid (1994) "Veiled vision/powerful presence: Women in post revolutionary Iranian cinema," in Mahnez Afkhami and Erika Friedl (eds), *The Eye of the Storm*. London: I. B. Tauris, pp. 131–50.

Naficy, Hamid (1995) "Iranian cinema under the Islamic Republic," *American Anthropologist*, 97: 3, 548–58.

Naficy, Hamid (2000) "Veiled voice and vision in Iranian cinema: The evolution of Rakhshan Banietemad's films," *Social Research*, 67: 2, 559–76.

Naficy, Hamid (2011a) *A Social History of Iranian Cinema: The Artisanal Era, 1897–1941*. Durham, NC: Duke University Press.

Naficy, Hamid (2011b) *A Social History of Iranian Cinema: The Industrializing Years, 1941–1978*. Durham, NC: Duke University Press.

Naficy, Hamid (2012a) *A Social History of Iranian Cinema: The Islamicate Period, 1978–1984*. Durham, NC: Duke University Press.

Naficy, Hamid (2012b) *A Social History of Iranian Cinema: The Globalizing Era, 1984–2010* (E-Duke Books Scholarly Collection). Durham, NC: Duke University Press.

Naficy, Hamid (2012c), "Neorealism Iranian style," in Saverio Giovacchini and Robert Sklar (eds), *Global Neorealism: The Transnational History of a Film Style*. Jackson: University Press of Mississippi, pp. 226–39.

Naficy, Hamid (2013) "The anthropological unconscious of Iranian ethnographic films: A brief take," *Anthropology of the Contemporary Middle East and Central Eurasia*, 1, pp. 113–25.

Najd-Ahmadi, Tara (2018) "The Incomplete: Art, Politics, and Remembering the Past," unpublished manuscript, based on presentation at *Counter-Memories: Memoryscapes in Iranian Cinema* conference, Basel.

Najmabadi, Afsaneh (1997) "The erotic *vatan* [homeland] as beloved and mother: To love, to possess, and to protect," *Comparative Studies in Society and History*, 39: 3, pp. 442–67.

Najmabadi, Afsaneh (2005) *Women with Mustaches and Men without Beards: Gender and Sexual Anxieties of Iranian Modernity*. Berkeley: University of California Press.

Nichols, Bill (1994) "Discovering form, inferring meaning: New cinemas and the film festival circuit," *Film Quarterly*, 47: 3, 16–30.

Nichols, Bill (2010) Introduction to Documentary, 2nd edn. Bloomington: Indiana University Press.

Nichols, Bill (2017) *Introduction to Documentary*. Bloomington: Indiana University Press.

Nooraninejad, Setayesh (2018) *The Writing Culture of Iranian Soldier during the Iran–Iraq War (1980–1988)*, Annual History Colloquium, Darwin, 27 October.

Nooshin, Laudan (2005) "Underground, overground: Rock music and youth discourses in Iran," *Iranian Studies* (special issue: *Music and Society in Iran*), 38: 3, 463–94.

Nooshin, Laudan (2018) "'Our Angel of Salvation': Toward an understanding of Iranian cyberspace as an alternative sphere of musical sociality," *Ethnomusicology*, 62: 3, 341–74.

Nooshin, Laudan (2019) "Windows onto other worlds: Music and the negotiation of otherness in Iranian cinema," *Music and the Moving Image*, 12: 3, 25–57.

Omid, Jamal (2004) *History of Iranian Cinema (1980–1991)* [Tarikh-e sinema-ye Iran (1358–1369)]. Tehran: Rozaneh.

Pak-Shiraz, Nacim (2017) "Shooting the isolation and marginality of masculinities in Iranian cinema," *Iranian Studies*, 50: 6, 945–67.

Pak-Shiraz, Nacim (2018) "Constructing masculinities through *Javanmards* in pre-revolutionary Iranian cinema," in Lloyd Ridgeon (ed.), *Javanmardi: The Ethics and Practice of Persianate Perfection*. London: Gingko Library, pp. 297–318.

Pang, Laikwan (2017) *The Art of Cloning: Creative Production During China's Cultural Revolution*. London: Verso.

Peberdy, D. (2011) *Masculinity and Film Performance: Male Angst in Contemporary American Cinema*. Basingstoke: Palgrave Macmillan.

Proctor, Rachel (2002) "Interview: Questioning the Mullahs," *Texas Observer*, <https://www.texasobserver.org/756-interview-questioning-the-mullahs/> (last accessed January 2020).

Rahimieh, Nasrin, and Dominic Brookshaw (eds) (2010) *Forugh Farrokhzad, Poet of Modern Iran: Iconic Woman and Feminine Pioneer of the New Persian Poetry*. London: I. B. Tauris.

Rekabtalaei, Golbarg (2019) *Iranian Cosmopolitanism: A Cinematic History*. Cambridge: Cambridge University Press.

Rice, Tom (2015) "Listening," in David Novak and Matt Sakkeeny (eds), *Keywords in Sound*. Durham, NC: Duke University Press, pp. 99–124.

Roddy, Michael (2014) "Iran's change at the top gives director cue to show social ills," Reuters, 5 September <https://www.reuters.com/article/us-filmfestival-venice-tales/irans-change-at-the-top-gives-director-cue-to-show-social-ills-idUSKBN0H015E20140905> (last accessed January 2020).

Rouch, Jean (2003 [1974]) "The Camera and Man," in Jean Rouch, *Ciné-Ethnography*, edited and translated by Steven Feld. London and Minneapolis: University of Minnesota Press, pp. 29–48.

Rugo, Daniele (2016) "Asghar Farhadi," *Third Text*, 30: 3–4, 173–87.

Rust, Stephen (2012) "The eco-cinema experience," in Stephen Rust, Salma Monani, and Sean Cubitt (eds), *Ecocinema Theory and Practice*. New York and London: Routledge.

Rust, Stephen, Salma Monani, and Sean Cubitt (eds) (2012) *Ecocinema Theory and Practice*. New York and London: Routledge.

Saberi, Iraj (2003) *25 Years of Iranian Cinema, Feature Films, vol I: 1979–1993* [25 sal sinema-ye Iran, film-haye sinemai, jeld-e avval: 1358–1372], Tehran: Muzeh-ye Sinema [Film Museum] va Bonyad-e Sinemai-ye Farabi [FCF].

Sadowski, Piotr (2017) *The Semiotics of Light and Shadow: Modern Visual Arts and Weimar Cinema*. London: Bloomsbury.

Sadr, Hamidreza (2002) *Against the Wind: Politics of Iranian Cinema*. Tehran: Zarrin.

Sadr, Hamidreza (2006) *Iranian Cinema: A Political History*. London: I. B. Tauris.

Saeed, Aqiqi (2015) *Under the Skins of the Tales: The Cinema of Rakhshan Banietemad* [Zir-e pust-e gesseh-ha: Sinema-ye Rakhshan Banietemad], Tehran: Rozaneh.

Sarris, A. (2011 [1977]) "The auteur theory revisited," in T. Corrigan, P. White, and M Mazaj (eds), *Critical Visions in Film Theory*. New York: Bedford/St. Martin's, pp. 354–61.

Saussure, Ferdinand de (2005) [1916]) *Cours de linguistique générale*, ed. Charles Bally and Albert Sechehaye, Paris: Payot.

Sayad, Cecilia (2013) *Performing Authorship: Self-Inscription and Corporeality in Cinema*. New York: I. B. Tauris.

Sciolino, Elaine (2000) "Runaway youths a thorn in Iran's chaste side," New York Times, 5 November, p. 3.

Scott, A. O. (2013) "Film review; An Iranian family facing conflict within and beyond," *New York Times*, 14 March, <https://www.nytimes.com/2003/03/14/movies/film-review-an-iranian-family-facing-conflict-within-and-beyond.html> (last accessed 24 September 2020).

Scott, James C. (1990) Domination and the Arts of Resistance: Hidden Transcripts. New Haven, CT: Yale University Press.

Shahla, Lahiji (2012) "Family in the cinematic works of Rakhshand Banietimad" [Khanevadeh dar asar-e sinnemai-ye Rakhshan Banietemad], *Iran Nameh*, 27: 1, 191–4.

Sharifi, Hamid, Mohammad Karamouzian, Mohammad Reza Baneshi, Mostafa Shokoohi, Ali Akbar Haghdoost, Will McFarland, and Ali Mirazazadeh (2017) "Population size estimation of female sex workers in Iran: Synthesis of methods and results," *PLoS ONE*, 12: 8, <https://doi.org/10.1371/journal.pone.0182755> (last accessed 15 July 2019).

Sheibani, Khatereh (2011) *The Poetics of Iranian Cinema: Aesthetics, Modernity and Film after the Revolution*. London and New York: I. B. Tauris.

Shohat, Ella (2001) *Talking Visions: Multicultural Feminism in a Transnational Age*. Cambridge, MA: MIT Press.

Silverman, Kaja (1988) *The Acoustic Mirror: The Female Voice in Psychoanalysis and Cinema*. Bloomington: Indiana University Press.

Simorgh (2015), "Conversation with Banietemad about *Tales*" [*Gofto-goo ba Rakhshan Banietemad darbare-ye film-e* Ghresse-ha], <https://seemorgh.com/culture/culture-news/234444> (last accessed 1 January 2020).

Smaill, Belinda (2012) "Cinema against the age: Feminism and contemporary documentary," *Screening the Past*, 34: 1–12.

Sohrabi, Naghmeh (2002) "To be heard: Of hope and despair: Rakhshan Bani-Etemad's *Our Times*," *The Iranian*, 23 January, <http://iranian.com/NaghmehSohrabi/2002/January/Film/index.html> (last accessed 24 September 2020).

Solanas, Fernando, and Octavio Getino (1970–1) "Toward a Third Cinema," *Cinéaste*, 4: 3 (Winter), Latin American Militant Cinema, 1–10.

Talattof, Kamran (2000) *The Politics of Writing in Iran: A History of Modern Persian Literature*, Syracuse, NY: Syracuse University Press.

Talu, Yonca (2015) "Interview: Rakhshan Bani-E'temad," *Film Comment*, 20 February, <https://www.filmcomment.com/blog/interview-rakhshan-bani-etemad/> (last accessed 1 January 2020).

Tapper, Richard (2002) *The New Iranian Cinema: Politics, Representation and Identity*. London: I. B. Tauris.

Tavakoli-Targhi, Mohamad (2001) *Refashioning Iran: Orientalism, Occidentalism and Historiography*. New York: Palgrave Macmillan.

Tavakoli-Targhi, Mohamad (2012) "The emergence of clerico-engineering as a form of governance in Iran," *Iran Nameh*, 27: 2–3, 14–17.

Varzi, Roxanne (2014) "A grave state: Rakhshand Bani-Etemad's *Mainline*," in Peter Decherney and Blake Atwood (eds), *Iranian Cinema in a Global Context: Policy, Politics, and Form*. Hoboken, NJ: Taylor and Francis, pp. 96–111.

Waldman, Diane, and Janet Walker (1999) *Feminism and Documentary*. Minneapolis: University of Minnesota.

Weidman, Amanda (2015) "Voice," in David Novak and Matt Sakkeeny (eds), *Keywords in Sound*. Durham, NC: Duke University Press, pp. 232–45.

Weissberg, Jay (2014) "Venice film review: 'Tales,'" *Variety*, 28 August, <https://variety.com/2014/film/festivals/venice-film-review-tales-1201292787/> (last accessed 1 January 2020).

Whittaker, Tom, and Sarah Wright (eds) (2017) "Introduction," in *Locating the Voice in Film: Critical Approaches and Global Practices*. Oxford: Oxford University Press.

Willemen, Paul (1986) "Voyeurism, the Look, and Dwoskin," in Philip Rosen (ed.), *Narrative, Apparatus, Ideology: A Film Theory Reader*. New York: Columbia University Press, pp. 210–18.

Willoquet-Maricondi, Paula (ed.) (2010) *Framing the World: Explorations in Ecocriticism and Film*. Charlottesville: University of Virginia Press.
Winters, Ben (2014) *Music, Performance, and the Realities of Film: Shared Concert Experiences in Screen Fiction*. London: Routledge.
Zeydabadi-Nejad, Saeed (2009) *The Politics of Iranian Cinema: Film and Society in the Islamic Republic*. London: Routledge.
Zeydabadi-Nejad, Saeed (2011) *The Politics of Iranian Cinema: Film and Society in the Islamic Republic*. London: Routledge.
Zeydabadi-Nejad, Saeed (2016) "Watching the Forbidden: Reception of Banned Films in Iran," in Malte Hagener, Vinzenz Hediger, and Alena Strohmaier (eds), The State of *Post-Cinema: Tracing the Moving Image in the Age of Digital Dissemination*. London: Palgrave Macmillan, pp. 99–113.
Zheng, Wang (1999) *Women in the Chinese Enlightenment: Oral and Textual Histories*. Berkeley: University of California Press.

Index

A Few Kilos of Dates for a Funeral (2006), 160
A Separation (2011), 62
Abdol Wahab, Mohsen, 141
Adineh, Golab, 18–19, 36–8, 43, 52, 80, 85, 128, 161
agency, 10, 97, 106–7, 116–17, 124, 127, 171, 184, 190, 220
Ahmadinejad, Mahmoud, 22, 63, 77, 88, 91, 166, 197
All My Trees (2015), 206–18
Anvar, Fakhreddin, 30
Army Nurse (1985), 173–84
Aslani, Farhad, 69, 71, 89, 166, 169
auteur, auteurship/authorship, auteurial, 9, 27–8, 32–3, 40, 104, 108, 127–8, 189–91, 204
Ayari Kianoush, 6, 34, 45, 50

Baran and the Native (1999), 24
Barghnavard, Shirin, 209, 211
Bazin, André, 44, 53, 151–2, 190
Beast's Chimney (1986), 34
Beheshti, Mohammad, 30–2
Beyzaie, Bahram, 32
Bordwell, David, 44, 59, 62, 64

Canary Yellow (1989), 36–7, 142
censorship, 31–2, 37, 49–54, 61, 70–5, 79–81, 86, 88, 92–3, 101, 103, 144, 149, 151
Centralization (1986), 21, 34, 191–6, 208–9
Chrysanthemums (1985), 34
civil society, 43, 53–4, 117

Dabashi, Hamid, 4, 5, 40–1
Deleuze, Gilles, 44, 45, 55, 112
Derakhshandeh, Pouran, 3
Divan, 58–9, 70–8
documentary, 7–8, 11, 16, 18, 21–2, 34–8, 43, 47–52, 58–78, 79–90, 104–14, 121, 128, 164–5, 189, 191, 194–8, 201–18, 219–32

Entezami, Ezzatolah, 32, 50

Farabi Cinema Foundation, 30–1
Farhadi, Asghar, 5, 62
Farhang, Dariush, 35
Farrokhzad, Forugh, 103, 111, 136, 189, 202
femininity, feminine, 40–1, 101, 103, 160–1, 174, 177, 182
film-farsi, 163, 167, 175
Foreign Currency (1989), 6, 22, 28, 38–9, 141–2

248 INDEX

Foroutanian, Shahrokh, 64
Forutan, Mohammad Reza, 51, 60
    79, 167
Foucault, Michel, 45–6, 190

General Department of Cinematic
    Affairs, GDCA, 30, 31, 35, 39
Gilane (2005), 7, 22, 109–12
Guardian Council, 106, 222, 226–7,
    231

Halimi, Mohammad Javad, Mr Halimi,
    35–6, 63–4, 168, 172
Hashemi, Faezeh, 48, 129
Hashemi, Mehdi, 35, 63, 168
Hashemi Rafsanjani, Akbar, 48
Hey, Humans (2016), 18, 209
hybridity, 37, 190

Iran–Iraq War, 6, 31, 39, 64, 109, 110–12,
    119, 121, 132, 143, 160
Islamic Republic of Iran Broadcasting,
    IRIB, Iranian National TV, TV, 17,
    34–6, 52, 224
Italian neorealism, 49, 135, 190

Jahel, 35, 163

Kar, Mehrangiz, 129
Keshavarz, Mohammad Ali, 32
Khachikian, Samuel, 27
Khatami, Mohammad, 22, 30, 43, 53–4,
    67, 104, 108, 143, 221–5, 231
Kia, Forugh, 7, 48, 52, 67, 80–7, 100–3,
    100, 115–49, 173–85
Kiarostami, Abbas, 40, 50, 51,
    118, 172
Kosari, Baran, 64, 73, 104, 109, 128, 165,
    166, 170
Kosari, Jahangir, 17, 34, 202
Kracauer, Siegfried, 44, 52

Lahiji, Shahla, 40, 129, 162–3, 175,
    240, 244
Lou, Nüer, 173, 178

Mainline (2006), 6–8, 19–21, 51, 57–8,
    62–4, 73–4, 77, 88, 141–3, 165, 171, 202
Makhmalbaf, Mohsen, 40
Makhmalbaf, Samira, 5
martyr, martyrdom, 6, 109, 110, 113,
    160, 163
masculinity, masculine, 4, 35–6, 41,
    160–4, 167–84
Mehrjui, Dariush, 27, 32–3, 189
Meshkini, Marziyeh, 40
Milani, Farzaneh, 98–9, 174–5, 179,
    181, 241
Milani, Tahmineh, 3, 5
Ministry of Culture and Islamic
    Guidance (MCIG), 16, 27, 30, 59,
    78, 166
Mirtahmasb Mojtaba, 8, 209, 211
Mostafavi, Farid, 6, 21, 34, 36,
    38–9, 166
Motamed-Aria, Fatemeh, 64, 109, 196
Moussavi, Mir Hossein, 30, 31
Mulvey, L., 6, 53, 123

Naficy, Hamid, 5, 28, 32, 37, 61, 98–101,
    114, 127, 137, 221
Narges (1992), 3–4, 7, 19–20, 27, 40,
    48, 59, 64–6, 68–9, 142, 207
National Iranian Radio and Television,
    NIRT, 15
neorealism, 37, 49, 190
Nichols, Bill, 3–4, 193, 212, 221–2
Nobar, Nobar Kordani, 7, 51, 70–4, 128,
    142, 150–8, 170–1

*Occupation of Migrant Peasants in the
    City*, 208
Off Limits (1988), 16–17, 33–4, 37–8, 58,
    62–4, 142, 168, 195, 207
Our Times (2002), 22, 98, 104–9, 195,
    219–32

Pahlavi, 28, 30, 33, 46
poetic, poeticism, 9, 49, 53, 58–9, 70–7,
    89, 97, 99–100, 103–4, 113–14, 127,
    136–7, 189, 191–3, 202, 221

Radan, Bahram, 64, 73, 109
Rasul, 50, 70–3, 142–58, 169
Razavi, Atefeh, 20, 48, 64
Rezaei, Habib, 58, 79, 164
Rezai, Mohsen, 23
realism, 3–5, 18, 43–50, 55, 59–70, 89–90, 98, 144, 165
resistance, 14, 30, 41, 47, 55, 78, 79, 87, 92–3, 97, 113, 161, 175, 185, 220, 224–6, 230–2
Rouch, Jean, 44

Sabbaghzadeh, Mehdi, 34
sacred defense, 33, 45, 110, 160
Sadrameli, Rasul, 6, 34
Saedi, Gholam Hossein, 58
Salur, Saman, 160
self-reflexive, reflexive, 11, 48, 58, 79–80, 86–7, 194–7, 201, 221
Sharifinia, Mehraveh, 60, 167
social realism, 37, 44–5, 58, 100, 142, 189–90, 205
subjectivity, subjective, 4, 99–103, 111–13, 117–19, 123–4, 133, 139, 174, 196
Sun Dwellers (1980), 34

Tales (2014), 8, 43, 57–60, 63–4, 66, 68–9, 73, 85–98, 159–61, 164–6
The Blue-veiled (1995), 18, 50–1, 70–3, 136, 140–58, 169–70
The Cow (1969), 189
The Eagles (1985), 27
The House is Black (1962), 111, 189, 202
The Legend of the Sultan and the Shepherd (1984), 35
The May Lady (1998), 10, 19, 21, 48, 51–2, 67, 80, 82–7, 100, 101, 103–4, 111, 115–39, 143, 173–85, 204–5
The Mourners of Bayal (1964), 58
The Tenants (1986), 27, 33
To Whom Do You Show These Films? (1993), 43, 85, 154, 195–7
Tooba, 7, 18–21, 39, 43–4, 48, 53–5, 60–72, 80–93, 120, 130–2, 161, 198
Touran Khanom (2018), 209

Under the Skin of the City (1996), 191, 201–4
Under the Skin of the City (2001), 21, 39, 42, 51–4, 60–9, 80–2, 84–9, 143, 167, 207

voice-over, 48, 97, 101–14, 120, 122, 127, 135–7, 181, 196–203, 221, 223, 226

We Are Half of Iran's Population (2009), 22, 197

Zarrindast, Alireza, 35
Zarrinpour, Bahram, 21, 36

EU representative:
Easy Access System Europe
Mustamäe tee 50, 10621 Tallinn, Estonia
Gpsr.requests@easproject.com